Reading Tourism Texts

TOURISM AND CULTURAL CHANGE

Series Editors: Professor Mike Robinson, *Ironbridge International Institute for Cultural Heritage, University of Birmingham, UK* and Dr Alison Phipps, *University of Glasgow, Scotland, UK*

TCC is a series of books that explores the complex and ever-changing relationship between tourism and culture(s). The series focuses on the ways that places, peoples, pasts and ways of life are increasingly shaped/transformed/created/packaged for touristic purposes. The series examines the ways tourism utilises/makes and re-makes cultural capital in its various guises (visual and performing arts, crafts, festivals, built heritage, cuisine etc.) and the multifarious political, economic, social and ethical issues that are raised as a consequence.

Understanding tourism's relationships with culture(s) and vice versa is of ever-increasing significance in a globalising world. This series will critically examine the dynamic inter-relationships between tourism and culture(s). Theoretical explorations, research-informed analyses and detailed historical reviews from a variety of disciplinary perspectives are invited to consider such relationships.

Full details of all the books in this series and of all our other publications can be found on http://www.multilingual-matters.com, or by writing to Multilingual Matters, St Nicholas House, 31-34 High Street, Bristol BS1 2AW, UK.

Reading Tourism Texts

A Multimodal Analysis

Sabrina Francesconi

CHANNEL VIEW PUBLICATIONS
Bristol • Buffalo • Toronto

To P.M.

Library of Congress Cataloging in Publication Data
A catalog record for this book is available from the Library of Congress.
Francesconi, Sabrina, 1976–
Reading Tourism Texts: A Multimodal Analysis / Sabrina Francesconi.
Tourism and Cultural Change: 36
Includes bibliographical references and index.
1. Tourism–Social aspects. 2. Travel writing. I. Title.
G155.A1F67239 2014
306.4'819–dc23 2013042301

British Library Cataloguing in Publication Data
A catalogue entry for this book is available from the British Library.

ISBN-13: 978-1-84541-427-6 (hbk)
ISBN-13: 978-1-84541-426-9 (pbk)

Channel View Publications
UK: St Nicholas House, 31-34 High Street, Bristol BS1 2AW, UK.
USA: UTP, 2250 Military Road, Tonawanda, NY 14150, USA.
Canada: UTP, 5201 Dufferin Street, North York, Ontario M3H 5T8, Canada.

Copyright © 2014 Sabrina Francesconi.

All rights reserved. No part of this work may be reproduced in any form or by any means without permission in writing from the publisher.

The policy of Multilingual Matters/Channel View Publications is to use papers that are natural, renewable and recyclable products, made from wood grown in sustainable forests. In the manufacturing process of our books, and to further support our policy, preference is given to printers that have FSC and PEFC Chain of Custody certification. The FSC and/or PEFC logos will appear on those books where full certification has been granted to the printer concerned.

Typeset by R. J. Footring Ltd, Derby

Contents

Figures	viii
Tables	x
Acknowledgements	xi

Introduction: Tourism and Travel	1
Tourism/Travel and Texts	3
Background Literature	7
Outline of the Book	8
The English Language and Tourism	9
1 Genre Analysis	11
Genre and Generic Integrity	11
Genre Maps and Colonies	15
Actors	16
Medium	20
Stage of trip	22
Mode	22
Communication function	23
Genre value	25
Lexico-grammar strategies	26
Summary	28
Generic Innovation	28
Forms of generic innovation	28
Reasons for generic innovation	31
Genre analysis of Wikitravel to South Africa	34
Conclusion	39

2 Systemic Functional Grammar	41
Systemic Functional Linguistics	41
The Ideational Metafunction	44
The Interpersonal Metafunction	49
The Textual Metafunction	53
SFL in Tourism and Travel Texts	56
SFL Analysis of a Tourist Brochure on Malta	57
Transitivity and Theme analysis	59
Mood analysis	61
Clause complex analysis	63
SFL in an Online Travel Diary Recording a Trip to Malta	64
Transitivity and Theme analysis	66
Mood analysis	67
Clause complex analysis	68
Conclusion	70
3 Visual Analysis	71
Vision	71
Visual Culture and Tourism	75
The Tourist Gaze	76
Visual Analysis and Pictures of Ireland	81
The ideational metafunction	82
The interpersonal metafunction	89
The textual metafunction	97
Summary	99
Non-pictorial texts	102
Conclusion	103
4 Aural Analysis	104
Sound	104
The words of sound: A lexical map	107
The Soundscape	108
Sound in Tourism and Travel Texts	116
A radio travel programme on England	116
A radio commercial promoting India	124
Summary	126
Conclusion	126
5 Multimodal and Intermodal Analysis	127
Semiotic Resources	127
Multimodality and Intersemiosis	129

Multimodal Tourism Communication	131
Clustering and Reading Paths	133
Visit Jamaica website homepage	136
Intersemiosis in Static Texts	139
Humorous British postcards	141
Intersemiosis in Dynamic Texts	146
The Air New Zealand safety video	149
Intersemiosis in Hypertextual Texts	154
The Visit Jamaica website structure	155
Conclusion	157
Afterword: Methods of Multimodal Analysis	158
Glossary	163
Bibliography: Genre-Based Critical Works on the Language of Tourism	166
References	173
Author Index	182

Figures

1.1	Generic description of a travel magazine	17
1.2	Generic description of an academic volume	18
1.3	Comic strip embedded in a postcard	30
1.4	Wikitravel webpage (http://wikitravel.org/en/South_Africa) on South Africa	36
2.1	The ideational metafunction	44
2.2	The grammar system of Transitivity	47
2.3	The grammar system of clause complex	49
2.4	The grammar system of Mood	52
3.1	Donegal: Glenveagh National Park	77
3.2	Sligo: Tree Tops Townhouse	83
3.3	Carlow: Kilgraney Country House	84
3.4	Map of Ireland	85
3.5	Represented participants in tourist and travel images	86
3.6	Representational structures	87
3.7	Donegal: Glenveagh Castle	88
3.8	Conceptual structures	89
3.9	Donegal: Loch Finn	89
3.10	Cork: Bantry Bay	90
3.11	Clare: Poulnabrone Dolmen	91
3.12	Contact	91
3.13	Dublin: Luttrellstown Castle	92
3.14	Size of frame and social distance	93
3.15	Perspective	94
3.16	Markers of modality	95
3.17	Reality principles	97
3.18	Information value	98
3.19	Salience	98

3.20	Framing	99
4.1	The soundscape	109
4.2	Interaction of voices	112
4.3	Reality principles	115
4.4	Parameters for soundscape assessment	116
5.1	The logo used by the official Maltese tourist board	132
5.2	The Visitjamaica homepage, www.visitjamaica.com	137
5.3	Barthes's framework for intersemiosis in static texts	140
5.4	Equal and independent relative status in visual–verbal intersemiosis	142
5.5	Unequal relative status with image subordinate to text	143
5.6	Relative status in visual–verbal intersemiosis	144
5.7	Logico-semantic relation in visual–verbal semiosis	144
5.8	The logico-semantic relation of locution	145
5.9	The logico-semantic relation of extension	146
5.10	Ranks for film analysis	147
5.11	The structure of the Visit Jamaica website, www.visitjamaica.com	156

Tables

2.1	Context, meaning and grammar in language	43
2.2	Processes in the grammar system of Transitivity	46
2.3	Functions and responses in the grammar system of Mood	50
2.4	Process types in the brochure extract	60
2.5	The systems of Clause complex and Taxis in the brochure extract	64
2.6	Process types in the post	67
2.7	The systems of Clause complex and Taxis in the post	69
3.1	Visual semiosis in the Irish pictures: The ideational metafunctional parameters	100
3.2	Visual semiosis in the Irish pictures: The interpersonal metafunctional parameters	101
3.3	Visual semiosis in the Irish pictures: The textual metafunctional parameters	102
4.1	Ranks scales in writing and speech	104
5.1	Transcription of the Air New Zealand safety video: Image track	150
5.2	Transcription of the Air New Zealand safety video: Sound track	152

Acknowledgements

I wish to thank all the people who have supported this work in various ways. In particular, I am deeply indebted to:

- Peter Legon and Martyn Ford of Lee Gone Publications, for allowing me to publish their postcards in Figures 1.3, 5.4, 5.5, 5.7, 5.8 (copyright LGP).
- Derek Cullen, of the Photography and Multimedia Department of Discover Ireland, for sending and allowing me to publish Figures 3.1, 3.2, 3.3, 3.4, 3.7, 3.8, 3.9, 3.10, 3.13 (copyright Fáilte Ireland).
- Gobind C. Bhuyan, Director of Indiatourism Milan, for sending the 'Incredible India' radio commercial (copyright Indiatourism).
- Malta Tourism Authority for allowing me to reproduce their official logo in Figure 5.1 (copyright MTA).
- Jamaica Tourism Board, for permission to publish their website homepage in Figure 5.2 and the website structure in Figure 5.11 (copyright JTB).
- Air New Zealand, for providing information on the ANZ safety video and allowing me to publish screen shots in Table 5.1.

Special thanks to Prof. Manuela Caterina Moroni (University of Trento, Italy) for the accurate and precious phonetic transcription of the radio text in Chapter 4, and to musician, composer and music teacher Dr Marco Benzi, of the Conservatorio di Bolzano (Italy), for providing valuable insights for the understanding of music dynamics in the 'Incredible India' commercial. I am also grateful to Paolo Chistè, Claudio del Frari and Anna Pallaver (University of Trento) for the multimedia support. Finally, I wish to thank Miechelle van Kampen for the language revision of the volume. Any inaccuracies are my own.

Introduction: Tourism and Travel

'The herd of reëchoing tourists had departed and most of the solemn places had relapsed into solemnity' (James, [1881] 1998: 319). Henry James's *The Portrait of a Lady* thus narrates the scene in Saint Peter's, when the protagonist, Isabel Archer, is left alone with her thoughts and the possibility to liberate a 'repressed ecstasy of contemplation'. The quotation expresses an explicit denigration of noisy groups of tourists unable to understand, appreciate and respect art.

The first authoritative traces of such an anti-tourist position are clearly visible from the 18th century, in the literary works of George Gordon Byron and William Wordsworth, who lamented the diffusion of travel practice. In a 1799 poem entitled 'The Brothers', Wordsworth gave voice to his disgust: 'These tourists, heaven preserve us!' Over the following decades, novels by Frances Trollope, Charles Dickens, Henry James and E.M. Forster reinforced and perpetuated this view (Buzard, 1993; Fussel, 1987) and represented 'the tourist' as a grotesque figure, living predictable 'touristic' experiences in commodified 'tourist' areas perceived through simplistic 'touristic' viewpoints (Buzard, 1993: 4). Through animal-related metaphorical images, tourists have been traditionally depicted as moving in 'droves', 'herds', 'swarms' or 'flocks' (Culler, 1989: 153), as the above quotation from James testifies.

Consistently, the tourist type has been shaped through systematic resort to 'touristic' literature (Boorstin, [1987] 1992). Forster's ironic narrator of *A Room with a View* thus observed Lucy Honeychurch's attachment to the Baedeker travel guide:

> Lucy [...] was reduced to literature. Taking up Baedeker's *Handbook to Northern Italy*, she committed to memory the most important dates of Florentine History. For she was determined to enjoy herself on the morrow. (Forster, [1908] 1995: 5)

Luckily, brave Miss Lavish is strongly committed to 'saving' the young woman from the highly popular German guide, for decades recognised as the unmistakable symbol of tourism:

> Tut, tut! Miss Lucy! I hope we shall soon emancipate you from Baedeker. He does but touch the surface of things. As to the true Italy – he does not even dream of it. The true Italy is only to be found by patient observation. (Forster, [1908] 1995: 8)

Tourist identity has thus been strictly connected to the choice of 'touristic' text genres and to 'touristic' modalities of text consumption.

Far from vanishing or being confined to literary pages, such feelings and attitudes are extremely common in contemporary society. In everyday formal and informal interactions, the lexemes 'tourist' and 'tourism' often carry negative connotations of superficiality and passivity. Anti-tourism positions are socially pervasive but are often psychologically curious, if not paradoxical. They are frequently taken in tourism discourse and even among tourists themselves (Culler, 1989; Francesconi, 2007, 2012). MacCannell asserts that 'tourists dislike tourists' ([1976] 1989: 9). Tourists look for the less touristic festival, search for secret corners and crave off-the-beaten-track itineraries. In Culler's terms, 'wanting to be less touristy than other tourists is part of being a tourist' (1989: 156, 158), as if an anti-tourism standpoint would exorcise the tourist identity, yet permit one to continue being a tourist.

Unfolding a dichotomic discourse, tourism condemnation goes hand in hand with travel celebration (Buzard, 1993; Fussel, 1987). Evelyn Waugh (1930: 44) observed that: 'Every Englishman abroad, until it is proved to be the contrary, likes to consider himself a traveller and not a tourist'. Accordingly, 'travel' is a responsible, sustainable, fulfilling activity practised by independent, curious and refined human beings moved by an authentic interest and passion for what is remote, ancient and authentic. Normally associated with a lost Golden Age, with distant lands and with a social elite, this practice is enhanced through connotations of superiority, heroism and intelligence (Turner & Ash, 1976).

Clearly, the anti-tourism standpoint configures more an ideological assumption than an ethical position. In tourism communication, the use of terms like 'tourist' or 'traveller' is not grounded on denotative meaning but on connotation. The semantic border between a tourist and a traveller is indeed more opaque than it appears and the attempt to find a clear distinction proves challenging. By considering sender profile, a 'tourism' text could be related to a tour operator as author and a 'travel text' to a holidaymaker as author. The distinction may rely on holiday type: a mass experience could be termed 'tourism', while an individual experience 'travel'. Third, communication function could be taken into account: while 'tourism' texts might be those illocutionary promotional items produced by the tourism industry in order to sell packages, 'travel' texts would refer to books, reports and diaries that narrate a holiday experience with an aesthetic purpose. Yet, numerous genres such as official and organisational documents or alternative and innovative printed or digital informative instances would not fit these labels and seem more in-between texts.

A further problem regards where these labels originate and whether they are self-attached. In this case, the connotational potential is extreme. The preference for one term or the other indicates more how the text codifier wants to position the text itself than what its content and style actually are, the same being valid for travellers. Generally, holidaymakers want to be perceived and defined as 'travellers' and all texts linguistically position themselves as 'travel' texts. Consistently, tourism texts address their readers as 'visitors', thus enacting an effective ego-enhancing strategy (Dann, 1996a). In turn, holidaymakers define other holidaymakers as 'tourists' and travel texts define similar texts as 'tourist' publications. The anti-tourism discourse thus traces a semiotic circuit that projects and perpetuates stereotyped visions of identity and otherness (Francesconi, 2007, 2012).

In this context, this work invites a less biased observation of contemporary tourism textuality, as expressing an important part of our life and society. It does not avoid denying the importance of going on holiday with a respectful attitude towards the host population and environment. To the contrary, it claims that superficial and simplistic labels hide and legitimise non-ethical behaviour (Hall, 2000). Epistemically, this blurred travel–tourism dichotomy fits into the postmodern horizon (Jameson, 1991), with an emphasis on anti-hierarchical de-differentiation between what is artistic production and what is commercial, between what is high culture and what is low culture, between what is elitarian and what is popular (Urry, 2002: 77). As for terminology, the present volume tries to avoid using the abused tourism–travel distinction and adopts both lexemes, when possible. One term is used when the category is less ambiguous, as in the case of the overtly promotional tourism brochure, albeit an opaque, open and questionable lexical border is acknowledged.

Tourism/Travel and Texts

The aim of this volume is to examine linguistic, textual and discursive dynamics enacted by tourism and travel texts. The focus is on the tourism and travel domain because tourism pervades contemporary society. This is a reflection of the impressive dimensions and growth of the tourism industry.

In 1950, the number of international tourist arrivals was 25 million; in 2007 it was just under 900 million and by the year 2020 arrivals are expected to reach over 1.56 billion (World Tourism Organization, http://www2.unwto.org). Europe is projected to be the top receiving area, followed by East Asia, the Pacific, the Americas, Africa, the Middle East and South Asia. Undeniably, tourism has become a global phenomenon (Meethan, 2001; Wahab & Cooper, 2001). Nonetheless, not all human beings are tourists and the right to tourism affirmed by the 1948 Declaration of Human Rights is far from guaranteed. Tourism is global because it carries implications for everyone, as a problematic process, reflecting the multifold complexities and tensions of our society (Cohen, 2004; Jamal & Robinson, 2009: 3; Urry, 1995; Urry & Rojek, 1997). We regularly experience tourist encounters, we systematically benefit from tourist facilities, we actively participate in a tourist economy and we constantly consume tourist signs (Francesconi, 2012).

Like actual tourist practices, tourist textual practices and genres are socially pervasive and ubiquitous, and have global reach and impact (Thurlow & Jaworski, 2010: 235). We encounter tourism and travel texts in our everyday life: while reading the newspaper (printed or digital), with its destination advertisements, while driving to work and looking at posters and billboards, while checking our inbox with emails from tour operators or travel booking engines, while chatting with friends, relatives or colleagues with travel anecdotes. On a broader scale, literary travel narratives, radio programmes and digital tourist pictures have a global circulation (Dann, 2012a, 2012b). From here derives the ideological potential travel and tourism texts have to influence and orient perceptions, ideas, values and actions (Mangiapane, 2010; Thurlow & Jaworski, 2010).

Acknowledging this discursive scenario, tourism texts cannot be snobbishly condemned as 'superficial' (Culler, 1989), much as tourism cannot be neglected as a 'frivolous, recreational activity' (Thurlow & Jaworski, 2010: 7), but deserve critical attention and scientific investigation. In the insightful essay 'The semiotics of tourism', Culler (1989: 159) has explained how tourism texts 'mark' a tourist attraction and function as signs to the signified: 'by giving information about it, representing it, making it recognizable'. In the form of brochures, signs, leaflets and postcards, 'the marker represents a sight to the tourist', expressing the semiotic structure of tourist attractions. Consequently, tourism is to be seen as a 'semiotically embedded service' (Thurlow & Jaworski, 2010: 7) and tourism text instances will be addressed in this volume as complex crucial sign systems representing and making sense of the world.

Text configuration patterns are deeply rooted in the socio-historical age in which they are produced and consumed, and of which they provide valid insights. Dating back to the 2nd century AD, Pausanias' 10-volume *Guide to Greece* offered a historiographic and erudite description of the Hellenic territory. During the Middle Ages, the *mirabilia* travel publications were strictly related to the pilgrimage routes to Rome or other European sanctuaries. They were meant to accompany the holy itinerary and, although focused on spiritual aspects, also advised the pilgrim which accommodation or eating options to choose or to avoid. The 18th-century travel book reflected the extended experience of the Grand Tour, as well as the educated, refined, literary taste of the aristocratic Grand Tourist. Starting from the second half of the 19th century, the travel guide marked the increased accessibility of travel and the need for handy, affordable travel help. Later, the ubiquitous glossy brochure signalled the establishment of a global tourist industry (Fodde & van den Abbeele, 2012; Leed, 1991). Albeit totally different in terms of purpose, style and content, all the mentioned texts share the printed medium as a common denominator.

Far from representing fixed, static and absolute entities, tourism texts are dynamic and constantly subject to innovation (Calvi, 2010). Texts ceaselessly proliferate, differentiate and interact, and thereby engender hybrid forms (Bhatia, 1993, 2004, 2010). Alongside traditional genres like the guidebook, brochure or postcard, forms like Wikitravel, the travel weblog and the app have more recently found their way into tourism communication. Contemporary tourism interaction is thus marked by the establishment of the digital medium and by its revolutionary impact on modes and forms of tourism and travel exchanges (Dann, 2007). Communication has become global, instant, informal, up to date and democratic. In fact, besides being systematically adopted by institutions, boards, operators, hotels and agencies (i.e. the business-to-client, B2C, sector), the internet has also enabled consumer-to-consumer (C2C) exchanges, as in the case of blogs (Fodde & van den Abbeele, 2012). In turn, digital communication has influenced traditional printed texts, with many brochures, guides and catalogues 'migrating' to the web to reduce printing costs and reach a wider audience.

Migration to the web is not the only aspect characterising contemporary tourism communication. Ranging from literary works to informative or promotional genres, all tourism and travel texts are becoming increasingly multimodal (Francesconi, 2012). Inscribing graphic, iconic and photographic items into the verbal texts, literary texts explore and experiment with new expressive solutions and subvert traditional generic conventions. The layout of travel guides is progressively innovative: they become more visual, fragment the text into a plurality of sections, divide the page into numerous clusters, adopt cross-referencing inside the page and between pages (Francesconi, 2012). Online or printed travel diaries and reportage are complemented by pictures, grids and maps in order better to illustrate what has been visited and could be visited by other travellers. Multimodality fulfils a plurality of semiotic, cognitive and emotional functions: it captures the readers' attention and engenders a positive mood and a pleasant psychological attitude; it assists concentration, performs emphasis and thus leaves a lasting mnestic trace.

Of utmost importance for all types of communication, these processes achieve more relevance for destination promotion, as promotional texts heavily rely on graphic solutions, visuals and sound effects in order to enhance destination branding (Ashworth & Goodall, 2012a, 2012b). The reason may be found in the promoted object – the travel and holiday experience – being a non-material commodity (Santulli, 2007: 45). While traditional advertising promotes *objects* to be bought, which can be inspected for purchase beforehand, a holiday cannot be seen before the actual tourist experience (Maci, 2007: 42). It is thus the main task of destination promotion to textually re-present the place (Francesconi, 2007: 44; Hall, 1997). Verbal, visual and audio effects are subtly combined in order to offer a multisensorial experience and shape an illusion of reality and reality fruition (Held, 2004: 260), further enhanced through hypertextual navigation. As modalities of text consumption in multimodal and hypertextual texts are more open (the recipient can skim the text, zoom the image, rewind the video or randomly surf the website), potential visitors can feel as if they can explore the (absent) destination and 'live the holiday' before leaving home (Francesconi, 2011c; Maci, 2007).

Acknowledging multimodality as a pivotal source of expression and semiosis in tourism discourse, the present volume invites the use of tools of multimodal analysis for the investigation of authentic domain-specific instances. Multimodal analysis has been developed from systemic functional linguistics (SFL), based on M.A.K. Halliday's perspective on language as doing things and as making meaning, both occurring in specific sociocultural contexts and being contextually determined (Halliday, 1978). Halliday explored three distinct ways in which language usage creates meaning: the ideational, related to the expression of content; the interpersonal, related to the sender–addressee interaction; and textual metafunction, related to internal and external textual cohesion. Drawing on SFL's distinction between writing and speech, multimodal analysis has extended this metafunctional framework both to visual and aural semiotic systems (including pictures, music and sounds) and to their modes and forms of interplay. Throughout the chapters, multimodal analysis will be applied to a range of tourism and travel text instances, such as pictures, logos, brochures, blogs, radio programmes and commercials, webpages, wikis, videos and postcards.

To sum up, this volume posits the following claims regarding the contemporary tourism and travel text scenario:

- the distinction between traveller and tourist is biased;
- the distinction between tourism textuality and travel literature is too simplistic;
- the identity of tourism and travel texts is fluid and hybrid;
- multimodality has proved crucial in the processes of change and innovation;
- multimodal analysis is feasible for tourism text examination.

Background Literature

This work aims to further integrate the disciplines of applied linguistics and English for specific purposes (ESP), from which it derives, into the multidisciplinary network of tourism studies. ESP is relevant to the tourism and travel domain as a specific context in which language is used and according to which communication strategies are enacted (Gotti, 2003, 2005, 2006). Psychological, sociocultural, economic and professional situational variables play a substantial role for language, textual and discursive configurations and need to be properly addressed.

As such, ESP is consistent with the domain of inquiry of tourism studies. Traditionally, tourism studies have been influenced by positivist and post-positivist paradigms, with a focus on economic aspects and based on quantitative research methods (Jennings, 2009: 684). Over time, social sciences and environmental sciences have approached tourism, redefining their object of analysis as complex, multifold and plural. The emergence in the 1980s of different paradigms, such as pragmatism, critical theory, constructivism and postmodernism, has implied the inclusion of qualitative and mixed methodologies. The ongoing discussion is characterised by multidisciplinarity and by a plurality of methods, approaches and strategies reflecting the heterogeneity of the object of study itself. A wider range of disciplines, such as anthropology, sociology, psychology, communication studies, media studies and linguistics, are addressing market segments like spa tourism, sex tourism, literary tourism and heritage tourism, and specific geographical areas, for instance tourism in Asia, China, the Middle East or South America.

The present scenario is characterised by what Urry (2002: 142) calls 'tourism reflexivity', which can be perceived through the observation of 'the institutionalisation of tourism studies', with the birth of departments, the organisation of conferences and the publication of a number of monographs, textbooks and journals. Among the most important journals on the topic are *Annals of Tourism Research: A Social Sciences Journal*, published by Elsevier and edited by John Tribe, the *Journal of Tourism and Cultural Change*, published by Routledge and edited by Mike Robinson and Alison Phipps, the *Journal of Travel Research*, published by Sage and edited by Richard R. Perdue, and *Tourist Studies: An International Journal*, published by Sage and edited by Tim Edensor and Adrian Franklin. All these publications are multidisciplinary in nature. The tourism centres and departments hosted by numerous universities worldwide are also multidisciplinary. Among research centres on tourism studies are the International Centre for Tourism and Hospitality Research at Bournemouth University (UK), the International Tourism Research Institute at the University of South Carolina (USA) and the Centre for Tourism and Services Research at Victoria University (Australia).

Tourism reflexivity is exemplified in this volume itself, being part of the Tourism and Cultural Change series published by Channel View Publications and edited by Mike Robinson and Alison Phipps. Previous works in the series have addressed other tourism texts, like *Official Tourism Websites: A Discourse Analysis Perspective* (2010) by Richard Hallett and Judith Kaplan-Weinger. In order to examine the official websites of Santiago de Compostela, Latvia, Estonia and New Orleans, the authors interwove tools from critical discourse analysis, multimodal discourse analysis and visual semiotic analysis.

This volume is the synthesis of 10 years of academic research and teaching in the field of tourism and travel texts. Some of the results of this experience have been disseminated nationally and internationally through papers, essays, articles, a co-edited book (Palusci & Francesconi, 2006) and two monographs (2007, 2012). Previously published observations and results substantially influence the present work; in particular, Chapter 1 heavily relies on the first chapter of *Generic Integrity and Innovation in Tourism Texts in English* (Francesconi, 2012). In all works, a range of tourism text genres like brochures, leaflets, videos, online diaries, guides, postcards and souvenirs have been examined, insofar as they frame and communicate a tourist site as sight. What has been particularly improved throughout the years is, on the one hand, an approach to tourism texts as expressing specific genres and, on the other hand, a methodological approach suitable for such instances. This second aspect is the focus of the present volume.

Outline of the Book

After introducing the multiple connections between tourism and texts within the dynamics of the tourist discourse system, the volume devotes Chapter 1 to domain-specific text genres. An open and fluid definition of 'genre' is acknowledged, with particular attention to processes of generic innovation and hybridisation, mainly, albeit not exclusively, derived from the affirmation of the digital medium. The ever-expanding variety of tourism and travel texts is described and mapped through the various parameters of actors, medium, stage of trip, mode, communication function, genre value and degree of language specialisation (lexico-grammar).

The next three chapters are concerned with methodology and consider verbal, visual and audio systems. Chapter 2 illustrates Halliday's SFL, assuming that linguistic forms are determined by their communication function and that they project meaning accordingly. The ideational, interpersonal and textual metafunctions are observed within a tourist brochure and an online travel diary.

The metafunctional approach to semiosis is then developed in Chapters 3 and 4, with specific grids for the observation of the visual and audio systems. Verbal language is, in fact, substantiated in writing and speech, which rely, respectively, on visual and aural semiotic systems. The first includes images, whereas the second concerns music and sound effects. Chapter 3 thus presents the grammar of visual design outlined by Kress and van Leeuwen (2006) for the analysis of tourist images promoting Ireland, while Chapter 4 is devoted to correspondent tools for audio analysis developed by van Leeuwen (1999) for voice, music and sound effects in a radio programme on England and a radio commercial promoting India.

Chapter 5 outlines the concept of multimodal intersemiosis and addresses semiotic systems as co-existing and interacting. First, it examines printed static texts, which realise meaning through the simultaneous co-deployment of visual and verbal items, thus following the logic of space. Second, it explores dynamic texts, which unfold in time and signify through sequential images. Third, it investigates hypertextual artefacts, which combine both logics and invite multiple, multidirectional reading paths.

User-friendly features have been systematically adopted for this volume. A glossary of key-words is included at the end of the volume and terms listed and defined are given in bold when used for the first time. A genre-based bibliography lists basic and up-to-date critical tools for the analysis of each text genre.

The English Language and Tourism

As seen in the outline of the volume's structure, a plurality of authentic tourism and travel texts from the English-speaking world are considered, ranging from England to Malta, through Canada and New Zealand, India and Ireland, to Jamaica and South Africa. Not surprisingly, this work results from academic research and teaching in a course on ESP, a flourishing field in English departments and applied linguistics. The role of the English language is pivotal to the present discussion, not only for academic but also for historical, sociocultural and economic reasons.

The social and global pervasiveness of English in the tourism sector is also due to historical, political and economic reasons. Far from being a homogeneous and de-differentiated code, it is plural and fluid, resulting from the historical process of language contact between the pre-existing local, national language and the language of colonisation. Expressing a linguistic and cultural identity, diatopic varieties like Scottish English, Canadian English or Maltese English therefore manifest traits of distinction on the levels of phonetics, lexis, morphology and syntax (Kachru, 1985; McArthur, 1998). More visible in spoken and informal situations, these are not particularly evident in English for tourism – both as ESP and as promotional code – since a more standard variety is preferred.

In this status of common code, English is used as a *lingua franca* for tourism. As such, international official documents and regulations are written in English, and travel instructions and procedures are given and processed in English. In addition, numerous tourism- and travel-related speech acts like hotel check-in and conversations among international travellers occur in English, the code being adopted as a language of opportunity, enabling language users of different backgrounds to communicate for professional, recreational and institutional purposes (Crystal, 2003; Maci, 2010). In order to be accessible and understandable to a plurilingual audience, English for tourism is simplified, in terms of lexical range and morpho-syntax complexity (Crystal, 2003).

Tourism promotion worldwide is also generally in English, both for reasons of opportunity – the already mentioned global reach it allows – and for its connotative richness. Regarding this second point, English has often been defined as a language of 'prestige', which associates products or services with values of 'cosmopolitanism', 'dynamism' and 'glamour'. For this reason, languages constantly borrow English terminology even if they do not need to (Pinnavaia, 2001). Albeit important in tourism and travel texts, this connotative aspect is not taken into consideration in the present volume but needs to be acknowledged, being central to numerous linguistic studies addressing English word-formation strategies and code-switching procedures in languages other than English.

Written in English on English texts, this volume thus observes the interweaving of tourism and travel discourses, multimodal configurations and the English language code as interweaving ideologically driven semiotic systems.

1 Genre Analysis

Genre and Generic Integrity

This chapter addresses tourism discourse through the notion of genre and through genre analysis. After briefly mentioning the development of the concept of genre throughout the decades, an open, fluid definition is acknowledged, with a focus on processes of generic **innovation** and **hybridisation**. Attention is paid to tourism texts and different classification models are illustrated, with varying emphasis on actors (sender, addressee), medium, stage of trip, mode, communication function, genre value and degree of language specialisation (lexico-grammar). The last section examines Wikitravel as exemplifying travel text innovation.

Tourism and travel textuality and language are substantially affected by the situational context they inhabit. Following Gotti (2006: 19), the language of tourism is taken as 'specialised discourse'. Frequently used and abused terms and formulae like 'restricted language', 'special language', 'codes' and 'microlanguage' seem inappropriate, as they suggest a relation of subordination to general language. Rather than a mere terminological issue, this choice acknowledges a more complex view of tourism and the language use it implies and is being implied by (Gotti, 2003, 2005, 2006). Identifying English for tourism as 'specialised discourse' foregrounds that it 'possesses all the lexical, phonetic, morphosyntactic and textual resources of general language' (Gotti, 2006: 19). Yet, as Graham Dann asserts, 'tourism has a discourse of its own' (Dann, 1996a: 2).

Discourse has been defined as 'language use in institutional, professional or more general social contexts' (Bhatia, 2004: 3). Going beyond linguistic forms *per se*, 'discourse' is language as that is shaped by and is shaping society and regulating individuals' interaction within that society. Accordingly, it is as social practice that discourse makes meaning (Jaworski & Coupland,

1999: 3). Specifically, the critical debate on discourse has traditionally unveiled the ideological component of discursive practices (Mills, 1997; Said, 1978). In his influential work *The Archaeology of Knowledge*, Foucault ([1969] 2002) defines discourse as expressing and negotiating ideologically rooted social viewpoints and value systems. In this light, it would be used as a means of control, manipulation and orientation of recipients' mindsets and behaviour. It is the task of discourse analysis to unveil ideologically based assumptions and communication strategies.

Discourse analysis can be variously conducted following a multiperspective model, considering text, genre, professional practice or social practice. Among these, **genre** is increasingly being assigned a substantial role in explorations of discourse and it is used here to understand tourism and travel specialised discourse. Throughout the volume attention will be paid to how discourse instantiates generic patterns into authentic texts such as websites, brochures, online diaries, postcards or videos.

Far from being unquestioned and unquestionable, the notion of genre has undergone systematic (re)conceptualisation throughout the centuries and is still an open concept. Ancient, medieval, renaissance, modern and contemporary models differently defined and applied generic forms as classification systems (Ragonese, 2010: 5). Derived from the Latin *genus*, genre was prominently used in classical philosophy. Drawing on Aristotle's *Rhetorics* and the recognition of the three official discourse practices – deliberative, forensic and epideictic (see e.g. Jonathan, 1984) – various positions grounded genre theories on predictable structural and stylistic constraints. In a literary context, Dante Alighieri illustrated the classic styles of tragedy, comedy and elegy in his *De vulgari eloquentia* ([1302–05], 1996). More recently, in the 20th-century debate, Northrop Frye (1957) identified in certain universal genres the key to organising the whole literary corpus. These positions have nourished a view of generic **integrity** (Bhatia, 2004), which relies on conventionalised and standardised stable patterns instantiating genre configurations in recurrent textual situations.

Over the centuries, this classification method has not been exempt from criticism. Anti-prescriptive and anti-regulatory positions towards genre, born in the aesthetic and cultural context of Romanticism, were maintained in the last century by intellectuals like Croce and Blanchot (see Ragonese, 2010: 5). These stressed the rigid and deterministic nature of generic classifications, ultimately perceived as undermining the comprehension of a text in its literary uniqueness.

However, it was Todorov ([1978, 1990) who underlined the importance of addressing genre as a 'negative imperative', a theoretical model that is meaningful only when and if displaced and deconstructed in diverse, specific and irreducible textual practices. As such, genre analysis is not to be taken as prescriptive but as descriptive (Chandler, 1997: 1) and it should observe the extent to which a text participates in a genre group, and questions, redefines and subverts it at the same time. Following this open and fluid interpretation of genre, Bakhtin (1986) proposed the generic notion of 'heteroglossia', suggesting that texts use a plurality of juxtaposed and interactive voices, thereby confirming the impossibility of rigid generic taxonomies.

In recent decades, the debate on genre has expanded enormously and incorporated varying positions. As reported mainly by Halliday (1978) and Kress (2003, 2010), the Sydney school has been developing a notion of genre as deriving from a systemic functional view of language (see Chapter 2), which could be fruitfully applied to educational contexts. The New Rhetoric School, including Bateman and Miller, emphasises social practice as shaping genres, with a focus on textual and contextual dynamics. Within the domain of ESP in applied linguistics, scholars like Bhatia (1993, 2002, 2004, 2010) and Swales (1990) have been addressing genre as a communicative event, occurring within a particular discourse community and following a specific communicative purpose or function.

Determining both generic content and form, the communication function is and has to be recognised by the expert members of the 'discourse community', that is, a socio-rhetorical group (Swales, 1990: 24). As Bhatia himself states (2004: 113), a communication function is not to be considered and treated as a 'definite and objective' criterion but as a flexible and dynamic one. Moreover, it is never isolated but needs to be recognised as composite and stratified (Martin, 1992; Swales, 1990). For instance, the functionally stratified title of a tourist publication should, at the same time, introduce a text, foreground the main theme and attract and capture attention. Yet, title stylistic and linguistic articulation is also flexible, as variously affected by text genre, target, medium, topic and position on the page or screen. Both aspects make the analytical process challenging.

Identifying communication purpose as the primary determinant of genre membership, Bhatia thus maintains that genre:

> essentially refers to language use in a conventionalized communicative setting in order to give expression to a specific set of communicative goals of a disciplinary or social institution, which give rise to stable structural forms by imposing constraints on the use of lexico-grammatical as well as discoursal resources. (Bhatia, 2004: 23)

Accordingly, the still crucial concept of generic integrity refers to a genre's standardised nature, to its recognisable structural and stable identity

(Bhatia, 2004: 113), which can be identified both by text-internal and text-external features. The former indicate textual, intertextual and contextual elements, while the latter imply discursive practices and procedures as well as disciplinary culture (Maci, 2010: 42). For example, the encoding of a letter of complaint regarding a holiday requires specific textual rules to be followed, such as the codification and placement of the sender's address, date, recipient's address, salutation, subject, body, greeting and enclosure. These factors may vary if the faster and cheaper genre of email is chosen, peculiarities of which are contextually determined.

Clearly, language analysts heavily rely on generic constraints to assess **texts**. However, a genre-based view of discourse addresses regularities in linguistic and stylistic behaviour not *per se* but as they are affected by the purpose of the communication. In Bhatia's terms, such features are defined in terms of 'typification of rhetorical action, regularities of staged, goal-oriented social processes, and consistency of communicative purposes' (Bhatia, 2004: 22). Three main levels of investigation can thus be identified (Bhatia, 1993):

- a structural level, aimed at the identification of a set of rhetorical moves;
- a textual level, concerned with the genre-specific use of linguistic features;
- a lexico-grammar level, focused on specific and recurring linguistic features.

Like the units in the previously mentioned letter of complaint, **moves** are textual segments fulfilling a specific function or 'functional stages occurring in a particular sequence' (Eggins, 2011: 58). This last concept of sequentiality implies the existence of a step-by-step text organisation. Travel reportage, for instance, shows a generic structure composed of title, subtitle, introduction, body text and conclusion, in this order. Each move follows distinct formal conventions. The title, for example, adopts nominalisation, wordplay and key-words to capture readers' attention and briefly refer to text content. At the same time, the article body text makes use of lexico-grammar strategies proper of the language of tourism, like superlative forms of adjectives, abundant and laudatory lexis and anaphoric syntactic structures (Belenguer, 2002; Berger, 2004; Canals & Liverani, 2010). Avoiding a distinction between right and wrong solutions, such a functional view of genre enables assessment of how and why some texts are appropriate while others are not. Appropriacy is seen in terms of the successful realisation of given communication functions in a given context (Eggins, 2011: 70).

In this three-level analysis, tourism text description enables the identification of aspects of similarity and difference between various genre instances.

It means that a particular text is similar to, reminiscent of, other texts circulating in their culture (Eggins, 2011: 55). In fact, genres are not isolated but are strictly interconnected, a concept exemplified by Bhatia through the well-known metaphor of the galaxy, according to which genres exist in **colonies**, like stars exist in galaxies, and colonies, like galaxies, interact with other generic star systems (Bhatia, 2002). Colonies – for example, promotional genres, introductory genres, academic genres – include similar genres with common features used within different discourse communities (Calvi, 2010: 15). Generic identity is thus negotiated within the mutual relations inherent in the colony. The following section outlines genre maps and colonies traced by scholars who have investigated tourism texts.

Genre Maps and Colonies

The critical debate on tourism and travel texts is increasingly exploiting and further developing conceptualisations and tools deriving from the field of genre studies (Bondi, 1999; Calvi, 2010; Francesconi, 2012; Maci, 2010). Yet, the ceaseless proliferation and innovation in specialised genre instances imposes a more complex and composite frame of reference. Notably, Calvi's multifunctional and multidimensional framework is based on the categories of genre families, macro-genres, genres and sub-genres, as follows (Calvi, 2010: 16):

- Genre **families** comprehend texts in a given socio-professional context with a similar communication purpose. The main genre families in tourism discourse are editorial (travel books, travel guides, travel and tourist magazines), institutional (official leaflets, brochures, websites, advertisements), commercial (hotel brochures, leaflets, advertisements, travel agent websites), organisational (tickets, bookings, cards, invoices), legal (regulations, norms), scientific and academic (critical volumes, articles, essays) and informal (travel blogs, travel chats).
- Defined by common communication purpose and medium, channel and sender, **macro-genres** include different genres, textual typologies and styles. Examples of tourist macro-genres are the brochure, the travel magazine, the travel catalogue, the webpage and the tourist guide, the latter including genres like itineraries, practical guides, maps and pictures.
- Either autonomous or embedded in macro-genres, **genres** are determined by communication and pragmatic function, formal distinctiveness and common language features. Among the wide range of tourist text genres are the practical guide, the descriptive guide, the itinerary, the travel

programme, the travel report and the advertisement. Other genres are tickets, bookings, contracts, cards, tourist regulations, travel reports, forums and travel blogs.
- **Sub-genres** are characterised on a thematic level. For instance, art, history, crafts, food and drink, nature, sport, events and entertainment are topics covered by most tourist texts.

According to Calvi and drawing on Bhatia's grid for the description of genre instances, the grid shown in Figure 1.1 describes the travel magazine as text macro-genre. Exemplified by recognisable titles such as *National Geographic Traveler Magazine*, *Lonely Planet Magazine*, *Afar Travel Magazine* and *Condè Nast Traveler*, the travel magazine can easily be described as part of the editorial family issued by a publishing house. It is, then, a macro-genre, identified as distinct in its printed medium (even though a growing number of magazines are also digitally available) and in its predominantly informative function. A plural and composite text, it includes genres like travel reports, destination advertisements and itineraries, which are distinctive in terms of form and language. More specifically, the genre of a report itself can be further described in terms of its thematic profile, since it can variously focus on geography, society, ethnography, nature, history and arts, sports or the economy, among others (Belenguer, 2002; Canals & Liverani, 2010).

A second example of generic description, illustrated in Figure 1.2, is given for the present volume. This text is part of the scientific family, being produced and used within the academic context and for research and educational purposes. It can subsequently be defined by printed medium and by educational function. Not homogeneous in its composition, it is a macro-genre, and it includes a list of contents, a list of figures, an introduction, five chapters, a bibliography and a glossary. Finally, the chapters focus on various topics of tourism and travel discourse, namely genre, verbal language, visual semiosis and so on.

As the considered text genres have revealed, a multifunctional and multidimensional framework encompasses a range of semiotically influential aspects, such as actors, medium, stage of trip, mode, communication function, genre value and lexico-grammar strategies. These shall be henceforth taken into account.

Actors

According to Gotti (2006), attention should first be given to the **actors** or agents involved in the communication system and to the roles and functions they play. In Calvi's framework, this component is particularly

Genre Analysis 17

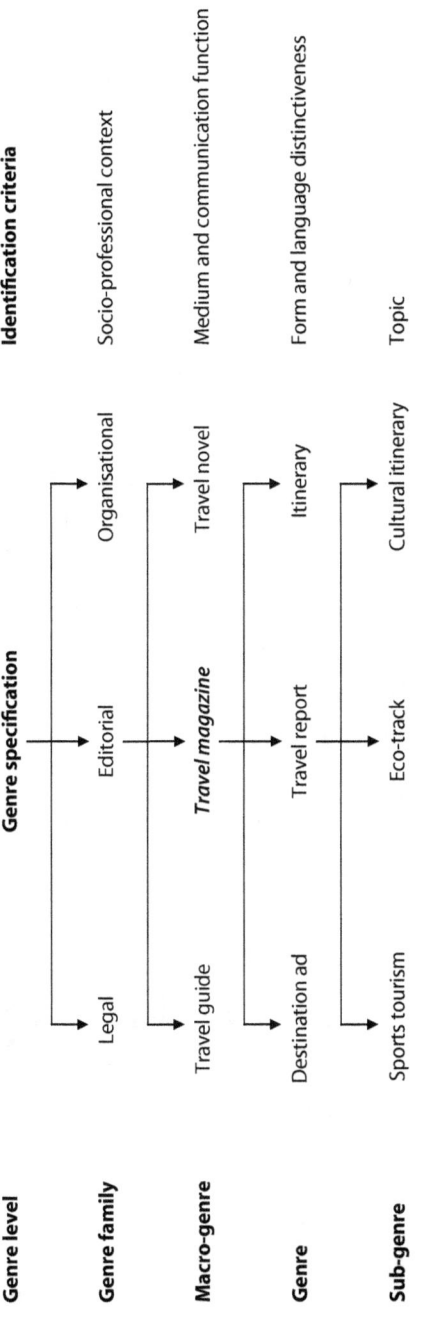

Figure 1.1 Generic description of a travel magazine

18 Reading Tourism Texts

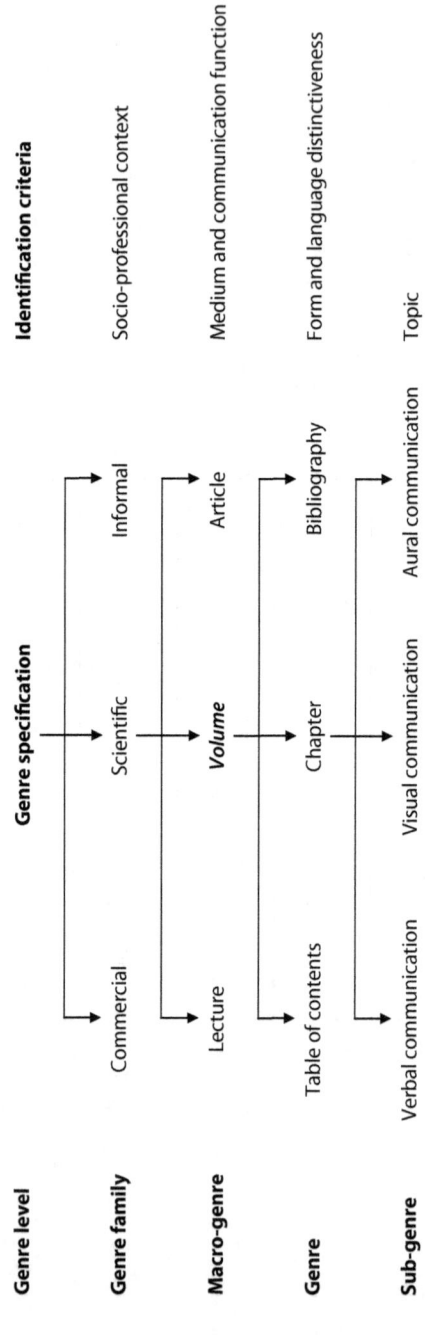

Figure 1.2 Generic description of an academic volume

relevant in the category of the family of genres, which relies on the message sender's profile. Gotti (2006: 20) claims that the language of tourism has a 'multi-dimensional nature' meaning that communication can variously occur between:

- specialists;
- specialists and non-specialists, in an educational context;
- specialists and a wider audience.

In the first case, formal tourist documents are produced, such as reports or projects. The second case includes textbooks, essays and manuals used to explain concepts and terms pertaining to the tourism domain. Exemplary texts for the third group are the reports published in travel magazines that I have already mentioned.

All three dimensions fit into what Calvi (2010) terms 'formal tourist texts': codified by tourist operators, they may be addressed to specialists or non-specialists in the tourism and travel domain. Formal texts can then be variously produced by institutional boards (regional, national and international), editorial (specialised or non-specialised publishing houses), academic institutions (research centres on tourism studies) or commercial institutions (tour operators). Notably, the substantial involvement of institutional bodies, both local and national, in tourism promotion places this communication domain within the wide range of promotional situations and testifies to the crucial role tourism is playing in regional, national and international business markets (WTO website and see Introduction).

Gotti's framework does not include a fourth level, whereby a mutual dialogue among non-specialists can occur (Calvi's 'informal' communication). This comprehends chats, word-of-mouth and blogs, and makes systematic use of general language, albeit with some specialised vocabulary pertaining to the tourism domain. However, Calvi (2010) predominantly locates informal texts in virtual spaces like Flickr, Pinterest, YouTube, Twitter, Facebook and TravelPod, where destination pictures, videos, itineraries, maps and travelogues are produced, shared and exchanged between users.

From a sociological viewpoint, the shift from formal to informal levels of tourism communication based on actors and their roles foregrounds what Dann has mapped as the systematic 'transition from monologue to more open forms of communication' (2012b: 62). Traditionally, he argues, tourist messages have been delivered following a top-down direction from sender to addressee, without any significant response or feedback. Among other genres, the brochure clearly exemplifies monological communication, being univocally delivered from the tourist industry to prospective tourists with an aim of destination-image formation and destination-choice determination (Francesconi, 2011b). More recently, forms of simultaneous or consecutive dialogue have developed within tourist discourse systems. Not only is a voice given to tourists, but also to the tourees. The latter group represents locals, the people who live in the visited places, who are generally obscured by the media and by the official tourist gaze (Dann, 2007: 17). On numerous occasions, tourist communication is now in fact a three-way process, configuring a trialogic interaction between actors. In such a case, real or digital situations are created in order to encourage an exchange of opinions, ideas, complaints and requests, as in 'meet the people' events, or co-presence and collaboration, as in the case of volunteer tourism.

However, Dann observes that the development from monologue to trialogue is not linear and unquestionable. Hence, highly monological forms of tourist communication tend to persist, and still exclude the voice of the Other and the performance of the 'mutual gaze' (Dann, 2007: 17). This is often for time- and money-saving reasons and due to 'vested interests and lack of openness to change' (Dann, 2012b: 68). Alongside its textual value, the 'mutual gaze' between visitors and local people is of pivotal importance for the enactment of ethical forms of hospitality (Derrida, [1997] 2000; Todorov, [1989] 1994). Host–guest power imbalance, in fact, may generate dangerous processes of occupation (if the guest is more powerful than the host) or inclusion (if the host is more powerful than the guest).

Yet, the categories of specialised and non-specialised actors do not identify unique and isolated senders or recipients. In real tourism communication, they often configure composite and stratified concepts. Within the tourism discourse system enacted, for instance, by a traditional printed text, the main actors are, on the one hand, tourist professionals in both the public and private sectors and, on the other, potential or actual tourists. At the most concrete level, the producers are the professionals writing the verbal texts and the photographers taking the pictures. On the next level, layout artists combine the verbal and visual units into more articulated pieces, like sections, pages, articles and advertisements. Moving up another level in the producer hierarchy, expectations and constraints are imposed by the public or private board, institution, operator or agency. A similarly layered situation characterises tourism events like festivals, fairs or performances, as well as digital texts like websites, virtual guides or travel communities (Danesi, 2002), albeit substantially influenced by medium-derived **affordances**.

Medium

In 1967, Marshall McLuhan's words 'the medium is the message' first underscored the pivotal importance of the support of communication in every meaning-making process. **Medium** has also been identified by Calvi as the second parameter of tourism and travel macro-genre identification, after that of sender. As the scholar herself claims (2010: 23), her multifunctional and multidimensional framework is to be considered as partial, since only written texts have been considered, given the scientific focus of the academic project. Printed materials are, in fact, the most traditional forms of tourism and travel communication, including the glossy brochure, the travel guide, the leaflet as well as the academic volume, the travel literary work and the transport ticket.

However, the range of tourism and travel texts is enormously wider, comprehending, for instance, numerous material items like souvenirs, which are massively produced and distributed by the tourism industry to confer materiality to the intangible holiday product. Magic snowballs and miniature monuments, alongside functional items like pens, pencils, mugs and t-shirts, are meant to fix and perpetuate the tourist gaze during the post-trip stage (Canestrini, 2001; Francesconi, 2005; Graburn, 1976; Stewart, 1984). Additionally, travellers can freely collect stones or shells to keep as memorabilia. They may also acquire local art pieces for display in their houses or, again, traditional food and drinks may be kept, shared and offered as souvenirs and gifts.

Besides material items, oral texts play a crucial role in tourism, starting from what Dann has called 'the most significant source of tourism communication', namely word-of-mouth (1996a: 147). Friends, relatives and acquaintances provide solicited or unsolicited information on the trip, based on their satisfying or dissatisfying direct experiences. Having no vested interest, they can then freely and spontaneously promote or demote a destination, express praise or criticism, or, in slightly different terms, through 'word-of-wish' or 'word-of-whinge' (Dann, 2012b: 60). Other aural texts are speeches given at conferences, academic lectures, holiday reservations by phone and radio programmes.

Also worth mentioning are the range of touristic events, comprising fairs, congresses, exhibitions, celebrations, festivals and performances, that, beyond receiving attention from the locals, attract increasing numbers of domestic and foreign visitors. Among many others, the well-known BIT Tourism International Exhibition, hosted yearly in Milan, counted in its 2013 edition 2000 exhibitors from 120 countries, 90,000 visitors, 60,000 trade professionals (44% of whom were travel agents, 15% involved in the accommodation sector and 10% tour operators) and 3500 journalists (see http://bit.fieramilano.it/en).

It is, however, the electronic medium that substantially characterises contemporary tourism and travel communication (Dann, 2007, 2012a,

2012b; Dann & Parrinello, 2007; Maci, 2007). Dann's early prediction that the language of tourism as a phenomenon that would increasingly become 'a language of cyberspace' (1996a: 6) is thus a reality. According to Internet World Stats (www.internetworldstats.com/), the number of internet users in the world had reached almost 370 million by the end of June 2012. Alongside official and private travel websites 'delivering' information in a traditional way with a low level of interactivity and participation, a significant process of 'informal' communication (Calvi, 2010), that is consumer to consumer (C2C), is developing in Web 2.0 with applications like social networking sites (Facebook), document-sharing websites (Flickr), travel communities (VirtualTourist) and wikis. Such forms are pervading and affecting the travel and tourism experience at all stages of the trip.

Stage of trip

Dann (1996a, 2007, 2012a, 2012b) has integrated the parameter of 'medium' into an insightful framework based on the **stage of trip**, meaning the stage at which a tourism text is consumed. Even though no clear-cut boundaries can be traced, the sociologist identified three general stages – pre-trip, on-trip and post-trip – and grouped text instances accordingly. The first group, which included brochures, perform a purely promotional function by orienting the readers' choices and preparing them for the experience through anticipation, most often by framing a notion of 'escape' from home. The second type, such as tourist guides and maps, are consumed during the trip because of their informational nature, while the third set, primarily postcards and souvenirs, serve the purpose of fixing and confirming the experienced trip in the reader's mind. On-trip promotional texts shape a notion of physical and spiritual 'renewal', whereas post-trip texts frame a discourse of 'reintegration' (Dann, 1996a: 140). The textual shape of such values is achieved through specific modal configurations.

Mode

Strictly interwoven with that of the material substance of medium, the concept of mode implies the semiotic resources used in the act of communication; there are, for instance, written, visual, audio and gestural modes (Kress, 2003, 2009, 2010). As for written texts, worthy of note are literary works like travel novels, poems and play scripts whose origin is not to be found in the tourism industry *per se* but which have nourished literary landscapes and generated the phenomenon of literary tourism (Robinson & Andersen, 2011). To give just two notable examples, the Lake District has attracted millions of visitors looking for literary, biographical and emotional traces of Wordsworth's and Coleridge's poems, and Stratford-upon-Avon would be unknown to most people without the biographical connection with Shakespeare. Besides literary works such as poems, novels and plays, written texts include academic and scientific articles, essays and volumes.

However, it is the visual mode, as Chapter 3 shall extensively argue and exemplify, that has played a substantial role in tourism experience and communication. The centrality, albeit not the exclusiveness, of the visual to the rituals of modern travel and tourism has been asserted by a number of critical voices in tourism studies, from MacCannell ([1976] 1989, 1992) to Urry (2002). The tourist picture, not surprisingly, is the symbol of holidays and few holidaymakers would leave home without taking a camera along. Similarly, no tourism promotional text would exist without a glossy picture. Worthy of note, the same picture projects different sociocultural meanings via the tactile properties of printed, digital or material media.

Monomodality is, then, a mere abstraction, all communication being multimodal (Baldry & Thibault, 2006; Kress & van Leeuwen, 2006; Lemke, 2002; Norris, 2004), and tourism and travel communication not being an exception (Urry, 2002; Urry & Larsen, 2011). Even the apparently monomodal word-of-mouth exploits the semiotic potential of numerous aspects of body language, like eye contact, posture and gesture, as interconnected with speech. In authentic texts, different modes interact, following either simultaneous or sequential logics of space and of time or, alternatively, of hypertextuality (see Chapter 5). Brochures, guidebooks, maps, flyers, advertisements, posters and billboards are examples of static texts, functioning through the logics of space. Examples of dynamic multimodal texts include soap operas, films or videos acting as travel motivators and generating the growing trend of film-induced tourism (Beeton, 2005; MacCannell, [1976] 1989: 4). By the means of modal configurations, all these instances variously achieve their communication function. This is the topic of the following section.

Communication function

In spite of their plural and diverse focus, Calvi, Gotti and Dann's grids have stressed the importance of the pragmatic **communication function** in determining a tourist text's genre (Maci, 2010: 48). Speech act theory (Austin, 1962; Searle, 1969) addresses the performative role of language and postulates that we 'do things with words' (Austin, 1962). Accordingly, three levels of action can be distinguished: the act of saying something, termed the 'locutionary' act; what one does in saying it, the 'illocutionary' act;

and what one does by saying it, the 'perlocutionary' act. This means that the communication instance says something (conveys content) and does something towards someone (states, invites, asks) in order to get something done by them (persuade, convince, provoke). Every utterance is simultaneously a locutionary, illocutionary and perlocutionary act – even though a single prominent aspect may be detected.

While acknowledging multifunctionality and functional hybridity, several predominant functions can still be identified in specific tourism texts. Within the tourism domain, for example, different text genres can be detected that fulfil the main communication functions of information and promotion; that is, they convey information about a site (history, culture, facilities) and convince readers to choose that site as their holiday destination. An ideal line could be traced from maximally informative tourism texts based on locutionary acts like travel terms-and-condition forms, to maximally promotional texts based on illocutionary acts like travel destination advertisements. Intermediate positions may be occupied by reports, mainly informative but with an indirect promotional function, and by mainly promotional but indirectly informative brochures (Francesconi, 2012).

Maci (2010: 102) significantly relates the pragmatic function to the trip-stage genres consumed. As such, pre-trip texts like brochures are mainly of a promotional nature, while on-trip texts like guidebooks are basically informative and instructive, and post-trip texts remind readers of the holiday experience. Similarly, communication function varies with reference to involved actors, tour operators being prominently concerned with persuading readers to visit a location, whereas travel writers are motivated by aesthetics. Although literary books are generally produced without the intention of influencing the reader's inclinations to travel, both literary authors and their works can shape a destination's image and its ability to attract visitors (Robinson & Andersen, 2011).

Pre-trip tourism promotion texts act primarily on 'push factors', namely psychological motivations for travel, such as the need for serenity, style, adventure and fun (Ashworth & Goodall, 2012a, 2012b; Dann, 1993). Via multimodal strategies like colour, music and poetic style, texts express these concepts and establish a positive attitude in the text recipient (Held, 2004). Through a process of 'indexical transfer' (Dann, 1996a; Santulli, 2007), the positive value is purposefully transferred to the recipient and finally to the destination, eventually pushing readers towards the to-be-visited site.

Worthy of note, tourism and travel texts are increasingly resorting to entertaining communication strategies (Held, 2004), especially at the post-trip stage. Traditionally, promotional texts have attempted to mimic a poetic style in order to weave a pleasant text and seduce readers. However, tourism texts are increasingly encapsulating humour in their messages (see Chapter 5). As an attention-attracting and attention-holding strategy, humour generates a positive attitude in text recipients, anchors positive emotions to the destination and enhances message memorability (Coleman & Crang, 2002; Crouch *et al.*, 2005; Davies, 2002; Pearce, 2009). As in the case of the aesthetic function, the entertaining function may be used either intentionally or unintentionally as a destination-enhancing strategy.

Genre value

Related to communication functions are the varying **genre values** these text genres adopt (Bhatia, 2002, 2004), namely the five general and 'basic forms' of linguistic communication (Enkvist, 1991; Maci, 2010; Ramm, 2000; Werlich, 1982), also defined by Bakhtin (1986) as the 'primary speech genres':

- the narrative, based on the telling of a story;
- the descriptive, based on space representation;
- the instructive/regulative value, aiming at the provision of instructions;
- the expositive, aiming at explanation;
- the argumentative, aiming at evaluation.

If moves are defined by textual sequencing and cognitive structuring (Bhatia, 2004: 60), genre values can be identified in terms of subject matter, theme, chaining strategies and preferred genre configuration.

Within the wide range of tourism and travel texts, the *narrative genre value* is predominant in travel books, diaries and word-of-mouth. The latter tend to follow a chronological line, presenting events as they unfold in time. Conversely, the former imply a manipulation of the plot, frequently using analepsis and prolepsis techniques alongside juxtaposed and intersecting diegetic plans. The narrative value may also be found in travel guides, but only in specific history sections.

As for the *descriptive genre value*, travel guides, reports and diaries often offer descriptions of some geographical areas like urban districts or natural scenery, but also of people and relations among these elements (Jack & Phipps, 2005). Descriptions in both travel books and brochures are carefully encoded, with a wide and varied vocabulary in the first case, and a more standardised and formulaic lexis in the second.

While absent in travel books, diaries and reportage, the *instructive genre value* is clearly visible in guidebooks, in particular in itinerary sections advising about tours, sights, events and eating and sleeping options. The verbal markers of this genre value are the imperative mood and sequential chains of temporal circumstances or processes, introduced for example with the words 'then', 'once' and after', which link steps in a procedure. Both within other texts (e.g. guides, catalogues and websites) and as autonomous, self-sufficient information printed on a single sheet or folded piece of paper, itineraries are characterised by short paragraphs, fragmented sentences and a high frequency of time prepositions and locutions (Maci, 2010: 88). Other examples of instructive genre value are word-of-mouth tips given to tourist readers on where to go on holiday, what to do, what to bring and when best to start queuing for something. For example, some guidebooks include pieces of advice and graphically present them in a separate box or as bullet points in a list rather than as a cohesive and extended paragraph.

However, genre values are never exclusive and isolated; they systematically combine and interact and appear in tourist and travel texts in hybrid forms (Bhatia, 2004; Fodde & Denti, 2008; Francesconi, 2012; Maci, 2010; Ramm, 2000). Enkvist (1991) observes that travel guides systematically interweave the descriptive and the instructive genre values in what he terms 'stop–look–see' text. This hybrid form suggests, at the same time, the direction, duration and intensity of the movement and of the gaze. It thus prescribes a sort of 'mobile gaze', whereby the sensorial experience of vision assumes a kinaesthetic component.

Particular to organisational, legal and institutional genres, the *expositive genre value* shows a certain presence in some guidebook sections that offer detailed, objective information like timetables, weather conditions and glossaries. Textually, this value is characterised by subjects appearing at the start of sentences (Fodde & Denti, 2008: 163).

The *argumentative genre value* can be easily found in some travel reports, where a balanced, critical gaze is cast upon a destination and both positive and negative elements are underscored and discussed. It is also used in travel books, diaries and guides. However, Myers (2010: 10) asserts that it is rarely present in online C2C texts: the immediacy and spontaneity of text codification would undermine the development of argumentative and counter-argumentative lines. This highlights the central importance of lexico-grammar choices to genre value configurations.

Lexico-grammar strategies

The multidimensional nature of communication has implications for **lexico-grammar** choices (see Chapter 2) and the degree of language specialisation. For instance, a highly specialised discourse based on conciseness, transparency, monoreferentiality, pre-modification, lexical density and depersonalisation (Maci, 2010: ch. 1) is adopted in written documents, professional meetings and telephone conversations between specialists, within what Swales (1990) terms a 'discourse community' of experts.

When specialists address non-specialists, discursive features of general language are mixed with specialised vocabulary. This regularly happens in travel agencies and hotels and at information points but also in radio programmes, tourist webpages and printed brochures (Gotti, 2006: 20, 21). An example of specialist–non-specialist communication is the following excerpt, from a 'terms and conditions' section made available online by the Canadian tour operator Rockymountaineer:

> The luggage or articles accepted and transported on the Rocky Mountaineer are subject to Rocky Mountaineer's luggage policy and conditions as set herein. Guests travelling on the Rocky Mountaineer are limited to two checked pieces of luggage per person (in addition to the carry-on overnight luggage required for the Red Leaf Service two-day rail tour portion on the Rocky Mountaineer). Total checked luggage weight per person is not to exceed 30 kg (66 lb). Each piece of luggage must have an identification tag attached to it, which includes name, return address and telephone number. (www.rockymountaineer.com/en)

The text clearly shows the use of a highly formal register, and specialised and monoreferential vocabulary, deprived of qualifying adjectivation. No linking adjuncts are used to make the text cohesive: it is meant only to convey information in a clear way.

A completely different language is adopted on a tour operator's website, an example of expert–non-expert communication, which aims to persuade readers to visit Canada:

> Vast and epic, an ideal self-drive or touring destination.
>
> Canada is a country of contrasts, with the picturesque streets of Quebec City, the high-rise towers of Toronto, the epic and amazing Niagara Falls and the ice fields and mountains of the west. (www.kuoni.com)

The style is here carefully selected for its connotative rather than denotative potential, with highly evocative terms, especially laudatory adjectives (Goddard, 2002; Leech, 1966; Meyer, 1994, 1999). The anaphoric syntax structure unfolds through a slow, relaxing rhythm and engenders a pleasant piece of writing that evokes a poetic style (Robinson & Andersen, 2011: 7). Interestingly, this style thus reflects the refined lexis and subtle syntax of travel writing, which deploys a wide range of emotional and evocative vocabulary together with sophisticated figures of speech, within a complex, accurate and varied sentence and paragraph system. It yet differs from literary travel writing in the systematic resort to euphoric language, superlative forms, interrogative and imperative structures and the abuse of clichés.

Finally, informal communication between non-specialists is characterised by conversational tone, substantial emotional component, less specialised vocabulary, and often inaccurate syntax, lexis and punctuation (Cohen & Cooper, 2004; Myers, 2010). As informal communication is typical of contemporary and digital tourism textuality, this last point will be further developed in the next section and in Chapter 2.

Summary

To sum up, the following parameters may be considered in order to examine tourism and travel texts:

- actors;
- medium;
- trip stage;
- mode;
- communication function;
- genre value;
- lexico-grammar strategy.

Clearly, some of these parameters, like lexico-grammar, allow the identification of a text's internal features, whereas others, like trip stage, address a text's external, discursive features.

Generic Innovation

Mapping tourism texts is difficult, not only because texts ceaselessly proliferate in number, but also because of their fluidity in their configuration patterns. The tourism and travel text genre scenario shows in fact a high degree of dynamism, in relation to both single generic instances and colonies of genres (Calvi, 2010; Dann, 2012a, 2012b; Gotti, 2006). The next section discusses how genre instances change, and the following section why they do so.

Forms of generic innovation

As Bhatia has observed in the last two decades (1993, 2002, 2004, 2010), one of the most fruitful factors enabling changes in the system of tourism texts is the interaction of different colonies. This form of generic innovation is termed **interdiscursivity** and can be viewed 'as a function of appropriation of generic resources across three kinds of contextual and other text-external boundaries: professional genres, professional practices, and professional cultures' (Bhatia, 2010: 36). Fairclough (1989, 1995) has diagnosed in contemporary communication a general, indeed massive tendency of 'commodification', or 'promotionalisation', whereby market discourse tends to invade and mould other areas. This is visible in cases where information text genres systematically adopt unnecessary glossy pictures, code-play, key-wording or dynamic clusters.

Interdiscursivity is not a homogeneous process. Generic innovation occurs within a variety of discursive processes and professional practices and results in the 'embedding', 'bending' and 'mixing' of generic norms in professional contexts (Bhatia, 2010: 35).

Through the process of **embedding**, an author uses a genre 'as a template to give expression to another conventionally distinct generic form' (Bhatia, 1997: 191). The example given by Bhatia is an advertisement written as if it were a poem, which readers still recognise as an advertisement. As for embedding in tourism and travel texts, Figure 1.3 shows a comic strip embedded on a postcard, designed by Martyn Ford and Peter Legon. This text functions within a communication context of 'postcarding' (Östman, 2004); that is, it is purchased, written on, adorned with a stamp, posted and then received and read by the recipient. It is chosen over standard competing postcards due to the unexpected and innovative presence of humorous sequential panels that involve and entertain recipients in a pleasant reading process. Generic innovation also affects the unusual self-mockery process: produced and distributed in the United Kingdom, the strip mocks the poor quality of British food, thus performing humorous self-representation. Generic embedding and self-mockery may be read as ego-enhancement and promotion strategies (Francesconi, 2011a, 2012).

Genre **bending** is a process of adaptation of an existing genre giving rise to a new genre with a different communicative purpose, through a process called 'repurposing'. Within tourism communication, it is now frequent to bend many editorial or official travel reports to promote products or services and/or to mix them with advertisements (Bhatia, 2004: 134). Another example will be discussed in the final part of this chapter, the new genre of Wikitravel. The text is meant to offer an open digital travel guide, with the purpose of guiding prospective travellers in their destination choice; it will be read as bending the Wikipedia encyclopaedia format.

In the third process, genre **mixing**, the genres involved are no longer distinguishable (Bhatia, 1997, 2004), as in the cases of 'docufiction' and

Figure 1.3 Comic strip embedded in a postcard (copyright LGP)

'advertorial'. Bhatia provides the example of the travel advertorial as a mixed genre, a hybrid form between editorial and advertisement. Presented as an editorial, this text genre displays a number of text-internal indicators of advertising genres of a visual and verbal nature, for example the inclusion of colourful and attractive pictures, logos, subheadings and systematic nominalisation. Similarly, content is expressed through a poetic style, avoiding negative elements and including only positive descriptions. The discourse community that the text addresses is clearly holidaymakers, who are attracted by a text that does not look like a standard advertisement.

Having discussed how genres change, the next section addresses why this happens.

Reasons for generic innovation

Motivations for generic changes are complex and multifaceted. Overall, generic innovations may either reflect the natural, spontaneous development of tourist and travel communication or may be induced by the tourism industry and planned by marketing experts (Calvi, 2010). Within genre colonies, some new genres are added because new media and modal configurations are useful, versatile or in fashion, while others are dropped because they are useless, ineffective or old-fashioned (Bhatia, 2004: 62). Notably, Bhatia (2004) adds a psychological and cognitive component into genre analysis: expert and purposeful manipulation of generic resources in tourism and travel texts enables one text instance to be fostered over competing texts through attractiveness, to overcome for a generally sceptical attitude towards promotional texts, and/or to suggest exclusiveness and social distinction to the audience.

As Chandler (1997: 3) argues, genres change because of authorial experimentation, economic factors, audience preferences, communication purposes and technological factors. These motivations never act in isolation but are always interconnected. A good example is the in-flight magazine, freely given by airlines to their passengers. Because of the economic recession and a drop in advertising sales, such texts 'are changing their own image in order to appear less marketing-orientated' (Maci, 2012: 200). This means some sections are being added, others eliminated and others redesigned to seem less touristy, while maintaining the text's attractiveness.

A curious instance of induced generic innovation due to audience preferences and communication purpose is the funny 'safety announcement'. I personally witnessed the power of such hilarious multimodal texts on a flight to Istanbul with the Turkish company Pegasus Airlines in September 2012. The creative in-flight safety announcement featured children as flight attendants giving instructions on how to properly use seat belts, oxygen masks and life jackets. Adopting an impeccable dress code, showing precise security movements and mastering an accurate specialised language, these miniature flight assistants communicated with unique energy and enthusiasm. As a result, the generic innovation proved to be an effective, attention-catching and attention-holding device: while security instructions are rarely listened to, all the passengers were literally captivated by the video. Eventually, this subtle textual technique can save lives (YouTube shows versions in English and Turkish).

Alongside these brilliant induced innovations, the natural development of tourism textuality in contemporary society is basically, albeit not exclusively, of a virtual nature and therefore falls into Chandler's category of technological transformation. The establishment and growth of digital communication and the internet within contemporary social interaction is having a revolutionary mutual impact on modes and forms of tourism textual exchanges (Dann, 2012a, 2012b; Dann & Parrinello, 2007). The internet presents the possibility for instant, free and democratic communication as well as greater exchange of information between geographically distant consumers (Wenger, 2008). As such, it has become a crucial component of tourism and of travel communication, with implications in terms of affordances, functions and actors' involvement. For instance, the same destination advertisement in printed form inside a specialised travel magazine or in digital form on a webpage addresses a different target group in terms of age, sociocultural profile, habits and interests; reaches the target in a different time frame; and adds to the destination different connotations in terms of prestige, exclusiveness and, most importantly, accessibility.

At the beginning of the digital age, numerous tourist texts experienced a 'migration' to the web (Calvi, 2010: 16; Garzone *et al.*, 2007) through a process of 'remediation' (Bolter & Grusin, 2000). Paper documents like leaflets, brochures and catalogues issued by institutional boards or private tour operators were made available in electronic form. This process eliminated printing costs and increased accessibility, especially for a younger, internet-savvy audience (Long & Robinson, 2009: 105). Remediation occurs in different ways and simple uploading maintains a first 'frozen' PDF version; this generates what has been defined as Web 1.0, a traditional online visual and verbal document, based on static textuality that is read by the internet user following a pre-established trajectory and without any participation or interactivity (Garzone, 2007). Alternatively, migration to the web can open up to hypertextuality and generate an HTML document (Hypertext Mark-up Language) that offers various menu-driven options for individual preferences and forms of fruition. Text content is pre-established but reading trajectories and reading modalities are decided by the user.

Importantly, word-of-mouth has been transformed on the internet into what Dann and Parrinello (2007: 12) have termed 'word-of-mouse', and is made globally and instantly visible via Web 2.0 applications like social networking sites, document-sharing websites, travel blogs, travel wikis and so on. 'Virtual' friends can freely promote or demote travel destinations on the basis of their direct experience. Coherent with the open nature of travel information, the 2.0 digital text shows a more 'open, collaborative and participatory' nature, with users not only surfing the net but also 'making things through editing, updating, blogging, remixing, posting, responding, sharing, exhibiting, tagging and so on' (Urry & Larsen, 2011: 59). An interesting example is the Schmap travel guide (e.g. www.london.schmap.com), an online platform where users ceaselessly add comments and proposals and make the guide more similar to a social network desktop. As a palimpsest, this online text features also a more traditional frame as background, where typical guide sections like 'restaurants', 'shopping' and 'to do' sections can be found.

Not only do tourism and travel digital texts circulate with incredible potential in terms of accessibility, but most tourist actions are now performed via the internet. Without leaving their desk and thus saving time, prospective travellers check flight availability at Expedia.com – the largest online travel company in the world – compare prices, book and then pay for their tickets. While on trips, an increasing number of holidaymakers organise their itineraries using travel apps like Tourist, Trip Journal, MTrip Travel Guides and programs installed on smartphones that offer immediate and specific information as needed. Both while on holiday and once back home, travellers share huge amounts of travel-related material on user-generated social networking sites like Facebook, in photo communities like Flickr and, more specifically, on travel-community websites like VirtualTourist (Dann, 2012a, 2012b). Moreover, travel-community websites are experiencing increased power in influencing the market. With more than 75 million travel reviews and opinions, the popular TripAdvisor site is consulted at the pre-trip stage by 60 million individual monthly visitors (www.tripadvisor.co.uk, accessed January 2013). It helps them organise their journeys and find the 'perfect' flight, accommodation, restaurant, landmarks and itinerary. At the post-trip stage, it then hosts their positive or negative comments as either satisfied or unsatisfied travellers.

The establishment of the electronic medium has substantially affected language use and developed what Crystal (2006: 255) terms **Netspeak**. As a distinct code located between writing and speech, it shows peculiarities in terms of morphology, lexis and syntax. When opening a webpage, one immediately notices that paragraphs, sentences and clauses are shorter, syntax is predominantly paratactic and the vocabulary range is restricted. Consequently, register is increasingly more colloquial, informal and direct. These features become more prominent in C2C digital texts: in online diaries, social network or chat posts, colloquialisms abound, exaggerated punctuation is used to personalise the text and formal inaccuracies are far from rare (Myers, 2010). The following extract from an online travel diary recording a trip to Toronto illustrates some of the linguistic and stylistic properties of Netspeak:

> Up early to get on a 9am hop-on, hop-off bus tour ... no I'm not keen, it's when the ticket is valid for and it takes 2 hours to do with out

getting off. This is my last day in a city for a couple of days - yippee! So with no energy left in my body,I sit in the already hot sunny morning on the top deck with no intention of moving or getting off at any of the stops. Toronto is a huge city and I'm certainly not seeing it on foot like some of the others. (Posted Tuesday, 5 July 2011 by kimrobinson Uk on the TravelPod website, www.travelpod.com)

This fragment immediately reveals distinctive features like parataxis, contracted forms, colloquialisms and formal and typographic inaccuracies, which could never be used in a printed text, be it of an institutional, organisational or editorial nature. However, the enormous impact of Netspeak is going beyond the virtual sphere and progressively affecting written language use and language in general. Even scientific oral and written texts like academic essays and lectures tend to progressively adopt a more informal tenor, sometimes admitting contracted, personal and informal solutions. Chapter 2 provides a more extended discussion of the verbal language of tourism and how it is affected by medium and by new technologies in particular.

Similarly, the layout of electronic pages is influencing the design of traditional printed texts (Kress, 2010), and tourist institutional, editorial and private bodies have subtly exploited its communication potential and strategies. New information technologies follow the visual aspect and the dominance of the screen to a greater extent, focusing more on how the message can be depicted and represented than on how it can be told and narrated (Kress, 2003: 3). According to this logic of the screen, the electronic page is governed by the logic of space-simultaneity and the co-occurrence of communication patterns on space. Meanwhile, printed communication is progressively adapting to such logic and is innovating its configuration. The contemporary verbal text participates in this logic and becomes part of the layout; that is, it first acquires meaning through its visual potential in terms of placement, size, typeface and colour choices.

Genre analysis of Wikitravel to South Africa

Having acknowledged in the two sections above the forms of generic change and the reasons for them, this section takes into account a specific innovative tourism text, namely Wikitravel. It seeks to describe and evaluate it as a text genre, observing its elements of integrity and innovation. In order to provide evidence of this process of generic innovation and integrity, examples are taken from the Wikitravel page on South Africa.

Having been a British colony from 1806 to 1931, South Africa has English among its 11 official languages, and widely adopts it in public and commercial life. The country is experiencing a surprising growth in tourism arrivals, quantified as an increase of 22% in international tourism receipts in the first nine months of 2012 (WTO website, accessed March 2013).

Established in 2003, Wikitravel presents itself on its webpage as 'the original, free, complete up-to-date and reliable worldwide travel guide' (http://wikitravel.org/en/Main_Page, accessed February 2013). It is the first 'premier travel wiki on the internet', with travel-related articles constantly added and edited by numerous authors around the world, named Wiki-travelers (Long & Robinson, 2009).

As the *Oxford English Dictionary* affirms, 'wikis are websites that allow any user to change or add the information it contains'. Within the wide range of digital texts, Wikitravel can be better defined as a C2C 2.0 wiki text, written by non-expert, unremunerated writers on the basis of their direct experience and on freely chosen sources. As such, Wikitravel is a 'collaborative' text, since different Wikitravelers can co-work to produce a unique, homogeneous virtual text, based on their travel experience. To this end, verbal clusters are visible on the screen page that explicitly ask internet users to provide further contributions and help the page grow. Worthy of note, they innovate tourism textuality in its democratic authorship. The open nature of Wikitravel thus refers to the potentially almost limitless number of its authors, its language versions and the fluid nature of its text. As a consequence of this plural and multiple author instance, it may potentially be extremely 'up-to-date and reliable', but this really depends on Wikitravelers' enthusiasm, rhythm, style and information sources. As a result, pages may also be partial, incomplete or out of date.

Wikitravelers may decide to use either their own language or English as a lingua franca (see Introduction). A multilingual text, the guide is thus available in several world languages, the number of which is constantly growing. In February 2013, the South Africa text (Figure 1.4) was in 16 languages, including German, Esperanto, Spanish, Suomi, French, Portuguese, Rumanian, Japanese, Russian, Swedish, Chinese and Hebrew. Yet, different Wikitravel versions do not provide automatic and equivalent translations of a source text. Some versions are longer and more complex, being the result of a more collaborative textuality or of more effort by one single author. This is generally the case with the English text, English being a global language used by most Wikitravelers.

Such open, fluid, incomplete identity evokes the source of this text, the online open Wikipedia encyclopaedia. As such, Wikitravel still maintains a high degree of generic integrity, showing a certain amount of Wikipedia properties and, in turn, of the scientific language traditional encyclopaedias adopt. These are in terms of content, structure and text development, with

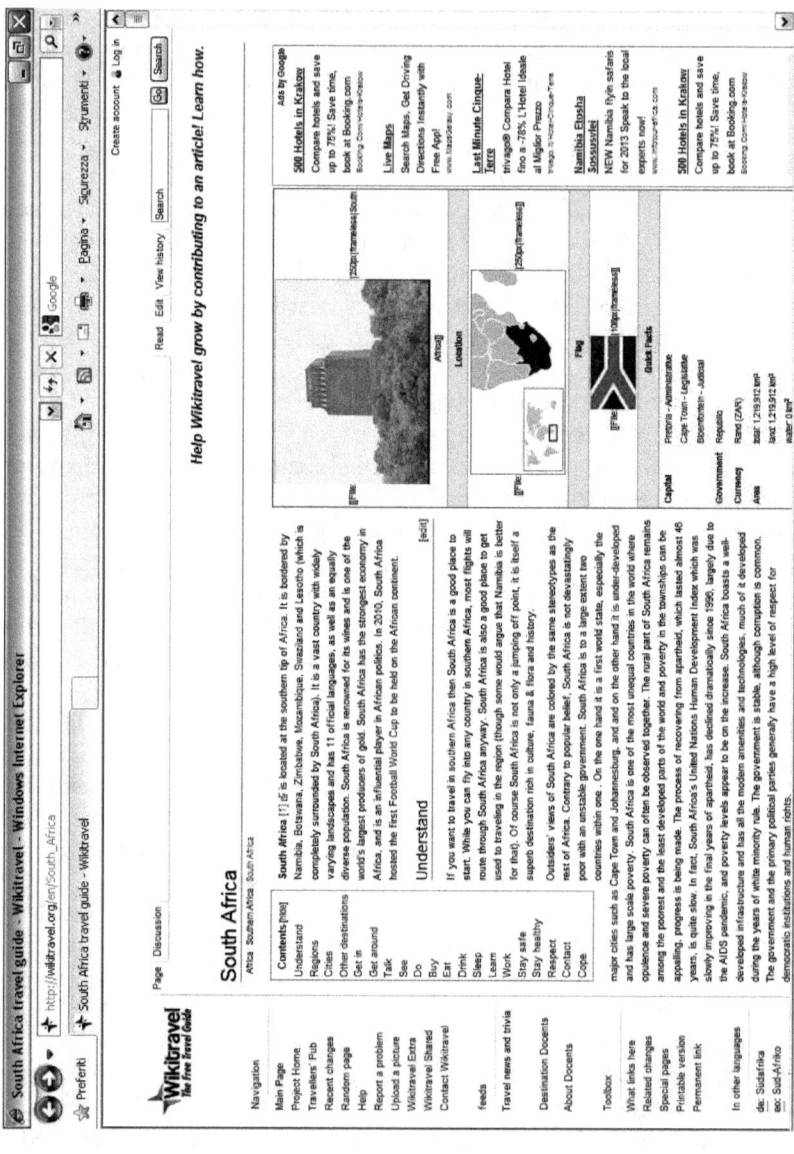

Figure 1.4 Wikitravel webpage (http://wikitravel.org/en/South_Africa) on South Africa (accessed February 2013)

a multilingual 'Contents' list and some thematic sections like 'see', 'buy' and 'eat', and with form and style conventions, like impersonal structures, formal register, controlled punctuation and scientific vocabulary. It is, then, an open, collaborative text, consistent with the wiki format, and travellers can constantly add, delete or modify the text. Questions then arise as to this hybrid textual identity, in between an encyclopaedia and a guide, a scientific, an editorial or an informal text.

Worthy of note, Wikitravel defines itself as a 'guide', thereby inscribing its textuality within a more pragmatic system of reference, implying a functional and interpersonal role that is absent in the Wikipedia encyclopaedia. Undoubtedly, Wikitravel could be accessed by future travellers for destination choice and holiday planning, profiting from medium-based affordances in terms of accessibility. In order to ascertain whether there is generic hybridity and to discuss the dynamics of integrity and innovation, some discussion of genre values is necessary. Which values are predominant? Which are absent? How are these used to achieve the given communication function?

First, the narrative genre value can be observed in relation to event narration within a temporal reference, exemplified in the following extract:

> They [the Bantu] displaced, conquered and absorbed the original Khoisan speakers, the Khoikhoi and San peoples. The Bantu slowly moved south.

Narrating the history of the Bantu people and in particular their migration movements, this passage is deprived of temporal chains that guide and sustain the reading process. The style is highly neutral and essential, being closer to scientific textuality than to travel literature.

On the South Africa Wikitravel page, the descriptive genre value is systematically used, as in the following passage depicting physical aspects of South African environments. Descriptive fragments use spatial chaining strategies like 'to the north' and 'to the south-east' as spatial circumstances in theme position:

> To the north of Johannesburg, the altitude drops beyond the escarpment of the Highveld, and turns into the lower lying Bushveld, an area of mixed dry forest and an abundance of wildlife. East of the Highveld, beyond the eastern escarpment, the Lowveld stretches towards the Indian Ocean.

Such linking solutions are adopted in the Wikitravel text to lead the message, to organise text development and to make the text cohesive (Fodde & Denti, 2008: 161; Ramm, 2000).

By means of the narrative and descriptive genre values, the digital guide performs its main function, namely to inform internet users about a geographical area. However, a traditional travel guide would enrich descriptions with qualifying adjectives, which are clearly absent in this excerpt. Again, the style is more of a neutral and scientific nature.

Interestingly, the hybrid device of 'stop–look–see' which Enkvist sees as peculiar of travel guides is absent in the South Africa Wikitravel page, which again maintains the generic integrity traits of encyclopaedias in terms of objective, scientific and impersonal style, and which lacks the interactive, dialogic component of tourism texts.

This feature leads to discussion of the expositive value. The following is an extract on the local climate, showing precise and documented information from competent scientific sources and expressed using a highly specialised language:

> South Africa has a generally temperate climate, due in part to being surrounded by the Atlantic and Indian Oceans on three sides, by its location in the climatically milder southern hemisphere and due to the average elevation rising steadily towards the north (towards the equator) and further inland. Due to this varied topography and oceanic influence, a great variety of climatic zones exist.

Undoubtedly, the expositive genre value is pervasive on the Wikitravel page, which abounds in objective graphs, tables and boxes with detailed and updated information. Once more, this aspect makes this text closer to an encyclopaedia than to a guide.

In the Wikitravel page on South Africa, an interesting section provides a detailed description of the country's extremely rich biodiversity, especially plant diversity. It is followed by this paragraph on the risks of climate change:

> Climate change is expected to bring considerable warming and drying to much of this already semi-arid region, with greater frequency and intensity of extreme weather events such as heatwaves, flooding and drought. According to computer generated climate modelling produced by the South African National Biodiversity Institute[75] parts of southern Africa will see an increase in temperature by about one degree Celsius along the coast to more than four degrees Celsius in the already hot hinterland such as the Northern Cape in late spring and summertime by 2050. The Cape Floral Kingdom has been identified as one of the global biodiversity hotspots since it will be hit very hard by

climate change and has such a great diversity of life. Drought, increased intensity and frequency of fire and climbing temperatures are expected to push many of these rare species towards extinction.

Remarkably, no textual marker relates this paragraph to the previous one and suggests the development of an argumentative line. No adverb or chaining strategy shows the emotional participation and position of the Wikitraveler with respect to such an important issue, and evaluation patterns are absent. Rather, the language is highly specialised, the register is scientific and the vocabulary is monoreferential. Once more, this conforms to the encyclopaedic style of Wikipedia.

To sum up, this text provides an interesting example of text hybridity. Being at the crossroads of different colonies, it brings the scientific and the editorial domains into contact, giving birth to a C2C informal text. Wikitravel is a digital text genre that combines written and visual modes, even though the written is predominant. Produced and consumed by the same interactants, it may be codified and decodified at different stages of a trip. While overtly expressing the pragmatic purpose of 'guiding' Wikitravelers in their travels, its textuality is deeply rooted in modes and forms of the informative scientific text it originates from, namely Wikipedia. The observation of adopted genre values proves that this instance is more grounded in a documentary, scientific, detailed informative role. Guide-specific properties like advice, tips and warnings on what to do and not to do and what to eat and not to eat are absent, but there is also evidently an interpersonal bond and a sense of solidarity among Wikitravelers. The use of genre values and linguistic features confirms this hypothesis. Significantly, then, Wikitravel, in terms of text genre, is open and collaborative thanks to the medium it relies on but traditional in the verbal strategies it features. Paradoxically, in this age when printed guides tend to adopt a variety of textual and verbal interactive, participatory strategies like tip boxes, personal pronouns and imperative forms, this digital genre seems more faithful to Wikipedia and shows a scientific, objective, neutral style.

Conclusion

This chapter has explored tourism and travel texts by the means of genre analysis. The first section has discussed genre, as reconceptualised throughout the centuries and as a still an open concept. A fluid and functional definition has been acknowledged for the present volume, paying particular attention to processes of generic integrity, innovation and hybridisation. The focus is on tourism texts and different classification models have been illustrated, with varying emphasis on stage of trip, medium, mode, actor (sender or addressee), genre value, communication function and lexico-grammar strategy (degree of language specialisation) as determining generic integrity. Finally, generic innovation has been discussed, with particular attention to motivations and forms of change. Examples of tourism texts, spontaneous and induced innovation and hybridisation have been offered, with a close examination of Wikitravel.

After this introduction to tourism and travel text genres, the following chapters examine verbal, visual and audio semiotic systems. Chapter 2 concentrates on verbal language within the frame of systemic functional linguistics.

2 Systemic Functional Grammar

Systemic Functional Linguistics

Having discussed genre conceptualisations and configurations in the previous chapter, this second chapter illustrates systemic functional grammar, addressing language as interconnected linguistic systems from which users choose in order to express meaning. In the final part, the model will be applied to tourism texts on the Maltese archipelago.

Following J.R. Firth's functional–semantic tradition, the social semiotic linguist Michael Halliday developed **systemic functional linguistics** (SFL), which is both a theory of language as social process used in everyday social interaction and an analytical methodology that permits the systematic description of language patterns (Eggins, 2011: 21). It makes four main theoretical claims about language, which will be discussed here:

- language is functional;
- language is contextual;
- language is semantic;
- language is semiotic.

First, Halliday's functional grammar asserts that linguistic choices are determined by their function in the linguistic system. Overall, functional theories of language seek to explain what language is and how it works by asking what functions it has fulfilled in society and how these are achieved through the language skills of speaking and listening, reading and writing. The evolution of language throughout the centuries is seen in this light as serving different human needs in everyday situations (Halliday & Hasan, 1985; Halliday, 2004).

Second, SFL addresses language use, that is, language as realised in social and cultural authentic contexts (Eggins, 2011: 81). Context cannot be thus ignored in text analysis, as it determines and shapes language and, subsequently, text genre configurations. More specifically, it is the recurrence of the situations in which we use language that generates the possibilities and constraints for text genre configuration. In turn, genres can be defined as consistent with respect to their context. The social context affecting language is realised through the three main dimensions of situations, or register variables: field, tenor and mode (Halliday, 1978; Halliday & Hasan, 1985; Halliday, 2004). These are defined as follows:

- **Field** indicates what the text deals with and covers the activity (the process that the interactants are engaged in) and the domain of experience (the topic).
- **Tenor** concerns the social role relationships between participants in the linguistic act in a given context, for example customer–salesperson, politician–public or friend–friend. Relations may be described in terms of power (equal, non-equal), contact (frequent, occasional) and affective involvement (high–low).
- **Mode** refers to the means of communication and regards the role played by language in the situation in which it operates, for example spoken or written language.

All these possible register variables have a direct and substantial impact on the language that will be produced and on the meaning it makes. As SFL is a functional–semantic approach to language, language is seen in terms of specific semantic functions, which leads to the following point.

Third, meaning potential in language is expressed through functional components called **metafunctions**, lines of meaning, which embrace the main, general purposes language is used for (Halliday, 2004: 29–31). The three metafunctions are:

- the **ideational**, aimed at representation of the environment;
- the **interpersonal**, referring to the actions of participants;
- the **textual**, related to the message.

Potential travellers or tourists as readers interact with a text in terms of all three metafunctions. They would first understand the text's processes, its participants and the circumstances referred to, as well as the relationship between one process and another, or one participant and another, which share the same position in the text. Second, readers would recognise the speech functions being used, whether the article, guide, brochure or online post is making an offer, providing statements, asking questions or commanding, as well as the attitudes and judgements embodied. Third, readers would appreciate the value of the message reported, or its relevance to the context in which it occurs, as well as the coherence between the different parts of the text (Royce, 2007: 66).

Since the various functions determine a grammatical structure, language is conceived as a system that integrates content and expression. In its meaning-making potential, language can be seen as composed of an upper level of content, known as semantics, an intermediate level of content, known as lexico-grammar, and a lower level of expression, realised via phonology and graphology (Eggins, 2011: 19; Halliday, 2004: 24, 25). Language, thus, follows a three-layered semiotic model based on:

- semantics ↔ (upper) level of content;
- semantics and lexico-grammar ↔ (lower) level of content;
- phonology and phonetics ↔ level of expression.

Fourth, all three metafunctions are found both at the level of semantics and at the level of grammar in systemic theory. In Halliday's systemic functional theory, language is seen as a set of features and a systemic grammar is the paradigmatic ordering of language, functioning as a network of interrelated options (Halliday, 2004: 22). As such, systemicists take the notion of choice, or opposition, to be of fundamental importance in understanding how language makes meaning (Eggins, 2011: 198).

The system of language deploys the units of sentence, clause, group, word and morpheme, which offer ranks for systemic functional grammar. In SFL, the clause, as a semiotic unit, has priority over the others and analysts examine how the choice of an item along the paradigmatic axis, its place in the clause unit or its combination with another item projects 'meaning'. Notably, systemic functional grammar is not seen as a list of rules: every grammar choice implies a choice from a set of options, and choices are not assessed as right or wrong but as appropriate or inappropriate to a particular context (Eggins, 2011: 20). Consistent with the view of genre analysis illustrated in the previous chapter, SFL elaborates not a prescriptive but a descriptive grammar (Eggins, 2011: 139).

To sum up, Table 2.1 shows the grammar systems that express the three metafunctions (which are developed in the following sections, with examples mainly from Wilson, 2000), related to the register variables.

Table 2.1 Context, meaning and grammar in language

Register	Metafunction	Grammar systems
Field	Ideational	Transitivity, taxis and logico-semantics
Tenor	Interpersonal	Mood and modality
Mode	Textual	Theme–rheme

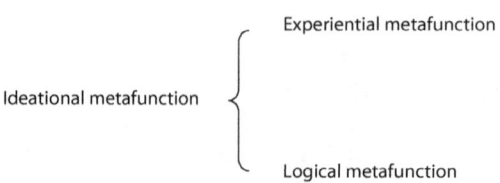

Figure 2.1 The ideational metafunction

The Ideational Metafunction

The register variable of 'field' is directly linked to the semantics of the ideational metafunction. In turn, the ideational strand of meaning is further divided into experiential and logical components (Figure 2.1). The experiential metafunction is concerned with clauses as representation of experience, while the logical metafunction refers to the logical structure of the **clause complex**.

The experiential metafunction is configured predominantly through selections in the grammar system of **Transitivity** in the clause network. Transitivity covers the interpretation and expression in language of different types of process and participant roles in the form of linguistic structures. It can have three elements:

- the process itself, realised by a verb;
- the participants in the process (persons, things or abstract entities), expressed by a nominal group;
- the circumstances of place, time and manner, articulated through an adverbial group or prepositional phrase.

Processes can be first divided between material processes and mental processes: while material processes typically express doing, happening and causing, like 'make', 'build', 'occur' and 'open', mental processes indicate perception, cognition and desideration, like 'hate', 'remember' and 'like'. In a material process, the participants are the 'actor' (the doer of the action), the 'goal' (the participant the process was directed at or extended to) and the 'beneficiary' (participants that benefit from the process). In a mental process, the participants are the 'senser' and the 'phenomenon'. The two sentences are examples of each type:

Malta	*offers*	*you*	*a memorable experience.*
Actor	Material process	Beneficiary	Goal

Travellers	*seek*	*an authentic island experience.*
Senser	Mental process	Phenomenon

A third group is composed of relational processes, which indicate states of being, rather than actions (Eggins, 2011: 237). It is divided into processes of attribution or identification: an attributive clause is about characterising, while identification is about defining. In a process of attribution, participants are termed 'the carrier' and 'the attribute', while in a process of identification they are labelled 'token' and 'value'.

Our islands	*are blessed*	*with a mild climate.*
Carrier	Process of attribution	Attribute

Gozo and Comino	*are*	*the sister islands.*
Token	Process of identification	Value

Alongside are the three subsidiary behavioural, verbal and existential types. Behavioural processes include bodily expressions and psychological states, verbal process express saying and communicating, while existential processes indicate the existence or occurrence of phenomena:

Visitors	*dream*	*Malta's sun and sea.*
Behaver	Process of behaviour	Phenomenon

Locals	*say*	*their homeland is hospitable.*
Sayer	Verbal process	Target

There	*is*	*a good restaurant*	*round the corner.*
	Existential process	Existent	

Table 2.2 summarises all the mentioned process types and participants.

Associated with processes and participants are circumstantial elements, which provide information on where, when, how and why processes occur. The principal ones in English are the following (Eggins, 2011: 223; Halliday, 2004: 263):

- location – indicates when and where, in time (temporal) and in space (spatial);
- extent – indicates duration (temporal) and distance (spatial);
- manner – indicates means, quality and comparison;
- cause – indicates reason, purpose, behalf;

Table 2.2 Processes in the grammar system of Transitivity

Process type	Category meaning	Participants
Material	Doing	Actor, goal, beneficiary
Mental	Sensing	Senser, phenomenon
Attribution	Attributing	Carrier, attribute
Identification	Identifying	Token, value
Behavioural	Behaving	Behaver
Verbal	Saying	Sayer, target
Existential	Existing	Existent

- accompaniment – indicates with whom the action is realised;
- matter – indicates topic, argument;
- role – indicates guise or product someone or something is or becomes.

Examples of circumstantial elements, respectively, of location in space and extent in time, manner, cause, accompaniment, matter and role are identified in italics in these sentences:

Malta is a breathtaking destination *in the middle of the Mediterranean.*

A lot [of boats] come through *during the night* as well.

Our friends reached Rabat *by bus.*

I reached the restaurant *thanks to the helpful passer-by.*

Sue visited Mdina *with some Canadian friends.*

As for accommodation, visitors were really satisfied.

They were visiting Valletta *as tourists.*

As text analysis shall reveal, in tourism and travel texts, the grammar system of Transitivity predominantly resorts to material processes expressing movement, mental processes indicating sensorial perception, and circumstances of spatial extent and location. The processes of attribution and identification, associated with circumstances of manner and role, also have a certain importance.

Figure 2.2 summarises how the grammar system of Transitivity is built.

Besides expressing experiential meanings about participants and processes, language users link these meanings into coherent and semantically

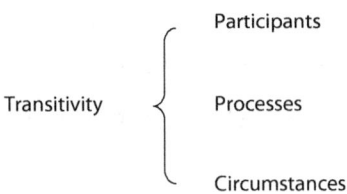

Figure 2.2 The grammar system of Transitivity

sequenced units (Eggins, 2011: 295). As such, the second part of the ideational metafunction is concerned with the logical structure of the clause complex. More specifically, two grammar systems govern logical relations: Taxis (or complexing) and Logico-semantics.

Taxis refers to how two or more adjacent clauses are linked together in certain systematic and meaningful ways (Eggins, 2011: 255; Halliday, 2004: 383). This builds a clause complex, which refers to both a grammatical and a semantic unit and which can show either a paratactic or syntactic relation. Parataxis occurs in cases of a relation of independency between adjacent clauses, while hypotaxis occurs in cases of dependency (Eggins, 2011: 258). Examples can be found in the following sentences, the first being a paratactic and the second a hypotactic clause complex:

> Malta has developed into a highly sought after location for international movie productions, *while Valletta's majestic Grand harbour welcomes cruise liner passengers from all over the world.*
>
> Our islands offer an impressive range of historical and cultural sites, together with a spectrum of activities, *making Malta a truly unique year-round holiday destination.*

In the first example, the two clauses are of equal weight and each one could stand alone as a complete sentence. In the second example, the second clause is hypotactically dependent on the main clause, the Head. In case of a single, unique clause, the clause unit is termed simplex.

A further alternative to a clause complex is embedding, which occurs when a clause functions within the structure of a group (Halliday, 2004: 426). If Taxis unfolds by expansion, embedding is thus realised by compression. The following sentences exemplify embedding in clause simplexes, the embedded clause appearing in double square brackets:

> Malta welcomes travellers [[who seek an authentic island experience]].
>
> The Archipelago has amenities [[you can't imagine]].
>
> Someone [[walking in the night]] helped them finding their way to the hotel.

In the first example, the defining Finite relative clause in brackets is embedded in the noun 'travellers', whom it post-modifies, acting as a Complement. In the second case, the Finite clause is embedded in the noun 'amenities' and post-modifies it. By contrast, the third sentence exemplifies a non-Finite clause embedded in the Subject and serving as a post-modifier. As for language use, Taxis can be generally seen as characterising spoken, informal writing, while embedding is associated with carefully written and formal texts (Eggins, 2011: 269, 270; Halliday, 1989). In tourism and travel texts, the former is typical of 2.0 communication, while the latter is more frequent in travel books, brochures and guides, but is also typical of tourist norms and regulations.

The second grammar system of the ideational metafunction is **Logico-semantic relations**, which refers to the types of meanings that allow adjacent clauses to project or expand on each other. Clauses may be related either through projection, where one clause is reported by another clause, or through expansion, where one clause develops or extends the meanings of another (Eggins, 2011: 254). As for the first, projected speech is called locution, whereas projected thought is called idea. The two verbs 'say' and 'think' in the following examples immediately clarify this distinction.

> Locals say *women stay at home because of high childcare costs.*
>
> The Maltese think *this is the happiest country to live.*

As for the second option, expansion, the three typologies of elaboration, extension and enhancement are identified. Elaboration implies restatement or clarification (introduced by 'in other words', 'for example', 'for instance'), extension realises addition or variation (with conjunctions like 'and', 'also', 'moreover', 'on the contrary', 'alternatively'), while enhancement expresses a semantic development in terms of time, comparison and cause. These three categories are exemplified in the following sentences:

> Malta is a microcosm of the Mediterranean, *that is it has absorbed traits from all its neighbours and conquerors.*

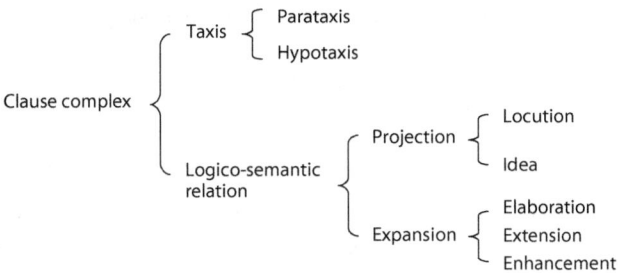

Figure 2.3 The grammar system of clause complex

Some linguists attribute the origins of Maltese to the Phoenicians' occupation of Malta in the 1st Millennium BC, *but most link it to North African Arabic dialects.*

Malta and its sister islands of Gozo and Comino offer you a memorable experience, *where moments of complete relaxation can be combined with exploration of the islands' many cultural, artistic and national treasures.*

As an example of elaboration, the first sentence above has a second clause that explains, via reformulation, the notion of 'microcosm' and is introduced by a linker, 'that is'. In the second sentence, the expansive typology is of extension, with a function of variation being expressed through the conjunction 'but'. The second clause in the third sentence further develops and clarifies the notion of 'memorability' in terms of physical regeneration and cultural enrichment; it thus realises enhancement. Figure 2.3 summarises the system of clause complex.

After illustrating the systems of Transitivity, Taxis and Logico-semantics in the ideational metafunction, the following section addresses the interpersonal metafunction and the grammar systems of Mood and Modality.

The Interpersonal Metafunction

According to SFL, the meaning of the clause can be considered as a form of action, as an interactive event projecting interpersonal meanings between participants. The semantics of interpersonal meanings are directly linked to context, more specifically to the register variable of tenor. Within the systemic functional model, language expressing interaction is structured in the grammar systems of Mood and Modality (Eggins, 2011: 183).

Table 2.3 Functions and responses in the grammar system of Mood

		Initiation	Expected response	Discretionary alternative
Give	Goods and services	Offer	Acceptance	Rejection
Demand	Goods and services	Command	Undertaking	Refusal
Give	Information	Statement	Acknowledgement	Contradiction
Demand	Information	Question	Answer	Disclaimer

Through the system of **Mood**, the clause is organised as an exchange between a speaker or writer and the audience, in which specific roles are played and assigned. The two main recognisable roles are giving and demanding. These can be further distinguished according to their relation to the commodity being exchanged, either goods and services or information. These two variables imply the four illocutory functions of offer, command, statement and question, as illustrated in Table 2.3.

The basic illocutionary forces are encoded by means of three syntactic Moods: declarative, interrogative and imperative. If interrogative, the clause is either polar interrogative (yes/no type) or content interrogative (wh-type).

In order to understand how the interpersonal metafunction is realised, clauses can be divided into two functional components, MOOD and Residue. MOOD indicates that the constituent of the clause is written in bold, while Mood describes the overall structure of the clause. It is the sequence in which they appear in the clause that establishes whether a statement is being made (as in the case of the following clause), a question is being asked, an offer is being made or a command is being given.

Sue	*prebooked*	*her visit to the Hypogeum.*
Subject	Finite	
MOOD		Residue

The MOOD element carries the argument and consists of the subject, the nominal group, and the Finite element, the verbal group. The verbal element (the first in the case of a verb group), the Finite, carries either tense or modality and consists of the semantic feature of the polarity (yes/no). For example, in the following sentence, the modal Finite carries a negative polarity:

Getting here	could not	be easier!
Subject	Finite	
MOOD		Residue

Non-Finite clauses are clauses that have not configured a tense or modal verbal element (Eggins, 2011: 154), as in the following examples:

Blessed with a mild climate, the Maltese Archipelago is a much beloved summer destination.

Alice asked the waiter for the bill, *smiling gently*.

Rather than choosing the main road, they drove up the hill.

Instead of phoning the hotel reception, Peter asked a passer-by.

Non-Finite clauses are by definition hypotactic, and can express elaboration, extension (third and fourth examples above) or enhancement (first and second instances). In order to understand the type of expansion non-Finite clauses represent, it is advisable to turn them into their most closely related Finite forms. The clauses in the following instances provide an interesting example:

Alice asked the waiter for the bill, *smiling gently*.

Alice asked the waiter for the bill *as she smiled gently*.

When the second clause 'smiling gently' is turned into the Finite clause 'as she smiled gently', it clearly shows an enhancing relation of time and manner.

In the system of Mood, the second important element is the **Residue**, composed of Predicator, Complement and Adjunct. The Predicator is the lexical part of the verbal group; in clauses like the following one, with one single verbal constituent, the Finite element conflates with the Predicator.

Our islands	offer		an impressive range of cultural sites.
Subject	Finite	Predicator	Complement
MOOD			Residue

As this clause shows, the Complement is normally a nominal group, with the potential of being a Subject.

Typically realised by an adverbial group or a nominal phrase, Adjuncts provide some additional but non-essential information. Modal Adjuncts are of two types: mood adjuncts and commentary Adjuncts. Mood Adjuncts express probability ('certainly', 'maybe'), usuality ('occasionally', 'never'), obligation ('apparently', 'of course'), inclination ('willingly', 'readily'), time ('already', 'soon'), degree ('quiet', 'hardly') and intensity ('really', 'ever'). Commentary Adjuncts express the speaker-writer's comment on the message, as both attitude and evaluation; examples are 'honestly', 'hopefully', 'provisionally' and 'as expected'. Besides modal Adjuncts, with interpersonal meaning, are conjunctive Adjuncts, with a textual function. Conjunctive Adjuncts provide cohesion inside a sentence, as in the cases of 'and', 'but' and 'so'. The following is an example of a mood Adjunct of probability:

Malta	*is*	*certainly*	*the perfect holiday destination!*
Subject	Finite	Mood Adjunct of probability	Complement
MOOD			Residue

Composed of MOOD and Residue, the grammar system of Mood is summarised in Figure 2.4.

Although polarity plays a considerable role in language use, utterances do not usually have a black and white configuration. Through the two grammatical sub-systems of modalisation and modulation, identified under the label 'modality', language allows us to temper the exchange by expressing degrees of either probability/usuality or obligation/inclination. When modality is used to argue about the probability or frequency of propositions, it is referred to as modalisation (Halliday, 2004: 147). What follow are examples of modalisation:

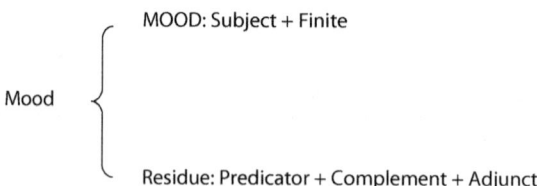

Figure 2.4 The grammar system of Mood

Sun-lovers are *never* disappointed by climate in Malta!

Boats enter Valletta grand harbour *incessantly*.

I *regularly* have coffee and pastizzi for breakfast.

When modality is used to argue the obligation or inclination of proposals, it is referred to as modulation (Eggins, 2011: 172; Halliday, 2004: 147). These sentences exemplify modulation, expressing different ways of informing or advising visitors to Malta or getting them to behave in a particular way:

You *must* carry your home driving licence, together with the International Driving Permit.

You *should* be aware that many Maltese drivers don't pay attention to speed limits.

You *can* book a trip to Sicily through most travel agents in Malta.

As the grammar systems of Mood and Modality have demonstrated, the interpersonal metafunction is concerned with interactants' relations. On the basis of the existing power dynamics (Martin, 1992: 29), interpersonal relations can be either vertical or horizontal and the two corresponding key tenor variables are of power and solidarity. In promotional texts, these distinct positions are blurred through subtle language manipulation and the staging of a pretended solidarity among author and recipients. In many traditional travel guides, like Baedeker, the author acts as an instructor and occupies a position of superiority, while more contemporary guidebooks, like the Lonely Planet series, establish a more equal author–reader relation. In travel books, reports and diaries, weak interaction is generally established, since the text is more concerned with a textual metafunction.

After illustrating the systems of MOOD and Modality in the interpersonal metafunction, the following section address the textual metafunction with the system of Thematisation.

The Textual Metafunction

Associated with the register variable of mode, the textual metafunction is realised when the clause gives a message and has a thematic structure. The textual metafunction is concerned with the verbal world, especially the flow of information in a text, and deploys clauses as relevant and coherent messages. Within clauses, mode is configured as foregrounding certain units, which then combine with others through continuity in the organisation of the clause and convey the message.

A two-part structure, a clause consists of a **Theme** accompanied by a **Rheme**: the former is the point of departure of the message and the prominent element, which is then developed by the latter. The Theme locates and orients the clause within its context (Halliday, 2004: 64). Generally a participant realised by a nominal group, the Theme may also be an adverbial group or propositional phrase complex; especially in these last two cases, it is foregrounded in speech by intonation. In the English clause, Theme depends on the position in the clause, and thus on Mood. An unmarked Theme (and Themes typically are unmarked) is when Theme conflates with structures in the first position of that mood class: Subject in a declarative, Finite in an interrogative, Predicator in an interrogative and a wh- element in a Wh- interrogative. A Marked theme, instead, is when Theme corresponds to any other constituent of the Mood system, for instance with an Adjunct (Halliday, 2004: 64). The following are examples, respectively, of unmarked and marked Thematisation:

Malta offers traditional and genuine hospitality.

For many centuries, Malta has welcomed travellers and visitors.

Marked and unmarked solutions may be chosen for semantic or stylistic purposes to foreground circumstantial information, or to add coherence or, again, to create a particular rhythm (Eggins, 2011: 320). This highly depends on text genres, communication functions, authorial experimentation and intended audience (see Chapter 1).

The grammar system of Thematisation is semantically related to the clause, intended as a system of information. Clause flow is organised starting from 'Given' and develops into 'New' informational elements. In other terms, a discourse-initiating unit normally refers to what is present in the verbal or non-verbal situation, maybe because it has been mentioned or written before and is uttered via anaphoric reference items such as 'it', 'this' or 'then'. In contrast, new information is not recoverable from the context. It is noteworthy that, albeit strictly connected, the given–new information structure and thematic structure do not conflate. In tourism texts, for example, the destination name may be positioned as Theme in order to connote it as familiar, reassuring and warm, or as Rheme to highlight its uniqueness, extraordinariness and diversity.

Within the fulfilment of the textual metafunction, two linguistic features are highly sensitive to mode variation: the degree of grammatical complexity and the lexical density of the language chosen (Eggins, 2011: 97). The first seems to be more related to speech and the second to writing (Halliday, 1989: 63).

Lexical density has been defined by Halliday (1989: 60) as the proportion of lexical items in a text. In other terms, the lexical density of a text can be calculated by expressing the number of content-carrying words (lexical items) in a text or sentence as a proportion of all the words in that textual unit. Content-carrying words include nouns, the main parts of the verbs (full verbs), adverbs, adjectives and numerals. Non-content-carrying words include pronouns, prepositions, determiners, conjunctions, and auxiliary and modal verbs, and are grammatical, structural and functional words. The following sentence opens a press release published on the WTO website:

> International tourist arrivals grew by 4% in 2012 to reach 1.035 billion, according to the latest UNWTO World Tourism Barometer. (http://www2.unwto.org, accessed 18 March 2013)

Out of 20 words, 15 are content-carrying words and 5 are non-content-carrying words. This means there are three times as many lexical words as there are grammar words. Compare this with a part of a BBC Radio 4 programme (analysed in Chapter 4), with the same number of words:

> The history of England is all around us, in the sense you don't have to travel far to find it.

Out of 20 words taken from this oral excerpt, 8 are content words and 12 are non-content words. Here, the proportions are in favour of grammar items. Hence Halliday (1978, 1989) observed that the lexical density of written texts seems to be double that of oral speech or, in general, texts with no possibility of feedback. In general, tourist text genres tend to show a high or very high level of lexical density (Stubbs, 1996: 74), with tourism reports and academic texts being extremely dense. Interestingly, lexically sparse texts tend to be syntactically intricate; that is, they typically have a high level of clause complexity.

Grammatical intricacy regards the complexity of language in terms of how many clauses are joined in a clause complex. It counts how many relations for parataxis or hypotaxis are established between clauses, while omitting embedding (see the grammar system of Taxis, described above). As already mentioned, embedding is considered an expansion within the constituents of a clause group, and not an external one (Halliday, 1978: 242). If one text displays a complex score of 1, it shows clause complexes of one clause each. A range of complexity scores is obtained from a text with several paratactic or hypotactic clauses. Interestingly, Castello (2001) asserts that the most important factor for establishing intricacy is not spoken and written discourse but consciousness. If the BBC spoken text quoted above demonstrates how speech can be controlled, an informal exchange of opinion on travel between friends is likely to show a fragmentary, highly complex structure unfolding, with false starts, repetitions, filled pauses and parenthetic remarks (Halliday, 1989; see also Chapter 4).

SFL in Tourism and Travel Texts

After observing the theoretical and methodological framework of SFL, questions should be raised as to its relevance to tourism and travel discourse. How can a tourist/travel text be decodified using the SFL model? What are the most significant genre-related language aspects? How do tourists/travellers as readers approach the tourism and travel text?

A systemic functional approach to tourist information texts in English has been taken by Castello (2001). In his corpus-based study, the researcher outlined some similarities and differences between the four genres of webpages, brochures, magazines and guides (Castello, 2001: 57–73). His findings demonstrate that websites, for example, are characterised by the lowest score for grammar intricacy in the corpus, while tourist guides present the highest. Imperative forms recur more systematically in brochures, with a similar frequency in magazines and websites, but with less frequency in tourist guides. An exception is the Lonely Planet guide, which constructs an informal and friendly tenor. Tourist guides also have the lowest score in terms of interrogative forms – again with distinct values for Lonely Planet – while the highest score is to be found in magazines. Significantly, brochures and websites show a similar average number of occurrences. Rare occurrence of expressions of modality characterises guides and brochures, while websites and magazines adopt this device very frequently. The same distinction emerges with reference to sentence complexity: brochures have the highest, whereas magazines and guides have the lowest level of minor and elliptical clauses. Castello's study confirms that the language of travel and tourism cannot be examined as a de-differentiated system and that a genre-based approach provides fruitful insights into functional regularities (see Chapter 1).

The following sections offer an example of tourism text analysis, namely a brochure and an online travel diary, with SFL tools. The text and genre are first introduced, drawing on the previous chapter, followed by microanalysis and grammar analysis at clause rank. Each text is analysed three times: the first time for Transitivity and Theme; the second time for Mood;

and the third time for clause complexing. While keys are presented for each analysis, texts have been divided into clauses, with embedded clauses shown within double brackets. As an exhaustive analysis is impossible in the space available, a selective analysis will be provided, which may still offer some insights into text interpretation.

SFL Analysis of a Tourist Brochure on Malta

Even in this age of 2.0 digital communication, the glossy pages of the brochure still symbolise one of the most recognisable and widespread tourism texts. Yet, within the generalised anti-tourism semiotic system (see Introduction), the brochure is generally associated with mass holidays and stereotyped perception.

Deeply rooted in the history of travel, the first brochure is commonly dated back to the work of Thomas Cook in the second part of the 19th century. Considered the pioneer of the package tour, the British Baptist minister started organising excursions for middle-class travellers of his parish, providing information on places of historic interest, transportation, food, lodging and shops (Leed, 1991). In order to materially collect such contents, Cook used the printing machines in his own print shop to compose an early form of brochure (Nielsen, 2001:12). Interestingly, the birth of the brochure can be identified in the attempt to enlarge social access to and democratise travel, a practice before confined to the world of the aristocracy.

After a century and a half, the brochure we know today is a more diversified text. It can be issued either by public institutions or boards and be part of the institutional genre family, or by private agencies and operators and be part of the commercial one (Calvi, 2010). In both cases, it is a B2C text, being produced by the tourism authority/agent and addressed to potential or actual tourists (see Chapter 1; and Francesconi, 2011b). In its printed form, it is freely available at travel agencies and tourist information offices; it is generally small enough to be carried around (Hiippala, 2012a: 99). In its digital version, it can be easily consulted, shared or downloaded. In fact, this text genre is increasingly made available online, in order to reduce printing costs and to instantly reach a wider audience. Remediated versions enable readers to choose different viewing options, zooming in and out, enjoying full-screen vision, select varying background images or music, and manipulating vision quality.

As for communication function, the brochure has been defined as 'a form of printed promotional material designed to communicate with existing or potential tourists' (Molina & Esteban, 2006: 1041). As the second target is predominant, the text genre is generally consumed at the pre-trip stage by potential holidaymakers for destination-image formation and destination choice performance (Molina & Esteban, 2006). It can be seen as multifunctional, as it is informative but mainly promotional. Acting as a tourist 'marker' (Culler, 1989), it establishes a particular significance of a site as sight and thus operates as a semiotic, cognitive and affective artefact (Hiippala, 2012a: 99). As such, it constructs a positive image of a destination as a holiday attraction worth visiting, beautifying and celebrating the physical place. In order to achieve this aim, it subtly combines catchy pictures and enchanting verbal language (Dann, 1996a; Ferreira, 2007; Ling Ip, 2008; Mocini, 2009).

The brochure is generally recognisable by its simple organisation, with a cover, a summary, a section for general presentation, one for tailored offers and, finally, terms and conditions (Francesconi, 2007). These show a functional pyramid structure, the first section, the cover, being the most attention-grabbing and persuasive – to be positioned at the top of the imaginary pyramid – while the 'terms and conditions' exclusively fulfil informative functions – serving as the pyramid's base. Internal sections like 'general site presentation' and 'tailored offers' gradually increase their informative function as they decrease the interpersonal one.

In order to examine SFL in tourism promotion texts, an insightful case is the 2009 *Malta, Gozo and Comino* brochure issued by the official Maltese tourist board, Malta Tourism Authority (MTA), and produced by the communications agency Media Consulta (Francesconi, 2011b). Retrieved by means of the Wordsmith Tools 5.0 software, the data show that the corpus is definitely small, consisting of only 2579 tokens, that is running words in the text (see Afterword). As a tourism text, the brochure is short compared to, for instance, the 118,645 tokens of the 2010 *Lonely Planet Guide to Malta and Gozo* (Wilson, 2010). The following is an introductory extract from the brochure:

The Maltese islands: truly Mediterranean

Blessed with a mild climate and set in crystal waters, Malta and its sister islands of Gozo and Comino offer you a memorable experience, where moments of complete relaxation can be combined with the exploration of the islands' many cultural, artistic and national treasures.

Long considered a microcosm of the Mediterranean and a favourite with travellers who seek an authentic island experience, our islands offer an impressive range of historical and cultural sites, together with a spectrum of activities, making Malta a truly unique year-round holiday destination.

Malta has managed to strike the right balance between traditional hospitality and a cosmopolitan spirit born out of millennial history of welcoming people from all around the region and beyond. Moreover, Malta has developed into a highly sought after location for international movie productions, while Valletta's majestic Grand harbour welcomes cruise liner passengers from all over the world.

The Maltese islands are just a few hours away from major European airports, and with the many scheduled, low-cost and charter flights linking Malta to a host of European and other Mediterranean countries, not to mention the excellent sea connection to Europe, getting here could not be easier! (Malta Tourism Authority, 2009: 2)

The text can be first observed in the fulfilment of the ideational metafunction via the grammar system of Transitivity, with reference to the register variable of field, and in the textual metafunction via the grammar system of Thematisation, with reference to the register variable of mode.

Transitivity and Theme analysis

Key. Processes: material (Pm), mental (Pme), attributive (Pa), identifying (Pi), behavioural (Pb), verbal (Pv), existential (Pe). Participants: Actor (A), Goal (G), Beneficiary (B), Senser (S), Phenomenon (Ph), Carrier (C), Attribute (At), Token (T), Value (V), Behaver (B), Sayer (Sy), Target (T), Existent (E). Circumstance of location (Cl), of extent (Cx), of manner (Cm), of cause (Cc), of accompaniment (Ca), of matter (Ct), of role (Co). Theme is underlined.

> <u>Blessed (Pa) with a mild climate (At) and set (Pa) in crystal waters (At), Malta and its sister islands of Gozo and Comino</u> (A) offer (Pm) you a memorable experience (G), where moments of complete relaxation (C) can be combined (Pa) with the exploration of the islands' many cultural, artistic and national treasures (At).
> <u>Long (Cx) considered (Pme) a microcosm of the Mediterranean and a favourite with travellers (Ph) who (S) seek (Pme) an authentic island experience (Ph), our islands (A)</u> offer (Pm) an impressive range of historical and cultural sites, together with a spectrum of activities (G), making (Pa) Malta (C) a truly unique year-round holiday destination (At).
> <u>Malta (A)</u> has managed to strike (Pm) the right balance between traditional hospitality and a cosmopolitan spirit (G) born (Pm) out of millennial history of welcoming (Pm) people (G) from all around the region and beyond (Cl). <u>Moreover, Malta</u> (T) has developed into (Pi) a

highly sought after location for international movie productions (V), while Valletta's majestic Grand harbour (A) welcomes (Pm) cruise liner passengers (B) from all over the world (Cl).

The Maltese islands (C) are (Pa) just a few hours away from major European airports (At), and with the many scheduled, low-cost and charter flights (A) linking (Pm) Malta (G) to a host of European and other Mediterranean countries (B), not to mention the excellent sea connection to Europe, getting here (C) could not be (Pa) easier (At)!

The grammar system of Transitivity provides interesting insights, as Table 2.4 summarises. The range of process types is rather restricted: out of a total of 16 process types, 6 items are attributive. This indicates that the text is fundamentally concerned with describing the Maltese islands in their tourist appeal. A second group is represented by material verbs, mainly referred to through metaphorically expressed actions, performed by the personified destination towards potential visitors. Everything it has is 'offered' to visitors, who are 'welcome'. As for participants, the archipelago is overtly mentioned five times, either as Actor or as Carrier, and once as Beneficiary. Alongside, the highest number of participants indicates the island's several pull factors, such as the climate, water, cultural and artistic treasures, natural sites, hospitality and transport services. Interestingly, the Beneficiary of Malta's beauties is termed the 'traveller', evoking a curious, active and non-massified attitude. The item 'tourist' is purposefully omitted, given its widespread negative connotation of superficiality and passivity (see Introduction).

This passage is divided into four short paragraphs. As for Theme–Rheme structure, a marked Theme is adopted very often, where Theme does not conflate with Subject in declarative sentences. Where a dependent clause preceded its main clause, a double Theme analysis has been carried out.

Table 2.4 Process types in the brochure extract

Process type	No.	Process type	No.
Material	7	Verbal	0
Mental	2	Behavioural	0
Attributive	6	Existential	0
Identifying	1		
Total number of processes: 16			

This realises a carefully written mode, in which the writer has planned the rhetorical development of the text. For instance, the first sentence shows subtle Theme planning, with two parallel dependent clauses in Thematic position. This kind of rhetorical syntax constructs a slow, pleasant and suspended rhythm. This is confirmed by the fact that the destination name is often Thematised, positioned and foregrounded as given, known and familiar. The Maltese archipelago is thus the most prominent element in the passage; the remainder of the message, the Rheme, is meant to sustain and document the destination enhancement.

Having observed the systems of Transitivity and Thematisation, the following section examines the system of Mood.

Mood analysis

Key. Subject (S), Finite (F), negative (Fn), modalised (Fms), modulated (Fml). Predicator (P), modulated Predicator (Pml), modalised Predicator (Pms), fused Finite and Predicator (F/P). Complement (C), attributive Complement (Ca), Adjunct (A), circumstantial (Ac), mood (Am), comment (Ao), polarity (Ap), vocative (Av), conjunctive (Aj), continuity (At). MOOD element of ranking (non-embedded) clauses is shown in bold, [[embedded clauses]].

1.i [[Blessed (P) with a mild climate (C)]] and (Aj) [[set (P) in crystal waters (Ac)]], **Malta and its sister islands of Gozo and Comino** (S) **offer** (F/P) you a memorable experience (C), 1.ii where (Aj) **moments of complete relaxation** (S) **can** (Fml) **be combined with** (P) the exploration of the islands' many cultural, artistic and national treasures (C).

2.i [[Long (Ac) considered (P) a microcosm of the Mediterranean and a favourite with travellers (C)]] [[who (S) seek (F/P) an authentic island experience (C)]], **our islands** (S) **offer** (F/P) an impressive range of historical and cultural sites, together with a spectrum of activities (C), [[making (F/P) Malta (C) a truly unique year-round holiday destination (Ca)]].

3. **Malta** (S) **has** (F) managed to strike (P) the right balance between traditional hospitality and a cosmopolitan spirit (C) [[born (P) out of millennial history (Ac)]] [[of welcoming (F/P) people (C) from all around the region and beyond (Ac)]]. 4.i Moreover (Aj), **Malta** (S) **has** (F) developed into (P) a highly sought after location for international movie productions (C), 4ii while (Aj) **Valletta's majestic Grand harbour** (S) **welcomes** (F/P) cruise liner passengers (C) from all over the world (Ac).

5.i **The Maltese islands** (S) **are** (F) just (Am) a few hours away from major European airports (Ac), 5.ii and (Aj) with the many scheduled, low-cost and charter flights (Ac) [[linking (P) Malta (C) to a host of European and other Mediterranean countries (Ac)]], not to mention (Aj) the excellent sea connection to Europe (C), **getting here** (S) **could not** (Fms) be (P) easier (Ca)!

The system of Mood is of interest in this passage. Given the fundamentally persuasive function of tourism texts, the construction of the clause as exchange between a sender and an audience needs to be discussed. Overall, the text is built of statements with a descriptive purpose articulated through the declarative mood, whose aim is to provide tourist information. This situates the reader in a potential role of acknowledger. Surprisingly, no interrogative or imperative forms are used to establish any dialogic interaction, so that no demand is apparently articulated.

Yet, the descriptive genre value makes use of some interpersonal strategies like the possessive adjective 'our' and the personal pronoun 'you', which create a boundary between author and reader. Fodde and Denti (2008, 2012) specify that personal pronouns are used to frame interpersonal closeness and intimacy in tourism texts. Furthermore, the conversational and friendly tone they establish reduces scepticism towards promotional messages (Dann, 1996a; Mocini, 2009). This choice reflects what Dann (1996a: 185) more broadly terms 'ego-targeting', a promotional strategy aimed at directly addressing readers and to single them out from the crowd, making them feel unique and distinct from the undifferentiated mass of customers. Coherently, verbs like 'to welcome' and 'to offer', jointly with the adjective 'welcoming' and the noun 'hospitality', confirm a friendly host–guest interaction.

By means of the system of modalisation, the author intrudes in the message, expressing extremely positive attitudes and judgements. Specifically, this happens through the double use of the Mood Adjunct of certainty, 'truly'. The same position is reinforced in the clause 'getting here could not be easier!', where the Finite modal operator 'could' in the negative polarity carries a meaning of certainty. Rather than tempering the statements, the systems of modulation and modalisation are thus used only to confirm the certainty of facts expressed through declarative sentences.

Having examined the system of Mood, the following section concentrates on Clause complex, as realising the ideational metafunction in its logical component and the textual metafunction as for grammar intricacy.

Clause complex analysis

Key: [[embedded clauses]], 1, 2, 3 parataxis, α β χ : hypotaxis, " locution, ' idea, = elaboration, + extension, × enhancement

> 1. [[Blessed with a mild climate]] and [[set in crystal waters]], Malta and its sister islands of Gozo and Comino offer you a memorable experience,
> α × where moments of complete relaxation can be combined with the exploration of the islands' many cultural, artistic and national treasures.
> 1. [[Long considered a microcosm of the Mediterranean and a favourite with travellers]] [[who seek an authentic island experience]], our islands offer an impressive range of historical and cultural sites, together with a spectrum of activities, [[making Malta a truly unique year-round holiday destination]].
> Clause simplex: Malta has managed to strike the right balance between traditional hospitality and a cosmopolitan spirit [[born out of millennial history]] [[of welcoming people from all around the region and beyond]].
> 1. Moreover, Malta has developed into a highly sought after location for international movie productions,
> 2. while Valletta's majestic Grand harbour welcomes cruise liner passengers from all over the world.
> 1. The Maltese islands are just a few hours away from major European airports,
> α + and with the many scheduled, low-cost and charter flights [[linking Malta to a host of European and other Mediterranean countries]], not to mention the excellent sea connection to Europe, getting here could not be easier!

As for Clause complex analysis, this text shows a high proportion of words to sentences. Only once is clause simplex present, in favour of a more frequent complexing. Within clause complexes, hypotaxis is preferred to parataxis. Interestingly, embedding is adopted eight times. This confirms the hypothesis of a carefully written text, unfolding with a slow, descriptive rhythm. It also mirrors Castello's findings (2001) on the high level of sentence complexity and intricacy in the brochure text genre. Table 2.5 provides some data on the two grammar systems of the ideational metafunction.

All lexico-grammar analysis in the brochure enables us to interpret the register variables of field, tenor and mode. As for field, the Maltese archipelago is described as an ideal holiday destination, rich in natural and cultural wonders that have attracted visitors for ages. The tenor is constructed as

Table 2.5 The systems of Clause complex and Taxis in the brochure extract

No. of words	193	No. of clause complexes	4
No. of sentences	5	No. of embedded clauses	8
No. of ranking clauses	8	Parataxis	1
No. of clause simplexes	1	Hypotaxis	2

an expert, informed, but friendly author, seeking to establish a personal exchange with the potential tourist through high affective involvement. The text is then a descriptive piece of writing, which has been carefully composed following the conventions of writing but which incorporates interactive strategies typical of conversation. This hybridity is pursued for the ultimate promotional aim of the text.

After observing verbal language behaviour in the brochure as B2C printed text, the following section examines a C2C Web 2.0 text genre.

SFL in an Online Travel Diary Recording a Trip to Malta

Online travel diaries are web-based travelogues written and shared by travellers while they are still on the road (Cappelli, 2008; Dann, 2007; Dann & Parrinello, 2007; Morrison, 2008; Myers, 2010). This relatively recent forum for travel discussion has dramatically invaded and subverted the world of travel communication, mainly due to electronic material support, allowing instant and global connections. The subtle definition of 'word-of-mouse' provided by Dann and Parrinello (2007: 12) effectively highlights this fruitful migration onto the web of the most spontaneous and immediate form of tourism communication, word-of-mouth. This type of travel narration is supported by the opportunity for reader feedback: any reader can react to a post, generating an open dialogue with a potentially limitless number of participants (Dann, 2007, 2012a, 2012b; Dann & Parrinello, 2007).

In fact, these digital entries are generally seen as telling the 'real', uncensored story, which positions them as credible, unmediated witnesses to the events, places, services or facilities they describe (Calvi, 2010; Dann, 2007, 2012a, 2012b; Dann & Parinello, 2007). Taken as more valid in their evaluations than professionally written travel guides or brochures, these travelogues are increasingly being consulted by would-be travellers when planning their holidays (Dann, 2012a, 2012b).

Online travel diaries may be of varying length and may be composed of one or more textual units called posts, archived inside the blog in reverse chronological order. The written text is generally complemented by a wide range of multimodal material, like photos and videos, chart trips and maps. Diaries are typically found in blogs, composite texts to be considered as travel macro-genres (see Chapter 1). Emerging only in the mid-1990s as a practice among professionals in computing science and engineering, the phenomenon of blogging is expanding and differentiating rapidly: a new blog is created every half a second (Myers, 2010).

Far from the sophisticated style and language of prestigious, classic travel books, spontaneous and impulsive electronic journals are written in a colloquial and immediate style (Antelmi & Santulli, 2012; Cappelli, 2008; Dann, 2007, 2012a, 2012b; Dann & Parrinello, 2007; Morrison, 2008; Myers, 2010), following the conventions of 'Netspeak' (see Chapter 1). On the one hand, online travel accounts are unedited texts, often displaying lexico-grammatical mistakes or incoherent sentences and an impoverishment of lexicon. On the other hand, they explore different possibilities of expression, creating a spontaneous and impulsive form of textuality, merging characteristics of written and spoken English (Crystal, 2006: 255).

The following is an exemplary text taken from the TravelPod website (www.travelpod.com), retrieved by entering the single keyword 'Malta', and organising the results in reversed chronological order. The chosen entry was posted from Valletta, Malta's capital city, on 17 November 2012, by US traveller 'Dmarek'. Taken from the 1700-word post, the following paragraphs are the central part of the text (the final part of the first paragraph has been cut in order for the extract to be about the same length as the brochure passage). Formal inaccuracies have been left unedited and unhighlighted, in order to exemplify the stylistic distinction of this text genre.

> Now it was time to leave the Mdina (the walled part of the the city) and enter Rabat - or so it seemed as if that were what I was doing. On my way out, I stopped at tourist info and picked up a map - to find out that Domus Romana was nearest to the Mdina so I went there first - it was included in my Heritage Pass. They had a quite modern exhibit - very nicely done I thought. [...]
>
> Now to follow the map to the Catacombs. I inquired at a souvenir shop and before I could even ask, the man told me to head down the street for the catacombs. Do I look ghoulish?? I was grateful for the help though. I hear something loud outside - probably a big boat. Nope, don't see one out there. I love the view from this room - I get to see all kinds of boats coming through - especially in the morning, but the hotel staff person says a lot come through during the night as well - waiting for the price of oil, or whatever, to rise. At least, that is what I thought he said.

With the tools of SFL, the text can be first observed in the fulfilment of the ideational metafunction via the grammar system of Transitivity, with reference to the register variable of field, and in the textual metafunction via the grammar system of Thematisation, with reference to the register variable of mode.

Transitivity and Theme analysis

Now (Cl) it (T) was (Pi) time (V) to leave (Pm) the Mdina (the walled part of the the city) (G) and enter (Pm) Rabat (G) -or so it (T) seemed (Pi) as if that (T) were (Pi) what (G) I (A) was doing (Pm). On my way out (Cl), I (A) stopped (Pm) at tourist info (Cl), and picked up (Pm) a map (G) - to find out (Pme) that Domus Romana (Cr) was (Pa) nearest to the Mdina (At) so I went (Pm) there (Cl) first (Cx) - it (Cr) was (Pa) included in my Heritage Pass. They (A) had (Pm) a quite modern exhibit (G) - very nicely done (Pm) I (S) thought (Pme). [...]

Now (Cl) to follow (Pme) the map (Ph) to the Catacombs (Cl). I (Sy) inquired (Pv) at a souvenir shop (Cl) and before I (Sy) could even ask (Pv), the man (Sy) told (Pv) me (Rv) to head (Pm) down the street (Cl) for the catacombs. Do I (Cr) look (Pa) ghoulish (At)¿¿ I (Cr) was (Pa) grateful for the help (Cc) though. I hear (Pme) something loud (Ph) outside (Cl) - probably a big boat (Ph). Nope, don't see (Pme) one (Ph) out there (Cl). I (S) love (Pme) the view (Ph) from this room (Cl) - I (S) get to see (Pme) all kinds of boats (Ph) coming through (Pm) -especially in the morning (Cx), but the hotel staff person (Sy) says (Pv) a lot (A) come (Pm) through (Cl) during the night (Cx) as well -waiting for (Pm) the price of oil, or whatever (G), to rise (Pm). At least, that (T) is (Pi) what I (S) thought (Pme) he (Sy) said (Pv).

The grammar system of Transitivity provides interesting insights into the understanding of the nature and function of this text. The significant presence of material, mental and verbal process types (Table 2.6) immediately reveals that the electronic travel journal text genre is completely different from the previous one, the narrative genre value being predominant here over the descriptive one. Narrated events like 'to leave the Medina', 'enter Rabat', 'hear something loud', among others, are focused on the narrator's cognitive and sensorial perceptions and actions. There are consistently less attributive processes than in the previous descriptive passage.

Both marked and unmarked Thematisation is adopted, showing a variety of solutions. However, such variation does not feature any lexical or syntactic parallelism or rhythmic patterning as in the brochure genre.

Systemic Functional Grammar   67

Table 2.6 Process types in the post

Process type	No.	Process type	No.
Material	13	Verbal	5
Mental	8	Behavioural	0
Attributive	4	Existential	0
Identifying	4		
Total number of processes: 34			

Generally, unmarked solutions are more frequent. This demonstrates a non-carefully written text, resorting to simple and immediate strategies. Having observed the systems of Transitivity and of Thematisation, the following section examines the system of Mood.

Mood analysis

Now (Aj) **it** (S) **was** (F) time (Ca) to leave (P) the Mdina (the walled part of the the city) (C) and (Aj) enter (P) Rabat (C)- or (Aj) so (Ca) **it** (S) **seemed** (F/P) as if (Aj) that (S) were (F/P) [[what (C) I (S) was (F) doing (P)]]. On my way out (Ac), **I** (S) **stopped** (F/P) at tourist info (Ac) and (Aj) **picked up** (F/P) a map (C) - to find out (F/P) that (Aj) **Domus Romana** (S) **was** (F/P) nearest (Ca) to the Mdina (Ac) so (Aj) **I** (S) **went** (F/P) there (Ac) first (Ac) - **it** (S) **was** (F) included (P) in my Heritage Pass (Ac). **They** (S) **had** (F/P) a quite modern exhibit (C) - very nicely (Ac) done (F/P) **I** (S) **thought** (F/P). [...]

Now (Aj) **to follow** (F/P) the map (C) to the Catacombs (Ac). **I** (S) **inquired** (F/P) at a souvenir shop (Ac) and (Aj) before (Aj) **I** (S) **could** (Fms) even (Am) ask (P), **the man** (S) **told** (F/P) me (C) **to head** (P) down the street (Ac) for the catacombs (Ac). **Do I** (S) look (F/P) ghoulish (Ca)¿¿ **I** (S) **was** (F/P) grateful (Ca) for the help (Ac) though (Am). **I** (S) **hear** (F/P) something loud (C) outside (Ac) - probably (Am) a big boat (C). Nope (Ap), **don't** (Fn) see (P) one (C) out there (Ac). **I** (S) **love** (F/P) the view (C) from this room (Ac) - **I** (S) **get** (F) to see (P) all kinds of boats (C) [[coming through (P) - especially (Am) in the morning (Ac)]], but (Aj) **the hotel staff person** (S) **says** (F/P) **a lot come through** (F/P) during the night (Ac) as well (Aj)- waiting (P) for the price of oil, or whatever (C), to rise (P). At least (Aj), **that** (S) **is** (F/P) [[what (C) [[I (S) thought]] (F/P) **he** (S) **said** (F/P)]].

The system of Mood is of interest in this passage. As already highlighted, the online diary is constructed of statements with a narrative purpose, the declarative syntactic mood being predominant over other solutions. Only a rhetorical question is present, whose value is more self-referential than dialogic. In fact, the passage is centred on the first person's acts, thoughts and perceptions, as the systematic occurrence of the first-person personal pronoun demonstrates. By the means of the system of modalisation, the author then intrudes in the message: examples are the mood Adjunct of probability 'probably' and the conjunctive Adjunct 'though'.

Having examined the system of Mood, the following section concentrates on Clause complex, as realising the ideational metafunction in its logical component and the textual metafunction as to grammar intricacy.

Clause complex analysis

1. Now it was time to leave the Mdina (the walled part of the the city)
2. and enter Rabat -
3. or so it seemed
α as if that were [[what I was doing]].
1. On my way out, I stopped at tourist info
2. and picked up a map
α -to find out
β that Domus Romana was nearest to the Mdina
3. so I went there first
α × -it was included in my Heritage Pass.
α ' They had a quite modern exhibit [[-very nicely done]]
1. I thought. [...]
Clause simplex Now to follow the map to the Catacombs.
1. I inquired at a souvenir shop
α × and before I could even ask,
2. the man told me
α to head down the street for the catacombs.
Clause simplex Do I look ghoulish??
Clause simplex I was grateful for the help though.
Clause simplex I hear something loud outside - probably a big boat.
Clause simplex Nope, don›t see one out there.
1. I love the view from this room
α = - I get to see all kinds of boats [[coming through - especially in the morning]],
β + but the hotel staff person says
γ " a lot come through during the night as well - [[waiting for the price of oil, or whatever, to rise.]]
Clause simplex At least, that is [[what [[I thought]] he said.]]

Table 2.7 The systems of Clause complex and Taxis in the post

No. of words	200	No. of clause complexes	5
No. of sentences	11	No. of embedded clauses	6
No. of ranking clauses	26	Paratactic relations	5
No. of clause simplexes	6	Hypotactic relations	10

As for Clause complex analysis, this text shows a high number of sentences, of which six are clause simplexes and five complexes. As embedding is adopted six times, the number of ranking clauses is remarkable. Within complexes, hypotaxis and parataxis coexist and interact, hypotactic relations being more frequent. Table 2.7 provides some data on the systems of Clause complex and Taxis:

Short sentences, simplexes and parataxis reveal a text unfolding through a quicker rhythm, based on a simple and more immediate structure. Given the digital medium, the online diary codification generally occurs on-trip, which implies freshness and spontaneity in content but basic structures and forms (Francesconi, 2012). As such, the text is a narrative piece of writing featuring a conversational style, typical of Netspeak, which blogs tend to maximally express. It shows weak paragraphing, unclear logical progression of ideas, predominant parataxis, restricted vocabulary range, frequent repetitions and use of colloquialism, alongside a limited range of grammar structures and uncontrolled punctuation. As for the system of Mood, sentences are predominantly statements and use the declarative mood. Only one interrogative sentence is present, which expresses a personal thought of the blogger and not a dialogic form of interaction.

Lexico-grammar analysis of the online travel diary has revealed interesting insights into the register variables of field, tenor and mode. As for field, the author, Dmarek, narrates a personal visit to Mdina and Rabat. The tenor is constructed as an enthusiast and curious traveller, wishing to share the tale of this Maltese experience with a potentially limitless number of readers with whom the writer has an equal power relation. The two considered texts, in fact, slightly differ in their communication functions. Using Eggins' terminology (2011: 74), the brochure text has a pragmatic motivation, since it has a clear, tangible goal to be achieved. In particular, it seeks to convince readers to visit the promoted destination. The online travel diary, instead, aims to share opinions, experiences and suggestions on the destination or itinerary.

Conclusion

This chapter has outlined the theory and the methodological framework of SFL. It has illustrated the register variables of field, tenor and mode, as interconnected with the semantic metafunctions and eventually realised at the lexico-grammar level. It has then considered these levels in a tourism brochure and an online travel diary and observed how semiosis is affected by medium-based affordances and modal configurations. From the multimodal viewpoint this volume adopts, verbal language makes meaning as expressed through writing or speech. These vary in terms of materiality, semantic properties, cognitive orientation and semantic potential, issues which will be addressed in the following chapters.

3 Visual Analysis

Vision

Acknowledging the ubiquity and power of images in Western contemporary society, this chapter discusses the role of vision in tourism and travel discourse. It first introduces vision from a diachronic perspective, considering modes and forms of image production over the course of the centuries and the relationship between reality and its visual representation. After locating vision within the circular and pre-systematised epistemic lens of 'the tourist gaze', it presents and exemplifies a framework of analysis for tourism and travel visual texts, adapting to the tourism and travel domain the social semiotic tools developed by Kress and van Leeuwen and discussing examples referring to Ireland. In that context, it finally mentions the visual system of writing.

'Human experience is now more visual and visualized than ever before', observes Mirzoeff (1999: 1), discussing the pervasiveness and power of huge numbers of images in Western industrial society. The contemporary domains of science, education, communication, politics, business and popular culture rely on visuality, mediated through a wide range of media, including paintings, prints, film, television, digital images and virtual reality (Sturken & Cartwright, 2009: 24–26). Travel is no exception.

Constantly produced, reproduced, manipulated and disseminated, images convey different meanings, engender diverse reactions and perform various communication functions (Sturken & Cartwright, 2009: 9). Rather than being univocal and predictable, their interpretation is a complex, multifold and fluid process, deeply affected by the contexts and conditions of codification and decodification. Visual meanings can be imposed, transferred or simply suggested. Accordingly, the viewing process can identify with, negotiate or reject the ideological position of the image (Berger,

1972; Jenks, 1995; Mirzoeff, 1998, 1999). In order to be able to understand, negotiate and subvert imposed meanings, viewers need to develop an image awareness.

Critical attention to this phenomenon is surprisingly recent. Although today a wide range of disciplines devote their attention to vision, the term 'visual culture' came into use in the disciplinary field of art history in the 1970s. In the 1990s cultural studies experienced 'the visual turn', with a specific emphasis on visuality. An increasing number of conferences, courses and publications gave visual culture the status of a central field of inquiry in the 1990s and early 2000s (Crouch & Lübbren, 2003: 2). Nowadays, journals like *Visual Culture in Britain*, *Visual Communication* and *Visual Culture*, among others, provide an insightful platform for critical debate, which is progressively expanding into multidisciplinary contexts and addressing multimodal and multimedia texts.

However, for much of the time, Western culture has considered written texts as the highest forms of intellectual practice and visual texts a lower form of expression. Mirzoeff (1999: 9) locates the origin of this hostility in Plato's thought. The Greek philosopher claimed that all the objects encountered in everyday life are simply bad copies of reality: visual reproductions were only partial and distorted illustrations of ideas. Plato's position has intensively influenced Western thought, which has sometimes expressed overtly iconoclastic ideas.

The most relevant epistemic turning point was *Discourse on the Method* by Descartes ([1637] 2006), which marked the beginning of modernity. The French philosopher explained that what the eye sees depends on the rays of light refracted by its lenses, which, in turn, create an inverted image on the retina. The upside-down image produced by the eye has nothing to do with the object seen because, in reality, it is interpreted by the mind. Consequently, the process of vision is reconfigured, and linked to the various desires of the viewer, the social relations between the viewer and what is seen, and its sociocultural context.

After Descartes, sight was considered 'the noblest of the senses, the most discriminating and reliable of the sensuous mediators between humans and their physical environment' (Urry, 2002: 146). Discussing the authority and legitimation of the medical gaze, Foucault ([1963] 1973) noticed how visual observation has been considered as the foundation element of scientific approaches to the world. This resulted in a connection between sight and intellectual investigation, in an overlapping of physical and mental explorations. Central to the cognitive implications of the visual paradigm, the etymological root of the noun 'idea' is to be found in the Greek verb meaning 'to see' (Jenks, 1995: 1).

The epistemic changes of Descartes's world vision and of the scientific revolution are closely linked to a technique of visual composition invented in Italy in the mid-15th century, that is, perspective. Making the single eye the defining centre of the visible world, perspective hierarchically organises elements according to the distance from the observer (Berger, 1972: 18). More than a strategy of composition, perspective substituted the divine with the human observer as the new perceptive and organising centre (Berger, 1972: 16). The plane receding towards a vanishing point also implied the configuration of depth. In fact, making two-dimensional images resemble three-dimensional reality, the invention of perspective was the answer to making works of art more realistic and objective (Sturken & Cartwright, 2009: 164).

Hence, the visual representation has been often taken as a substitute for the items being represented. This impasse has been foregrounded in the thought-provoking 1929 *The Treachery of Images* by the Belgian surrealist painter René Magritte. Accompanying the careful drawing of a pipe is the clearly visible and steady writing: 'This is not a pipe'. Such artwork casts light on the arbitrary relation between signifier and signified, between the object and its representation, be it visual or verbal. And, last but not least, reminds the viewer that the painted or written pipe cannot be smoked!

In Western culture, the history of visuality and the relation between visual representation and reality is strictly connected to the history of image production and deeply affected by technology. In fact, the symbolic forms created by visual media are so substantial that people become dependent upon them for their knowledge of the world. Before the mechanical era, an image was unique in time and space and had a precise role. Singularity constituted what Benjamin ([1936] 1969) called its 'aura', a kind of sacred value. The original image was then authentic and authenticity could not be reproduced without losing that auratic value. Authorship and ownership were transparent concepts, the painting, fresco or drawing being univocally attributable to their author. In that context, the role and meaning of the image were fixed and codified within the given context of its fruition. For example, a religious painting inside a cathedral was meant to impart a precise moral lesson and the portrait of a nobleman in his villa had to celebrate his aristocratic status. Conventions and strategies of symbolic representation were adapted to these specific purposes.

In the early 19th century, the invention of photography had a revolutionary impact on the history of visuality. On the one hand, it gave maximum expression to the myth of mimetic rendering of reality. On the other hand, it subverted the image auratic value through reduplication and dissemination (Benjamin, [1936] 1969). As for the first point, a mechanical rather than human device was accepted as a guarantee of truth and its result was read as an unmediated copy of reality. In public or private, official and unofficial settings, photographs were taken as objective, documentary, incontrovertible proof of the occurrence and/or existence of something (Sontag, [1971] 2002: 5). This view has not completely faded in contemporary society, which partly still accepts and uses photography as a mimetic form of expression. Obviously, a high degree of subjectivity is involved in the act of taking a photograph. The adoption of a specific viewpoint, the process of framing, the technical manipulation of light, colour and distance are all strategies that variously inform the visual semiotic process. A powerful medium of reality modification, the camera has been described by Sontag as performing an 'aggression', 'appropriation', 'control' and even 'negation' of the object (Sontag, [1971] 2002: 5). This concept will be developed and examples will be given in the following sections.

As for the auratic value, the episteme dramatically changed with the age of mechanical reproduction of works of art and with the invention of photography (Benjamin, [1936] 1969). In their initial stages of development, photographs were prohibitively expensive, required bulky equipment and were taken by a few experienced photographers, who controlled the circulation of images (Robinson & Picard, 2009: 5). But then photography experienced progressive mass production and mass circulation, which further exploded in the 1980s with the emergence of the digital image.

The difference between photography and digital imaging derives from a technical distinction. While analogue images bear a physical correspondence with their material referents and are defined by properties along a continuous scale (e.g. tone and brightness), digital images are mathematically encoded as information on a digital chip (Sturken & Cartwright, 2009: 139). Thanks to that basic information, which can be endlessly reproduced, no difference exists in the quality of the copies of digital images. Any discussions about image originality and uniqueness become nonsense. What is noteworthy, though, is their infinite potential in terms of accessibility, storage, manipulation, uploads, downloads and transmission (Mirzoeff, 1999; Sturken & Cartwright, 2009: 212).

As a consequence of massification, pervasiveness and power, visual media play a dominant ideological role. Today, images are central to the mainstream commodity culture, which is based on constant production, promotion and consumption of goods (Sturken & Cartwright, 2009: 266). Since visual communication intimately connects representation and reality (Urry, 2002: 77), advertising uses images to shape sociocultural values and ideologies to persuade potential clients. Visions of freedom, purity, relaxation, intimacy, style and glamour can be variously articulated and systematically transmitted through mass media.

The sociocultural world we inhabit is hence a 'society of the spectacle' (Mirzoeff, 1999: 63), centred on the spectacularisation of consumerism. People in this spectacular society are so obsessed with the idea of accumulating products that in the end they buy only their image. It is precisely in this context that the anthropologist Urry defines tourist sites as 'centres of spectacle and display' (2002: 85). Acknowledging this label, the following section explores the multiple connections between visuality, tourists, travellers, holiday sites and their visual representation and promotion.

Visual Culture and Tourism

While on holiday in Florence at the *Pensione* Bertolini, Forster's ([1908] 1995) well-known and beloved character Lucy Honeychurch absolutely wants a 'room with a view': only a room overlooking the Arno will make her travel experience meaningful. The centrality of the visual to the rituals of modern travel and tourism has been asserted by the sociologist MacCannell ([1976] 1989) in his pioneer study on tourism and developed subsequently into more focalised literature in the field. As Jenkins (2003: 309) puts it, 'tourist consumption is primarily visual': visiting equals seeing; a tourist site is a 'sight' and what needs to be visited is a must-see, a *sehenswürdigkeit* (Francesconi, 2007, 2012). Accordingly, must-see hit parades are proudly displayed by travel guides, websites and blogs to clearly advise on the top five or top ten spots visitors absolutely have to see.

It is such destination sights that travellers look for, capture and consume through pictures and videos (Crouch & Lübbren, 2003). Aware of this necessity, destination people in many ethnographic tours ask to be paid in order to be photographed. Among the Mursi in southern Ethiopia, local people are used to asking for the corresponding value of a Kalashnikov bullet to let travellers take a picture of lip-plate women and body-painted men (Aime, 2000: 35). To the eyes of those people, travellers are picture-taking human beings.

Not surprisingly, then, photography was invented during a tourist experience. In *The Pencil of Nature* (1844–46), William Henry Fox Talbot relates that the idea of photography came to him in 1833 while making some sketches of the landscape at Lake Como, where he was spending some time during his Grand Tour. Through this medium, the Grand Tourist managed to perpetuate the act of contemplation, to crystallise the act of sightseeing and save it from time passing and distance in space (Francesconi, 2007: 47; Schaaf, 2000; Urry & Larsen, 2011: 164).

After almost two centuries, Sontag observes that, today, 'it seems positively unnatural to travel for pleasure without taking a camera along'

([1971] 2002: 9). Travelling equals photographing. The camera, she explains, enables tourists to capture, mark, fix and take control of the following time and of the 'exotic' space. The 20th century has been marked by a 'kodakisation' of the world (Urry, 2002), the Kodak camera having symbolised this organised and obsessive visual consumption of spaces. Paradoxically, the tourist picture, be it printed or digital, is not a means but an end in itself: 'travel becomes a strategy for accumulating photographs' (Sontag, [1971] 2002: 9).

Travel not only equals seeing, but also showing that one has seen. Seeing and ways of seeing are thus inextricably related to being seen and ways of being seen (Urry, 2002: 125). To socially and tangibly testify to the Grand Tour experience, classical statues were displayed by rich British aristocrats in their gardens, while contemporary living rooms proudly exhibit pieces of ethnic art, not to mention the huge numbers of pictures tourists bring home to inflict on relatives and friends in 'conspicuous display' (Robinson & Picard, 2009: 2). Travel is undoubtedly a 'marker of status' and status is subject to the never-ending process of confirmation. Nowadays, dynamics of vision and the configuration of visibility have partially migrated to the web, which offers global and instant display. In virtual photography communities like Pinterest and Instagram and social networks like Facebook and Twitter, digital images are constantly being uploaded, tagged, shared, disseminated and pinned. Undoubtedly, the virtual narration of holidays and the subsequent social visibility is becoming a winning strategy for identity and status acquisition and confirmation (Francesconi, 2012).

The Tourist Gaze

The tourist picture plays a crucial role in 'the tourist gaze', the model of tourist perception of the destination extensively examined by Urry (2002). Far from an immediate and impulsive sensorial process of perception, sightseeing is deeply affected by previous visual narratives and enacts all the individual tourist expectations, experiences and memories. In the scholar's own words:

> What is sought for in a holiday is a set of photographic images, which have already been seen in tour company brochures or on TV programmes. While a tourist is away, this then moves on to a tracking down and capturing of those images for oneself. And it ends up with travellers demonstrating that they really have been there by showing their version of the images that they had seen before they set off. (Urry, 2002: 129)

Figure 3.1 Donegal: Glenveagh National Park (copyright Fáilte Ireland)

More than the breathtaking landscape of Glenveagh National Park in Donegal, Figure 3.1 illustrates the process of sightseeing, showing the subject, object, direction and moment of the tourist gaze. Enacting a process of identification with the represented human beings, the visual text invites interactive participants to enter the scene, enjoy that panorama, from that particular viewpoint, at that particular moment and take a picture. A circular process, the tourist gaze is generated by and generates self-perpetuating modes and forms of vision.

The gaze, then, functions as a lens which (de)codifies new images, working with filters, carefully planned and framed by the tourist industry. By the means of multiple, pervasive and mobile cultural mediators such as brochures, guidebooks, websites, videos and postcards, imagery enables the tourist and travel industry to assert power over the viewer (Crouch & Lübbren, 2003: 9). The tourist gaze thus proves to be a profitable strategy of social control (Urry, 2002: 10), capable of turning viewers into visitors.

Curiously enough, the circular process continues with locals adapting to the rules and needs of 'the tourist picture'. In their clothes, houses, food and dances, the locals 'stage' (MacCannell, [1976] 1989) what tourists believe to be authentic and traditional or, better still, what tourist catalogues and travel literature have shaped as such. For instance, defined as 'mysterious' and 'magic', the Mali people of the Dogon partly adapt to this simplistic label for economic purposes and use traditional clothes and arms only for ethnic tourist pictures. Conversely, when they do their spiritual dances, they are happy to use dusty, discoloured t-shirts and Adidas shoes. They even cover their cement houses with earth, knowing that this is what tourists crave for and take pictures of (Aime, 2000).

The concept of the self-perpetuating circularity of the gaze confirms the slippery border between travel photographs and tourist photographs (see Introduction). While on a trip, travellers tend to reduplicate those tourist pictures seen on brochures or websites that have shaped their gaze. Are these travel or tourist pictures? Moreover, holidaymakers put their efforts into realising scenic holiday pictures, not so much to display their technical expertise as photographers but to render a positive image of the visited destination. The breathtaking picture is to be proudly displayed and exploited as an ego-enhancing strategy and a marker of status. In turn, some tourist pictures, especially in catalogues promoting alternative forms of travel, increasingly try to look less touristy and glossy, in order to appear more 'reliable'. Both tourist and travel pictures thus tend to overcome a naturalistic representation of reality and to beautify and enhance the site with positive emotions, feelings and connotations.

The circularity of the tourist gaze implies its prescription by pre-trip texts, which tend to advise which gaze to cast, how to perform the process of vision on the different contextual conditions. In her analysis of travel guides, the semiotician Giannitrapani (2010: 51) has described various ways in which the visitor can view a city and travel guides predefine this gaze. She has identified either partial or global gaze.

(1) A *partial gaze*, based on a horizontal, dialogic, personal relationship between the gazer and the tourist space, captured in its individual parts. The partial gaze can be either dynamic or static, as follows:

- A *dynamic* gaze can be first identified, which follows the rhythmic development of the itinerary. While walking through the urban streets, the visitor constantly looks around, casting and accumulating quick and sudden glimpses, performing a non-focused gaze. The viewer, then, has an active role, which derives from his/her movement and from the established dialogic gazer–gazee relation. This is verbally exemplified in the following excerpts, taken from the itinerary sections of the *Lonely Planet Guide to Scotland* (Wilson & Murphy, 2009: 24–26, *passim*):

> Continue to Dumfries (p178) and make a short side-trip to see spectacular Caerlaverock Castle (p180).
>
> After a look at romantic Kisimul Castle and a circuit of the island take the ferry to South Uilst (p400).
>
> Skye and Outer Hebrides (p389) are probably your best bet for spotting otters in the wild.

- Alternatively, the partial gaze may be *static*. Of a certain duration, this analytic and attentive process adopts a logic of composition of the sight process. This means that it may have different degrees of focalisation and be addressed to a detail, a portion and/or a whole item. In the process of vision, the tourist is static and has a passive role, because it is the scene that captures his/her attention (Giannitrapani, 2010: 53). An example can be seen in the following Wikitravel description of Edinburgh Castle. The building is seen from the outside, where the sloping forecourt called the Esplanade lies, and the static sightseeing process progressively focuses on the gatehouse, the statues, the motto and the ditch:

> The gatehouse at the head of the Esplanade was built as an architecturally cosmetic addition to the castle in 1888. Statues of Robert the Bruce by Thomas Clapperton and William Wallace by Alexander Carrick were added in 1929, and the Latin motto *Nemo me impune lacessit* is inscribed above the gate. The dry ditch in front of the entrance was completed in its present form in 1742. (www.wikitravel.org/en/scotland)

(2) A global form of perception, the topographic gaze is based on the strategy of the map. This gaze does not concentrate on figurative details, but observes the city from a bird's eye angle, which is inaccessible to the traveller. Far from a neutral form of visual representation, the map selects, organises and then conceptualises space as highly cohesive (Giannitrapani, 2010: 62). What follows is a verbal expression of the topographic gaze, across the use of geographical coordinates:

> [Scotland] has a 60 mile (96 km) land border with England to the south, and is separated from Northern Ireland by the North Channel of the Irish Sea. It is surrounded by the bracing waters of the North Sea to the east, and the North Atlantic Ocean to the west and north. (www.wikitravel.org/en/scotland)

A totalising gaze, the panoramic gaze is static and unfolds along a vertical line. Accessible to the traveller, it is cast by vantage points like towers, skyscrapers or mounts. It is systemic, conceptualises the location as an abstraction and implies an impersonal relationship between the gazer and the gaze. To this vertically oriented process I would include the horizontal dimension, a panorama, or 'scenery', also being visible from a distant viewpoint but from the same level. Some interesting examples of panoramic vision are offered in the following excerpts from the *Lonely Planet Guide to Scotland* (Wilson & Murphy, 2009: 26, 29), with a suspension of time and still landscape appreciation:

> In April and May Scotland's glorious scenery is set off by snow lingering on the mountains.

> In theory you could cover this spectacular 475-mile route in two days, but allowing time to stop and enjoy the scenery and the seafood makes two weeks a more realistic estimate.

These different forms of visual perception and fruition realise the ideational metafunction in language and, as the quotations show, are verbally represented through specific processes (verbs), participants (nominal groups) and circumstances (adverbial groups or prepositional phrases). Vision-related processes are mental processes indicating perception, implying the participant as the 'senser' and 'phenomenon'. Circumstantial elements basically indicate manner.

As the quoted passages demonstrate, the tourist gaze upon Scotland has been moulded by the aesthetic ideologies of the picturesque, the sublime, the gothic and, most generally, by the Romantic movement. Neglected and desolated ruins, rough and irregular traits, autumnal and foggy views have been unmistakable traits in the representation of the green Scottish landscape (MacLellan & Smith, 1998). Over the centuries, ancient myths and legends, and popular songs and movies have shaped and perpetuated a tourist gaze that is still present in contemporary travel guides and in a range of multimodal materials.

Yet, the paradigm of the tourist gaze is far from being unquestioned. Since its codification in 1990, it has been criticised for its monomodal and univocal perspective, that is, for the exclusiveness of the visual mode and of the tourist viewpoint. Over the past decade, Urry has extensively revised the concept, adopting a more open, integrated, inclusive theoretical and analytical framework (Urry & Larsen, 2011). Different sensorial experiences (e.g. the auditive, the gustatory, the olfactory and tactile) and various actors (e.g. tourees) have been acknowledged as co-participating in tourism discourse (Dann, 2012a; Urry, 2002; Urry & Larsen, 2011). Overcoming what Dann has termed the 'ocular-centrism' of tourism, sightseeing has thus been broadened to include complementary stimuli, as specific gesture and gaze in tourist spaces analysed by Jaworski and Thurlow (2009). Yet, vision is still acknowledged as the organising sense and, in this new light, the revised paradigm of the tourist gaze still offers fruitful insights into tourism and travel textuality.

Central in all promotional messages, visuality achieves even more importance in tourism promotion, due to the non-material commodity being promoted (Santulli, 2007: 45). As the holiday cannot be directly seen before the actual tourist experience, it is the main task of destination promotion to textually re-present the place, to have tourists feel as if they could see the holiday before leaving home (Francesconi, 2007: 44; Maci, 2007: 42). In fact, destination advertisements systematically use images to make the site seem 'visible' (Held, 2004: 259), to provide evidence of its existence and value, and thus authenticate both the sight and the promotional message (MacCannell, [1976] 1989). Acknowledging the pivotal role of visuals and visuality in tourism communication, proper analytical tools are necessary to critically observe the meaning-making visual process. The discussion of such tools is the focus of the following section.

Visual Analysis and Pictures of Ireland

Adopting and adapting the tools of SFL and the metafunctional system, Kress and van Leeuwen (2006) have developed an extremely useful framework for visual analysis, a simplified version of which will be hereafter applied to the tourism and travel discourse. This chapter is concerned with the unveiling of apparently neutral and transparent strategies of visual representation, which hide ideological attitudes and ultimately enact persuasive communication functions in visual travel and tourism texts. Examples will be presented of photographs featuring natural and artificial Irish sites, produced and distributed by the Irish official tourism board, Fáilte Ireland, which retains the rights over the images.

The ideational metafunction

In order to evaluate the ideational function of a visual act (i.e. the expression of content), attention should be devoted to participants and representational structures. As for the first, two kinds of participants should be distinguished: the 'interactive participants', that is, the real image producer and viewer; and the 'represented participants', that is, the people, places, events and things depicted in an image (Kress & van Leeuwen, 2006: 47). In the case of the considered promotional tourism discourse, the context of text production and reception is disjointed and the interactive participants cannot be co-present, as in the case of face-to-face communication (Kress & van Leeuwen, 2006: 114–116). Relations between them are then represented, rather than enacted, and will be analysed in the section below devoted to the interpersonal function.

Far from a transparent process, participant representation in tourism photography involves ideological acts of inclusion as well as exclusion: poverty, waste and death are usually obliterated by the tourist gaze (Urry, 2002: 129), in favour of exotic, tropical, unspoilt sites. This partiality is sometimes subverted in digital travel texts, with some blogs being concerned with objective site representation, and in travel pictures complementing travel reportage.

Alongside natural and artificial elements, human beings need to be evaluated. Dann (1996b) outlines a framework of analysis and invites observation of their presence, role and interaction in tourist pictures. If the visual space does not feature any human presence, the interactive participant has an **invitation** to enter the represented natural or artificial space, which seems to be waiting to be visited. This regularly occurs with the presentation of paradise islands. If humans are featured, attention should be paid to their distinct roles as hosts or guests. In general, when guests appear on tourist images, they are enjoying themselves, consuming spaces, facilities, products, events. An example is the mental process represented in Figure 3.1, showing the couple acting as Senser, admiring the Donegal landscape, playing the role of Phenomenon. In tourist pictures, human participants as guests tend to respond to standard and stereotyped canons: young, beautiful, heterosexual couples with blond-haired and blue-eyed smiling children. When hosts are depicted, they look happy and welcoming and are busy in some local/traditional/indigenous activities to be appreciated by visitors (Cohen, 1993). On the rare occasions that hosts and guests are staged together, they have distinct roles and fulfil different functions of servant/guide/interpreter/waiter/bus-driver versus master/to-be-satisfied visitor. In this case, the image stimulates in the tourist-viewer a process of **identification**.

Figure 3.2 Sligo: Tree Tops Townhouse (copyright Fáilte Ireland)

The Irish pictures made available by Fáilte Ireland contrast with this scenario: for example, Figures 3.2 and 3.3 show everyday scenes of Irish social life with human participants as Actors. In pictures, Actors are generally the most salient participants, and can be identified by various effects such as size, placement, focus, colour and light (Kress & van Leeuwen, 2006: 59). Local people are shown having tea and chatting in an indoor and in an outdoor picture. The Irish pictures thus partly deconstruct the clear-cut guest–host distinction shaped and perpetuated by traditional tourism texts. They show local people as happy and sociable beings, whose identity is not to be defined at the service of tourists.

Figure 3.3 Carlow: Kilgraney Country House (copyright Fáilte Ireland)

Under the category of 'things' as represented participants in tourist visuals, abstract images like maps, graphs or logos need to be included. Figure 3.4 displays an official tourist map of Ireland. This is a conceptual, analytical text, since it does not narrate a story but describes physical spatial relations and the relative location of these items – that is, how these items, as participants, fit together to build a whole (Kress & van Leeuwen, 2006: 50). Via the visual medium, this highly detailed topographic text displays the distribution of Irish settlements, as divided into cities, large towns and villages. It thus enacts a relational process of attribution, with Ireland

Visual Analysis 85

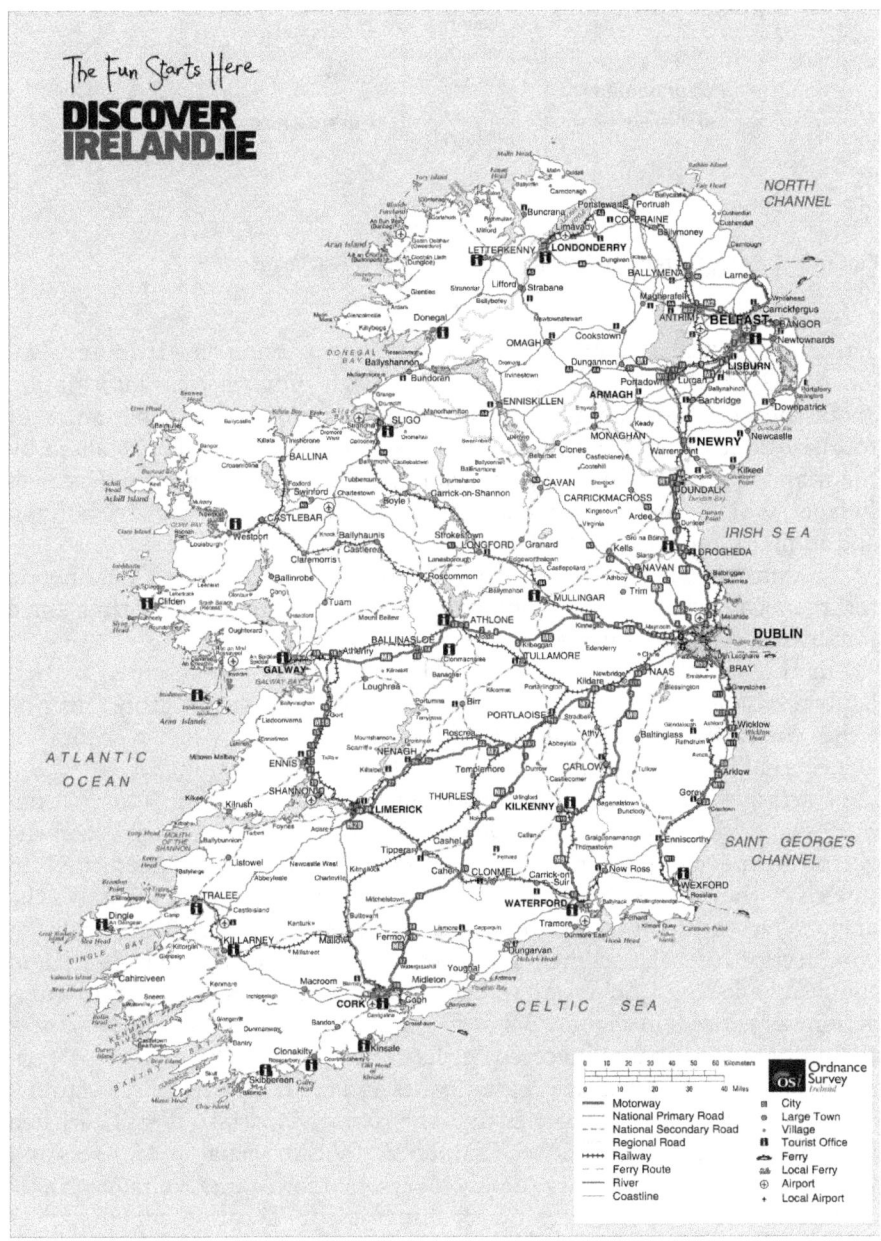

Figure 3.4 Map of Ireland (copyright Fáilte Ireland)

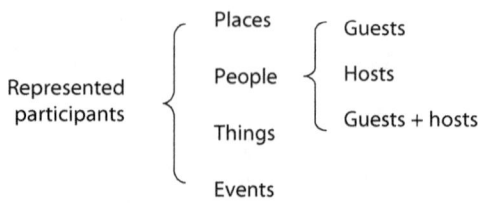

Figure 3.5 Represented participants in tourist and travel images

acting as the 'Carrier' and elements on the map acting as 'Attributes' (see Chapter 2). Addressed to prospective visitors, it provides clear information about the island, air and maritime transport systems and on the location of tourist offices. Interestingly, the exclusive informative function realised by the map is partly balanced by the caption 'The Fun Starts Here. Discover Ireland', which positions the text along a more emotional discursive horizon and fulfils an interpersonal role.

To sum up, Figure 3.5 illustrates Kress and van Leeuwen's parameters for the evaluation of represented participants, integrated with Dann's framework for tourist images.

In the realisation of the ideational metafunction, represented participants are organised across 'representational structures'. Structures may be either 'narrative', if they display the unfolding of actions or events, or 'conceptual', if they feature stable class, structure or meaning.

Narrative structures generate various processes (Figure 3.6). 'Action' processes are expressed through vectors originating from Actors. When the vector is an eye-line, as in Figure 3.1, 'reactional' processes are enacted. In this case, the couple acts as Reacter and the gaze they cast generates the diagonal vector upon which the whole visual text is constructed. Typical of comic strips, 'verbal' and 'mental' processes are signalled through speech and thought balloons. 'Conversion' processes represent a circle or human interaction, as is done in Figures 3.2 and 3.3, where vectors mutually connect the human participants involved in the conversation. The process of 'geometrical symbolism' excludes participants and contemplates only vectors.

Realised by the main participant, the narrative pattern is still enriched by circumstantial elements (see Chapter 2). Within visual texts, Kress and van Leeuwen (2006) identify mainly locative circumstances, circumstances of means and circumstances of accompaniment. Locative circumstances occupy a prominent position in travel and tourism texts, since they provide information concerning the setting of processes. This is visible in Figure 3.7 with the natural elements of water, woods, mountains and sky acting as

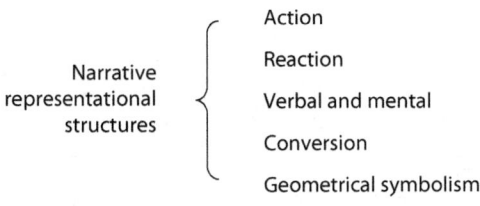

Figure 3.6 Representational structures

locative circumstances and surrounding Glenveagh Castle. Far from being blurred or out of focus, these elements are maximally contextualised, represented in detail and help to shape the castle as attractive. Consistent with the function of such images, the represented landscape is generally foregrounded through size, placement, light or colour effects. Yet, the function of such images is less descriptive than evocative, less naturalistic than symbolic.

Aimed at the representation of participants' stable identity, in terms of class, structure or meaning, conceptual structures include 'classificational', 'analytical' and 'symbolic' processes (Figure 3.8). The first group is typical of scientific or academic texts and is frequent in graphs, grids and trees displayed on printed and digital reports, plans and projects shared among a community of experts. Analytical texts represent part–whole relations and include topographical and topological texts, exemplified by the already mentioned topographic map in Figure 3.4. Differently, symbolic processes are frequent in travel magazines, catalogues and brochures, since they represent what the participant means or is. In turn, two types of symbolic processes can be identified: 'attributive' and 'suggestive' symbolic processes. The latter are relevant to the present discussion, since they depict participants in their timeless, frozen, universal value: human beings in their typical mood, places in their typical atmosphere. An insightful example is Figure 3.9, depicting the typical Irish landscape, with the loch, the mountains and the sheep captured in the typical gloomy, misty and cloudy weather and atmosphere. That particular scene has and frames a generalised and universal value, and represents Irishness. The same is true for Figure 3.7, with the architectural and cultural element of the castle near the loch informing a proper visual cliché of the Irish environment. Similarly, Figure 3.10 features Bantry Bay at sunset: the particular illumination de-emphasises details, which become irrelevant to the meaning of the whole scene. Central backlight generates extreme lighting conditions in Figure 3.11, which transfigure the whole scene and confer to Ireland qualities of magic, preciousness and extraordinariness.

Figure 3.7 Donegal: Glenveagh Castle (copyright Fáilte Ireland)

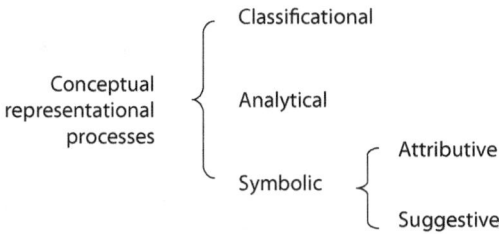

Figure 3.8 Conceptual structures

Figure 3.9 Donegal: Loch Finn (copyright Fáilte Ireland)

The interpersonal metafunction

In order to analyse the performance of the interpersonal function and the sender–addressee interaction, the following levels have to be observed: contact, size of frame, social distance, perspective and modality. **Contact** refers to whether represented participants look directly at the viewer or not (Kress & van Leeuwen, 2006: 117–121). In the former case, a situation of 'demand' is created: contact is established through the main participant's

Figure 3.10 Cork: Bantry Bay (copyright Fáilte Ireland)

direct gaze at the viewer, who is explicitly invited to interact with various feelings of disdain or desire, among others. Interestingly, Figure 3.3 enacts a dynamic process of contact: out of the three laughing represented participants, one is gazing at the pair on the doorstep, one away and the third at the interactive participant, demanding participation in the pleasant conversation. In the last case, no contact is made and the picture frames a notion of 'offer': the viewer becomes the detached, invisible onlooker and the represented participant the object of the gaze (Kress & van Leeuwen, 2006: 126). This function of offer is clearly visible in Figure 3.1 featuring Glenveagh National Park and in Figure 3.3 featuring Kilgraney Country House in Bagenalstown.

A different contact is established through the Ireland map in Figure 3.4, where the objective visual text, deprived of emotive involvement and subjectivity, encodes a function of offer, while the demand act is articulated through the caption. The visual system of contact (Figure 3.12) corresponds to the linguistic system of speech acts, based on the offer–demand polarity (see Chapter 2).

The second parameter of the interpersonal function, **size of frame**, derives instead from film language and is defined in relation to specific

Visual Analysis 91

Figure 3.11 Clare: Poulnabrone Dolmen (copyright Fáilte Ireland)

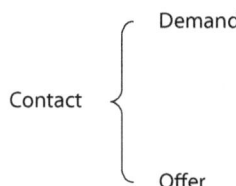

Figure 3.12 Contact

Figure 3.13 Dublin: Luttrellstown Castle (copyright Fáilte Ireland)

sections of the human body displayed on the screen. In 'close-ups' only the head and the subject's shoulders are depicted; in 'medium shots' the subject is cut off at the knees; and in 'long shots' the human figure is fully represented (Kress & van Leeuwen, 2006: 124). A medium shot is adopted in Figure 3.3, while Figures 3.9 and 3.10 are based on a long frame and Figures 3.11 and 3.13 on medium–long size. As a consequence of distance, different social relations between interactive participants can be distinguished (see Figure 3.14). More specifically, a scale can be identified of **social distance**, ranging from 'close personal distance', an intimate social relation where the viewer can grasp the object of the visual text, to a 'public distance', a social distance between strangers, passing through intermediate levels of 'far personal distance', the distance at which personal interests can be discussed, 'close social distance', the distance at which social business occurs, and 'far social distance', typical of formal and impersonal business interactions (Kress & van Leeuwen, 2006: 124). An example is the medium shot in Figure 3.2, which establishes a personal distance between the object and subject of the gaze: the viewer's position could allow him/her to sit in an armchair, drink tea and join the relaxing conversation of the group.

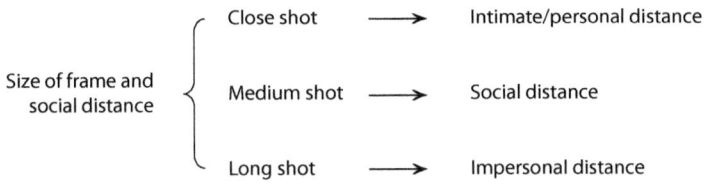

Figure 3.14 Size of frame and social distance

This system can obviously be applied to the representation of objects and of the environment. At 'close distance', the most frequent one, the object is partially shown; at 'middle distance' the object is fully represented; while at 'long distance' an item is totally depicted but out of reach, to be contemplated. Even the landscape can be seen from within, from a 'middle distance' with a foreground object, or from a 'long distance', for example from the air (Kress & van Leeuwen, 2006: 128). Once more, Figure 3.1 provides an insightful example, the tourist viewpoint being positioned within the landscape, immersed in the green Irish Glenveagh National Park. Conversely, Glenveagh Castle and the surrounding landscape in Figure 3.7 are seen from a longer distance, the viewpoint being positioned outside the frame.

Besides contact, size of frame and social distance, **perspective** enables the visual to establish a relationship between the interactive participants. Two types of images can be identified in Western culture. In 'subjective' images the viewer can look at a picture only from the specific viewpoint offered by the image-producer, while in 'objective' ones no specific viewpoint is adopted. While the latter is exemplified by the map of Ireland in Figure 3.4, all other instances represent subjective images.

Unsurprisingly, tourist pictures systematically adopt subjective images, since interpersonal relations between interactive participants are crucially important for the construction of the tourist gaze. Predominantly, high, eye and low angles are used (Figure 3.15). In a 'high-angle' image, interactive participants are positioned as having power over represented participants. By contrast, in a 'low-angle' image represented participants have power over interactive participants. An in-between position is expressed via 'eye level', with a point of view of equality and a relationship of involvement being encoded (Kress & van Leeuwen, 2006: 129–140). The general rule is that frontality enacts maximum involvement, while an oblique angle expresses detachment. Among the Irish pictures, a high angle is adopted in Figure 3.7, showing Glenveagh Castle from a vantage point of superiority: encoding

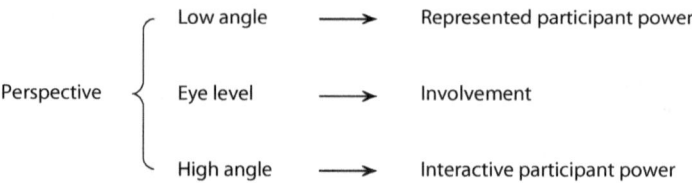

Figure 3.15 Perspective

Giannitrapani's panoramic gaze (2010), it invites a reassuring act of contemplation. Featuring an exterior view of Luttrellstown Castle in Dublin, Figure 3.13 provides an example of low angle, positioning the viewer in a relationship of inferiority to the castle, which is thus conceptually enhanced as fascinating, majestic and imposing. Differently, Figure 3.3 implies an eye-level view, establishing a relation of equality between the interactive participants and shaping the represented environment as welcoming and hospitable. Overall, the most frequent perspective strategy of eye level is adopted in Figures 3.1, 3.2, 3.3, 3.9, 3.10 and 3.11.

The last parameter fulfilling the interpersonal function is **modality**, concerned with the representation of truth or falsehood, certainty and doubt, credibility and reliability. In verbal language, these values are realised by modal verbs like 'can', 'may' and 'must' (Halliday, 1978; see Chapter 2). Negotiated within a social context and intertwined with power dynamics, modality cues are highly motivated signs and need to be properly questioned.

Various markers frame modality in visual texts and are concerned with colour, light and space representation (Figure 3.16). There are three that directly relate to colour: saturation, differentiation and **modulation**. In a monograph on the language of colour, van Leeuwen (2011) has developed and integrated his previous research and observed the social use of colour for expression and communication. Albeit used to denote specific people, places and things, or classes of them, as in the case of flags, brands and uniforms, or to create coherence in texts through chromatic repetition, coordination or contrast, colour is mainly used to perform interpersonal meanings. Modern interior design colour consultants exploit colour to reflect the house owner's personality, values and interests, while in public spaces like workplaces, schools and shops it is highly valued for its effects on workers, students and customers. While acknowledging sociocultural differences, many manuals and websites (among others, Gage, 1993, 1999) nonetheless give specific colour associations. Red evokes vitality and dynamism, fun and joy, but also a commanding and rebellious attitude. Orange conjures up

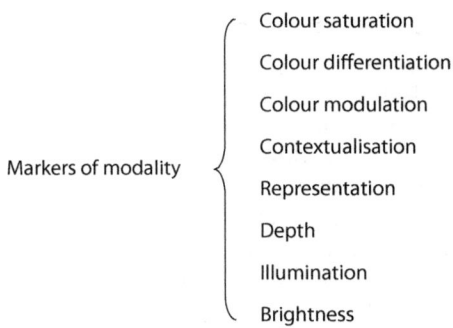

Figure 3.16 Markers of modality

notions of communication and inspiration, a festive and helpful attitude, yellow symbolises a creative and cheerful, young and bright mood, while green reminds us of nature and adventure, but also patience and relaxation. While blue inspires depth and freedom, peace and education, authority and formality, purple evokes a vain and luxurious attitude, a solemn and royal atmosphere, an intelligent and artistic spirit.

In this social semiotics of colour, van Leeuwen (2011) has outlined a descriptive theory, grounded on the 10 parameters of value, saturation, purity, transparency, luminosity, luminescence, lustre, temperature, modulation and differentiation. As this new grid is too big for the present discussion, only some parameters are taken into account. The most relevant seem to be those present in the grid previously outlined by Kress and van Leeuwen (2006), namely saturation, differentiation and modulation. First, 'colour saturation' indicates chromatic intensity and vividness and is expressed through a scale running from full colour saturation to its absence. The chromatic solutions in Figure 3.13 (reproduced here in black in white, but originally with an intense blue sky) are a good example of intense, saturated colours. Second, 'colour differentiation' can be measured on a scale that goes from a wide, varied palette of colours to monochrome. For instance, the original versions of Figures 3.3 and 3.7 revealed a high colour differentiation, which expresses vital social connections in the first and a vibrant landscape in the second. Conversely, a more restricted range of cold colours like blue and violet were used to connote Bantry Bay in Cork in Figure 3.10 as a peaceful and serene landscape. Third, 'colour modulation' refers to the adoption of various chromatic tints and shades as opposed to flat and unmodulated colours. In order to confer a notion of warm hospitality, the colour version of Figure 3.2 adopted a range of warm colours, from yellow, cream, to brown.

A fourth marker of modality, 'contextualisation', refers to the detailed representation of background or its absence. A good example of maximum contextualisation is offered in Figure 3.9, where the Donegal landscape around Loch Finn is clearly and accurately represented. This picture also shows a high level of representation, a marker characterised by the extreme representation of pictorial details to its maximum abstraction. Fifth, 'depth' is a criterion to be evaluated on a scale from maximally deep perspective to its absence. For example, depth is effectively expressed in Figure 3.1, where the three horizontal foreground, mid-ground and background layers can be distinguished as grass, loch, mountains and sky. In tourism and travel texts, this frequently adopted modality cue frames a notion of invitation and access to the to-be-explored location.

Finally there are two light-related markers: 'illumination', concerned with the presence of a specific source of illumination focusing on the represented participants, and 'brightness' related to the intensity of light (Kress & van Leeuwen, 2006: 152). Warm or cold illumination highly depends on its intensity (hard versus soft), source (natural versus artificial) and direction (diffuse versus direct). In the case of natural sunlight, special effects are created across the use of sunrise, daylight or sunset, with specific implications for the framing of the tourist gaze. Set in Clare, Figure 3.11 features warm light deriving from natural sunlight: the Poulnabrone Dolmen is captured at sunset, with rays of light coming from the very centre of the dolmen, engendering an effect of magic. As for direction, various effects of emphasis are achieved through background or foreground lighting, through front, side, back, under or top light, or through multidirectional light. Another example of the effect lighting can achieve, here through warm light, is offered by the Loch Finn landscape portrayed in Figure 3.9, connoted as romantic and sublime. Conversely, cold light is visible in Figure 3.1, in which the northern landscape evokes misty, gloomy settings. A high level of brightness is visible, for example, in Figures 3.7 and 3.13, while there is low–medium brightness in Figures 3.1 and 3.2. To sum up, colour, light and other markers of modality are listed in Figure 3.16.

Importantly, modality is realised through the interaction of these parameters. In the end, the integrated use of such modality cues encodes a certain representation of reality; that is, it expresses different **reality principles** or orientations (Figure 3.17). The main ones are *naturalistic*, *sensory* and *abstract* (see Chapters 2 and 4). The first orientation is expressed when reality is depicted in the most faithful way possible, with, for instance, a naturalistic palette of colours, naturalistic colour modulation and differentiation, and naturalistic distribution of shade and light. Yet, more than naturalistic and faithful portraits of reality, what travel and tourist images

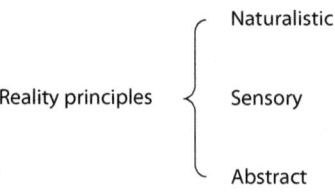

Figure 3.17 Reality principles

seek to construct are affective meanings, where the pleasure principle plays a dominant role. This explains the widely exemplified predominance of a sensory coding orientation, with the picture expressing feelings, emotions and moods to the viewer. The abstract modality configuration shows a process of decontextualisation, idealisation and essentialisation: the visual configuration achieves an analytic dimension and impersonal stance. The map of Ireland in Figure 3.4 exemplifies this last orientation.

The textual metafunction

Distinct from the ideological and interpersonal metafunctions, the textual function refers to the way the elements of a picture are integrated in order to create a meaningful whole. The compositional nature of images is characterised by three interrelated systems: information value, salience and framing (Kress & van Leeuwen, 2006: 177).

Still pictures adopt the code of spatial composition since all the elements are simultaneously co-present on the page or screen, while other dynamic texts, like movies, dance and radio programmes, make use of the code of temporal organisation (see Chapter 5). The principle of **information value** in spatial composition regards the meaningful location of elements, according to specific 'zones' (Figure 3.18). More precisely, already-given information is on the left side, while a new message is on the right side, a pattern of organisation that reflects the theme–rheme information structure of the English clause (see Chapter 2). The vertical line can also be exploited as a meaning-making device: 'on the top' is the most salient and/or ideal part, and 'on the bottom' more specific and practical information is given. Visual composition, alternatively, may be structured along the dimensions of 'centre', the most crucial part of the image, and 'margin', subordinated to the central one(s) (Kress & van Leeuwen, 2006: 195–199), as clearly visible in Figure 3.11 where Poulnabrone Dolmen is foregrounded, being placed at the centre of the visual space.

Information value is also an integration code, concerned with cohesion and coherence, and with how elements in a composition are balanced by

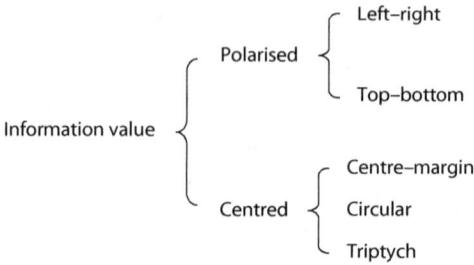

Figure 3.18 Information value

the means of colour, size and framing devices. In many tourism and travel pictures, composition mainly derives from perspective. As in Figure 3.7, *dispositio* and the projected compositional meaning are strictly related to the viewer's standpoint.

The second textual principle, **salience**, refers to the capacity depicted elements have to give more importance to some elements than others and consequently to attract viewers' attention, regardless of their position (Figure 3.19). In the aural system, this is achieved, for example, via duration or loudness or, again, via the use of stressed syllables or accented notes (see Chapter 4). Not objectively measurable, visual salience results from factors like size, sharpness of focus, tone and colour contrasts, placement, perspective and the presence of human figures or cultural symbols (Kress & van Leeuwen, 2006: 212). There is no doubt that bigger, foreground, enlightened elements draw more attention to themselves than small, background, dark items. In the corpus, it is through backlight that Figure 3.11 achieves the most salience, while depth is the most salient element in Figures 3.1 and 3.9, perspective in Figures 3.7 and 3.11, tone and colour contrast in Figure 3.13 and human presence in Figures 3.2 and 3.3.

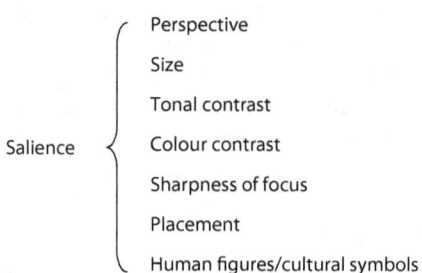

Figure 3.19 Salience

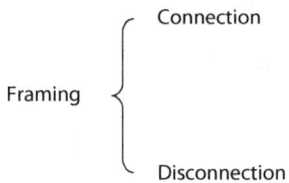

Figure 3.20 Framing

Finally, **framing** (Figure 3.20) refers to connecting or disconnecting devices within the image (Kress & van Leeuwen, 2006: 203). In a visual text, framing is strong when an element is presented as a separate and distinct element; it tends to be stronger in vertical compositions and weaker in horizontal compositions (Kress & van Leeuwen, 2006: 204). Achieved in writing through punctuation and in speech through pauses (see Chapters 2 and 4), framing presents some units of information as separate and can be obtained through (dis)continuity of colour, (dis)continuity of shape, frame lines, represented participants and empty space. It can also be realised by salient represented participants, as in Figure 3.9, where the curved, sinuous borders of the loch emanate in the surrounding natural environment, by human gazes as in Figure 3.3, or again in the vertical and diagonal lines in Figure 3.11. Light can be an element either of discontinuity, as in Figure 3.7, or of continuity, as in Figure 3.1, emotional effects and projected meanings being clearly different in the two texts.

Summary

Tables 3.1–3.3 summarise, respectively, the ideational, interpersonal and textual metafunctional parameters in the Fáilte Ireland pictures. Clearly, metafunctions and metafunctional parameters have been separated in the analysis in order to facilitate their explanation. Semiosis in genuine texts is more complex, multifaceted and slippery than presented here and all the above-mentioned functions overlap and act simultaneously. The same picture projects different meanings on the basis of: the co-text it is associated with; its material support; and its context of fruition. As for co-text, Chapter 5 will discuss the notion of clustering, describing the functioning of the picture within the broader space of the page or screen in interaction with other pictures or writing. Medium and context have been introduced in Chapter 1. Hence, meaning is deeply affected by the printed, digital or material support and subsequent constraints and possibilities, and by where, when and how the visual text is consumed.

Table 3.1 Visual semiosis in the Irish pictures: The ideational metafunctional parameters

Figure	Represented participants	Structural processes
3.1	Natural, human	Narrative reactional
3.2	Artificial, human	Narrative conversion
3.3	Artificial, human (natural)	Narrative conversion
3.4	Abstract	Analytic attributive
3.7	Natural, artificial	Symbolic suggestive
3.9	Natural (artificial)	Symbolic suggestive
3.10	Natural	Symbolic suggestive
3.11	Natural, artificial	Symbolic suggestive
3.13	Natural, artificial	Symbolic suggestive

Table 3.2 Visual semiosis in the Irish pictures: The interpersonal metafunctional parameters

	Contact	Size of frame	Angle	Colour	Context	Representation	Depth	Illumination	Brightness
3.1	X	Long	Eye	Cold colours	Max.	Very detailed	Max.	Cold light	Low-medium
3.2	X	Medium	Eye	Warm	Max.	Detailed	Max.	Warm	Low-medium
3.3	Yes	Medium	Eye	Contrast	Max.	Detailed	Medium	Cold	Normal
3.4	Symbolic modality								
3.7	X	Long	High	Contrast	Max.	Detailed	Max	High	Medium/high
3.9	X	Long	Eye	Warm	Max.	Detailed	Max.	Warm	Medium/high
3.10	X	Long	Eye	Almost absent	Max.	Very relevant	Max.	Warm	High
3.11	X	Medium-long	Eye	Warm	Low	Very relevant	Medium	Warm	Medium/high
3.13	X	Medium-long	Low	Saturated	Max.	Detailed	Max.	warm	High

Table 3.3 Visual semiosis in the Irish pictures: The textual metafunctional parameters

	Information value	Salience	Frame
3.1	Diagonal	Depth	Diagonal
3.2	Central	Human presence	Triangle
3.3	Low-right	Human presence	Triangle
3.4	Vertical		
3.7	Low central	Perspective	Horizontal
3.9	Central	Depth	Curved
3.10	Central	Tonal contrast	Horizontal
3.11	Central	Backlight	Horizon, vertical + diagonal
3.13	Central	Tonal contrast + perspective	Pyramid

Non-pictorial Texts

Albeit immediately associable to the sensorial experience of sight, pictures are not the exclusive visual text genre within tourism and travel discourse. Material culture heavily relies on three-dimensional texts, mainly perceived via sight. For example, in the case of souvenirs, sight can interact with touch for miniature items, with touch and smell for scented candles, and with touch, taste and smell for food items. A further visual semiotic resource to be considered in tourism and travel discourse is writing. If aspects of content like lexico-grammar have to be analysed following SFL frameworks, expression-related features require tools deriving from visual analysis.

The visual component of verbal language plays a substantial role in the meaning-making process via the systems of typography and layout (Kress, 2009; Stöckl, 2004). Typography mainly refers to the visual appearance and style of written units. As Stöckl (2004: 11) asserts, 'what intonation, speed and rhythm are to speech, typography is to writing'. Different choices of font, *style*, colour and Size capture and hold the attention and evoke distinct emotions and connotations, mainly related to the travel and tourism typology these represent. Size is sometimes increased as an attention-grabbing strategy, bold type is used to achieve emphasis, colour is added as a mood creator and the particular font used raises specific connotations: **Comic Sans** would be preferred to describe a trip for families with children, while **Bookman Old Style** would better fit a cultural holiday. The compositional parameter of layout is more concerned with patterns of placement, the Latin rhetorical function of *dispositio* and composition of the page space according to the aforementioned rules of information value. No doubt, the larger title of a travel report would fail to make meaning if positioned at the bottom of the page. Chapter 5 provides examples of the system of writing as integrated with other systems in order to make meaning in tourism and travel texts.

Conclusion

This chapter has explored the interconnections between visuality, travellers, tourists and space representation. Central to the semiotic process of the tourist gaze, visuality has been addressed as a non-neutral, ideological destination representation strategy. Given this, critical visual awareness needs to be developed and analytical instruments need to be properly mastered. A toolbox has been offered that may be valid for the decodification of visual tourism and travel texts or, more generally, the visual component of multimodal texts. Drawing from social semiotics, the toolbox enables viewers to understand how the tourism visual text conveys a message, establishes a codifier–decodifier relation, and achieves internal and external cohesion.

4 Aural Analysis

Sound

This chapter addresses the semiotic system of sound, based on sound materiality and on the logic of time. First, it defines the soundscape as the co-existence and interaction of speech, music and sound in a sound system. Second, it outlines a descriptive analytical framework for the mapping of sound resources, considering sound perspective, time and rhythm, interaction of voices, melody, voice quality, timbre and modality. Third, it concentrates on the use of sound resources within the tourist and travel communication system with an analysis of a radio programme and a radio commercial.

From a multimodal perspective, language makes meaning in its visual and audio modal configurations, and needs to be examined accordingly. Thus this fourth chapter relates to Chapter 2, since it further develops verbal language, here as speech, and complements Chapter 3 in its reference to verbal language as writing.

At the level of content, speech shares numerous aspects of lexis, syntax and grammar with writing (see Chapter 2), since both are modes for expressing linguistic meanings (Halliday, 1989). In order to enact the meaning-making process, both speech and writing function as a network of interrelated options. In speech, the phonological rank scale is composed of intonation phrase, foot, syllable and phoneme; the intonation phrase corresponds to the clause, the foot to group, the syllable to word and the phoneme to the letter or grapheme, as illustrated in Table 4.1.

Table 4.1 Ranks scales in writing and speech

Writing	Clause	Group	Word	Grapheme
Speech	Intonation phrase	Foot	Syllable	Phoneme

Yet, speech also makes meaning via the materiality and the resources of sound at the level of expression. Sound, the aural material of speech, is entirely different from the graphic material of writing: the former relies on the phonological system, while the latter relies on the graphological one. Not only is sound materiality diverse: a piece of speech needs time to unfold its constituent phonemes one after the other and the ear needs time to perceive sound. In contrast, a picture shows all the represented participants, colours, light effects and vectors at the same time and realises its meaning within the space borders of its frame. Consequently, the two distinct sensorial experiences of hearing and vision, as well as speech and writing, follow distinct logics of time and of space: the visual text projects meaning via simultaneity, while the aural text expresses its semiotic potential in consequentiality (Kress, 2009: 58; and see Chapter 5).

As for reception, if writing is received via the physiology of sight, speech is received via the physiology of hearing, and these two sensorial experiences differ significantly (Kress, 2009: 55). Auditory perception depends on the ability to detect sound vibrations through the ear. Vibrations are then transformed into nerve impulses that are processed by the brain, primarily in the temporal lobe.

Sound production and reception are marked by the co-presence of sound codifier and decodifier. In speech, the hearer can talk back and interact, as the first example in this chapter will show. This form of exchange is absent in images and writing, which need a temporal gap between the two moments of codification and decodification. The establishment of technologies of recording has partly modified this fact and a distinction exists between live and recorded programmes. In the case of recorded programmes, text codification is temporally distinct from broadcasting and simultaneity occurs between hearing and broadcasting time. As for feedback, broadcast audio texts like radio programmes can have a feedback from individual text recipients via telephone calls to the radio station itself, for example.

Speech may be associated with semiotic resources sharing these textual, discursive and contextual aspects, namely music and sound (van Leeuwen, 1999). Within a multimodal frame of reference, rather than being treated as following a code, aural semiotic systems are seen as carrying a meaning potential to be expressed through choices (see Chapters 2 and 3). Aural choices may be either intentional, as in the case of voice loudness in public speeches, or non-intentional, like natural birdsong or traffic noise. Some audio choices have a more universal value, such as police or ambulance sirens indicating emergency. Others are linked to religious, cultural or social contexts (van Leeuwen, 1999: 8), like the muezzin's song in the Islamic faith, calling to prayer and worship at given hours, five times a day. Accordingly, the paradigmatic patterning of oral options may imply different degrees of conventionality and standardisation.

Regardless of such semiotic richness, orality has often been defined in negative terms throughout the history of communication, as grounded on the lack of the technologies of writing. An opposition has been identified between refined and superior 'societies of the eye' and tribal and inferior 'societies of the ear' (McLuhan, 1967; Ong, 2002). In turn, societies of the ear have sometimes strongly opposed literate technologies adopted by societies of the eye. As Crystal argues (2006: 2), the Church defined newly invented printing as a satanic act, which would disseminate uncontrolled ideas, undermine the social order and bring damnation. Arguments against writing were first developed in Plato's *Phaedrus* through the voice of Socrates, who condemned the practice as inhuman, as based on the objectification of thought that can ceaselessly repeat the same things. In Western society, Socrates has been identified as marking the passage from oral to written society, his thoughts having been written down by Plato (McLuhan, 1967).

In his celebration of oral cultures, Ong (2002) foregrounds their additive, aggregative, emphatic and participatory foundation, which defines speech actors as active agents. Not surprisingly, McLuhan (1967) argues that in the contemporary electronic age a second orality is re-emerging because of the affirmation of audio-visual technologies like radio, television and the telephone relying on audio as the prominent or important system. Established after McLuhan's work, 2.0 media further enhance interaction, often with extremely reduced time lags between production and reception, and adopt a conversational lexico-grammar that makes the communication act and, more specifically, written language close to speech (as in Netspeak). In social network communication, for instance, graphic conventions like spelling and punctuation, capitals and spacing, repeated letters and emoticons are adopted in order to express what intonation, loudness and melody do in speech (Crystal, 2006). Such a conversational style has been denounced by purists as menacing and contaminating standard language, testifying to the ideological foundation of the battle between orality and literacy.

Similarly, language variation within speech phenomena is also connoted. For example, what is commonly labelled as 'standard English' and associated with 'Queen's English' or 'BBC English' is highly valued as a prestige variety, related to the accent known as Received Pronunciation. Described as relying on social distribution, it is prominently associated with education and high social class. Alongside social distribution, regional distribution is highly influential in spoken language: a dialect is in fact often related to a particular accent, and a speaker using a regional dialect is likely to use the corresponding regional accent. Partly conscious and partly unconscious of their linguistic identity and of the linguistic dynamics they enact, speakers negotiate more or less prestigious styles according to situational context and to intended purpose (van Leeuwen, 1999: 76).

As such, sound has sociocultural meaning and makes meaning in situational communication systems. However, van Leeuwen argues (1999: 190), a metafunctional approach does not work for mapping semiosis in the sound system, given that there is less specialisation of sound resources in comparison to visual or (written) linguistic ones. The semiotics of sound has not (yet) reached the same levels of abstraction and functional structuration as other codes. Given the focus of the present volume on images and words in tourism and travel texts, this chapter seeks to provide some insights into the aural component of wording and of its meaning potential in general, while references to music and sound effects provide evidence of the complexity of this semiotic process and further enrich the discussion.

The words of sound: A lexical map

In tourism and travel texts, the verbal description of auditory sensorial experiences is less articulated than the visual counterpart, from both conceptual and expressive viewpoints. It has already been argued that a hotel room 'needs' to have a view, that holidays 'need' to offer breathtaking scenarios and that those elements are systematically given visibility in brochures or on websites (see Chapter 3). When visitors look for the presence of a view, they also ask for the absence of sound, for *the sound of silence*. Silence is an important pull factor that accommodation can offer to its visitors, and is associated with the push factors of relaxation, serenity and tranquillity. Tourism and travel texts thus weave an isotopy of sound, verbally represented through specific processes, participants and circumstances. On a website promoting farm and cottage holidays in the Isle of Man, the accommodation section thus presents the Ballacricket Farmhouse:

> Nestled deep in the countryside in the South of the Isle of Man at Ronague, Ballacricket offers peace and tranquillity while remaining in the heart of the island. (www.isleofman-direct.co.uk)

With the key terms of 'peace' and 'tranquillity', the sensorial auditory perception intermingles with psychological and physiological states of wellbeing.

If present, the auditory dimension is always emphasised and sound is specifically connoted: hotels, resorts and farmhouses promise a 'breathless', 'absolute', 'unforgettable' 'silence'. From the same webpage, the following excerpt shows how the promoted holiday is meant to offer a multisensorial experience, where sight, hearing and taste combine:

> Idyllic and picturesque, enjoy walking up to fantastic views, sounds of surrounding wildlife and fresh home grown produce.

The 'sounds of surrounding wildlife' resonate with the tones of a local, traditional and genuine lifestyle.

As for verbal processes, the two most frequent lexical items are 'to listen' and 'to hear', the first indicating a conscious, attentive, active, prolonged process of perception, and the second a more spontaneous, passive, unconscious, immediate action. An interesting exemplification of this distinction is given in the following passage, taken from an online travel diary from a trip to Toronto, posted by Josmercier on TravelPod on 23 March 2010:

> When you are in a new environment, you always try to assess as much information as you can. To do that, you taste new food, you try new sports but most of all, you listen at every sound, accent, word and language you can possibly hear. The first detail that really impress me was the fact that the languages I can hear around is not only French nor only English, the main languages we hear are the Chinese ones such as Cantonese and Mandarin – I guess. (www.travelpod.co.uk)

In this extract, the auditory perception is presented as crucially important for the understanding of the sociocultural identity of Toronto as a multicultural city, where the Asian community is of growing importance. Remembering to ignore formal inaccuracies that are constitutive of blogs (see Chapter 1), we can point to the second sentence: 'you listen at every sound, accent, word and language you can possibly hear'. The invitation is to pay attention, namely to 'listen' to the languages one may casually encounter, namely to 'hear', in such a culturally rich and diverse environment. Sounds, thus, make meaning: they tell stories, evoke emotions and frame soundscapes. The object of the hearing/listening process is yet far from simple. It is in fact a complex and composed auditory system, which the following section addresses.

The Soundscape

In everyday formal and informal situations, different types and degrees of sounds co-exist and interact. Sounds are thus never isolated and autonomous: a number of natural and artificial sounds co-occur, from different sources and in different directions, and with different degrees of relevance

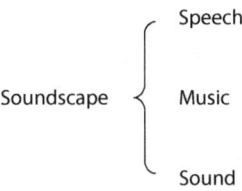

Figure 4.1 The soundscape

to actual or potential listeners. This composite semiotic system has been termed the **soundscape** by van Leeuwen (1999, 2009) and is made up of speech, music and other sounds (Figure 4.1). These derive, respectively, from human, musical and non-musical instruments, that is natural or artificial sources. Rarely fixed and static, the soundscape is normally fluid and dynamic: the presence, relevance and interaction of sounds constantly change over time, either spontaneously or as a result of sound manipulation.

In order to describe sound systems, van Leeuwen (1999) has outlined a sound semiotic theory and an analytical framework based on six parameters: sound perspective; sound time and rhythm; interaction of voices; melody; voice quality and timbre; and modality.

First, **perspective** is determined by the relative loudness of simultaneous sounds in a soundscape. The system of perspective places simultaneous sounds in a hierarchy and positions them into groups at different distances from the listener so that the sounds acquire varying degrees of importance, or significance, for the listener. Accordingly, the soundscape can be divided into three zones (van Leeuwen, 1999: 23):

- figure, positioned in the foreground, at a close distance;
- ground, positioned in the mid-ground, at a middle distance and acting as support;
- field, positioned in the background, at a far distance.

In particular communication situations like tourism promotion, soundscapes may follow a recurring schema. In a tourist video, the voice-over in the foreground generally acts as figure and mainly performs an ideological metafunction, while the soundtrack creates the atmosphere, and mainly performs an interpersonal function. In spontaneous settings, however, perspective is not a fixed but a dynamic condition: sounds may vary in absolute or relative loudness and therefore in priority to the listener. The opposite of perspective sound is immersive sound, which makes the listener feel immersed in and integrated with the environment.

Importantly, the combination of loudness and distance determines a range of possible social relations between sounds and listeners in terms of intimacy and formality. Van Leeuwen (1999) has identified a scale from intimate social distance, to personal, informal, formal and, finally, public distance. Clearly, aural social distance as deriving from loudness corresponds to visual social distance as determined by size of frame (see Chapter 3).

Today, the technologies of amplification and recording have undermined the links between social distance and actual proximity and made the two semiotic variables independent. It is noteworthy that the only difference between the system of perspective and the system of social distance is that the latter applies to single sounds, while the former applies to simultaneous sounds and has relative rather than absolute levels (van Leeuwen, 1999: 24).

After perspective, the second parameter outlined by van Leeuwen is that of **time** and rhythm. Time may be either measured or unmeasured. In the first case, the stream of time is divided into measures of equal duration and marked off by a regular pulse. The duration of these measures determines the tempo, which may be andante, moderato, allegro or adagio, among others. For instance, andante derives from the Italian 'walking' and indicates the pulse rate of an average male adult walking at an easy pace: sound unfolds at a fairly slow speed. Each measure begins with a pulse, a sound that is stressed, made prominent by loudness, pitch, relative duration or any combination of these (van Leeuwen, 1999: 26).

Measures are grouped together in phrases, of up to seven measures, marked off from each other by boundaries, bringing changes in the regular pulse rhythm. As frames, phrases identify units of interaction or moves (see Chapter 1) in a speech or music act. Advertising jingles on television or on the radio adopt call and response patterns in speech act organisation, usually with a male voice as the leader and a choir of female voices as the followers. The leader then represents the seductive salesman or role model and the choir members repeat the brand name or slogan in a catchy chorus, to represent the customers who are seduced by the salesman or follow the lead of the role model (van Leeuwen, 1999: 36). Alongside the identification of speech or music acts, rhythm has a framing role (Kress & van Leeuwen, 2006: 214), visually achieved by various systems like colour, light and composition. In music or speech, the aural flow is sometimes interrupted by a pause, a rallentando. Avoiding a continuous flow realised by equally timed rhythmic cycles, these junctures compose distinct sound units that show various degrees of (dis)connection.

Time and rhythm also serve affective and cognitive functions, since tempo establishes the human/biological aspect of an affective relationship to time. Rhythmic patterning evokes 'the regular sound of the mother's heartbeat in the womb', 'the vital processes of the body' and has 'an enhancing effect on neuronal circuits in the brain' (Cook, 2001: 125). Besides offering a pleasant affective situation, rhythmic regularity implies comfortable recognition and reassuring predictability on the cognitive level (Cook, 2001: 235). It thus sustains recall, which explains the value of metrical poetry as the foundation of orally transmitted tradition. The same magical rhythmic resonance grounds the already mentioned advertising jingles (van Leeuwen, 1999: 65; McLuhan, 1967: 19).

In *The Discourse of Advertising*, Cook (2001: 233) asserts that more than the denotative power of communication, advertising texts exploit the substance and means of language, 'playing' with 'the sounds and rhythms, meaning and grammatical patterns'. The 'patterning of sound', he explains, 'lends a text an extra dimension which reinforces, contradicts or adds to its linguistic meanings, or interpretations of them' (Cook, 2001: 125). Among sound patterning examples, phonetic, phonological aspects may be chosen and appear with syllabic, rhythmic or rhyme solutions. Alliteration occurs through the repetition of initial sounds in two or more different words across successive sentences, clauses or phrases (Trask, 1998: 15), as in the 'Incredible India' slogan of the Indian campaign that will be considered in the final part of the chapter. Immediate sound juxtaposition in two adjacent words plays a fundamental cohesive function; here it builds a unique verbal chunk composed of qualifying adjective + destination noun. Via the prosodic repetition of the close front unrounded vowel [i], both lexemes are emphasised and made memorable. The qualifying adjective achieves salience and memorability attached to the noun, and the destination is remembered as incredible. In other cases, the phoneme is repeated more than twice and provides the sentence with a rhythmic flow, giving a connotation of comfortable and pleasant familiarity to the message, as if it were a sort of lullaby.

The third parameter, **interaction of voices**, can be either sequential, by turn-taking, or as simultaneous, by speaking, playing or making noises at the same time. Types of simultaneous interaction are unison, where all participants produce the same sound; plurality, in which different voices and instruments intertwine; or dominance, based on one dominant voice and supporting voices (see Figure 4.2). An interesting example of sequentiality is in the previously mentioned advertising jingle with a leader and chorus. The chorus, as reactor, may: repeat all or most what the initiator has said/sung (imitation); repeat only the final line, in a process of emulation; give a distinct, formulaic answer like a yes or no clause; or, finally, produce a distinct but fully stated response, supporting or contrasting with the initiator's phrase. In general, a high segregation between the initiator's and reactor's

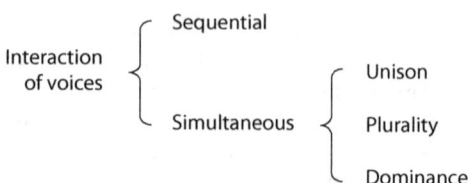

Figure 4.2 Interaction of voices

moves expresses symbolic distance, while partial overlapping signifies social closeness. In an academic conference, for example, turn-taking may occur but would be highly codified, listeners being supposed to raise their hand before talking. At the opposite extreme, speakers in an informal chat take turns in a spontaneous way and frequently overlap.

The parameters of perspective, time and rhythm, and interaction are realised by choices from all the sound resources available in a given context, among which are selections of melodic means. **Melody**, the fourth parameter identified by van Leeuwen, is defined by the *Dictionary of Phonetics and Phonology* as 'the sequence of pitch values in a speaker's voice within a particular utterance' (Trask, 1998: 220). Like colours in a visual system (see Chapter 3), it is strictly related to emotions: joy is expressed through a wide pitch range at high pitch level and a lively tempo; tenderness is realised via high pitch level, narrow pitch range, medium tempo and soft, slightly nasal and labialised voice; and anxiety is expressed through mid-pitch level, extremely narrow pitch range and breathy, tense voice (van Leeuwen, 1999: 95–97).

Alternatively referred to as tone group, tone unit and tone, the intonation phrase has been variously analysed and classified in its melodic structure based on pre-head, head, nucleus and tail. As such, it results from a combination of pitch movement, pitch range and pitch level. These pitch features can characterise sound acts or sound settings, the former also called sound gestures and the latter sound textures. Generally related to human activities or actions like a crime in a movie, acts or gestures are varied and develop and change in time, while settings or textures are more static and homogeneous and indicate non-human environmental states and processes. The two typologies can be isolated or combined; in the second case, they may be organised according to perspective, mutually foregrounded or backgrounded (van Leeuwen, 1999: 69).

The fifth parameter, **voice quality** and timbre, is multidimensional. Traditionally, voice was thought of as marking individual or social identity (van Leeuwen, 2009: 68) and was not conceived as a semiotic resource. More recently, a vocal semiosis started to be developed and speech started being defined as interlocking the material and experiential as well as the semiotic and the social. Rather than pairs of binary opposites, voice qualities are graded phenomena (van Leeuwen, 1999, 2009), carrying experiential meaning potential. The most important aspects to be considered are:

- Tension, with voices going from tense, alert, constrained, self-controlled to lax or relaxed. In general, tense or stiff segments are characterised by greater muscular tension, more vigorous and extensive movements of the tongue, lips and jaw, greater duration and greater subglottal air pressure than their lax correlates (Trask, 1998: 352).
- Roughness, to be described on a scale from rough (expressing friction) to smooth. For example, the rough voice by Marlon Brando in *The Godfather* intensely connotes the character and makes him highly attractive (van Leeuwen, 2009: 76).
- Breathiness, with heavy breath expressing excitement. Breathiness encompasses hoarse, rough, rasping, clean, smooth and well-oiled voices. For example, in commercials, a breathy, soft voice is adopted to suggest intimacy and to give the message a sensual and erotic appeal (van Leeuwen, 2009: 76).
- Loudness, ranging from a maximally soft to a loud voice.
- Pitch register, with varying degrees of height. A professional singing voice is generally characterised by rapid slight variation in the pitch and volume of the voice (Trask, 1998: 376).
- Vibrato or plain voice.

Hence, voice quality and timbre play a substantial role in determining social distance in this age of amplification technologies manipulating loudness. In order to indicate 'personal distance', the sound of the voice needs to include qualities such as a 'relaxed' voice and 'low pitch', together with low volume. To this end, professional speakers and actors change their voice according to the situation they are involved in: radio speakers' voices become higher and tenser while reading the news, while female voices promoting a perfume in a commercial become lower, and more whispery and breathy (van Leeuwen, 1999: 26).

Importantly, speech sounds can derive their semiotic potential from materiality and from associations with certain accents, but mainly from their articulation. In fact, vowels can be described in terms of frontality (front, back), height (high, low) and aperture (large, small), and consonants their degrees and modes of blocking, constricting and restricting the airstream (plosive, fricative and, for fricative, rough or smooth). For example, many slogans exploit the highly evocative power of the voiceless alveolar fricative [s] sound, which has relaxing, sensuous and seducing connotations (Francesconi, 2007). In terms of manner of articulation this sound is produced by directing air flow through a groove in the tongue at the place of articulation and directing it over the sharp edge of the teeth, causing high-frequency turbulence. The phonation type is voiceless, which means it is produced without vibrations of the vocal cords. Conversely, plosive consonant segments like the bilabial [p] or [b], where the articulation involves the complete closure of the vocal tract and the subsequent sudden release of the trapped air, confer a connotation of intensity, dynamism and energy. Phonation type is voiceless for [p] and voiced for [b].

The last parameter outlined by van Leeuwen (1999) is **modality**, judgements concerning mirror the frame for visual analysis. As already mentioned for verbal and visual codes, modality refers to the degree of truth assigned to a given sound event and is to be seen as presentation or representation. Modality is realised through a combination of the following parameters:

- Pitch range is to be perceived on a scale going from monotone to a maximal pitch extent. For example, highly reduced pitch ranges, as in monotone chanting or machine speech, reduce the level of human emotion. As for semiotic potential, a wide pitch range expresses excitement, surprise, anger, while a narrow pitch range conveys boredom, misery.
- Durational variation unfolds from a single standard length of sound for all the sounds in a sound event to various degrees of duration. Uniform sound duration like news reading on television suggests authority and objectivity, while purposefully extended sounds add an emotional value, as the two audio texts analysed in the second part of this chapter will demonstrate.
- Dynamic range implies the presence of a single level or various degrees of loudness, where variations in volume indicate self-expression and establish interpersonal meanings and relations, as opposed to flat and regulated volume.
- Perspectival depth, ranging from flat to layered music, signals the composite nature of a soundscape as comprising interactive background and foreground sounds. In movies, some sounds in the background, like footsteps, are often amplified to increase the emotional effect.
- Degrees of fluctuation are achieved from a completely steady sound to vibrato (maximally deep and/or rapid fluctuation). Lack of vibrato can mean restraint and relaxation, whereas high levels of vibrato suggest a strong expression of emotion. Vibrato can also be observed as increasing or decreasing and as making meaning accordingly.

- Degrees of friction can be measured on a scale ranging from maximally smooth to maximally rough sound and suggesting pure, clean or dirty sounds. Some degree of friction indicates a naturalist modality.
- Absorption range is to be perceived on a scale ranging from maximally dry to maximally spacious, reverberating, resonating sound. Absence of resonance may indicate intimacy, while echo and reverb may create an effect of exposure or entrapment.
- Degrees of directionality unfold on a scale ranging from a single human voice on a stage, say, to 'wrap-around' sounds, surrounding sounds, like environmental sounds and music.

Based on these parameters, three modalities of reality representation can be identified to represent how true and real they are: abstract sensory, naturalistic and sensory (see Figure 4.3). First, the abstract sensory modality interlocks abstract representation and emotive effect. For instance, classical music is modally configured through rationalised pitch range, rationalised wide durational range, wide loudness range, reduced friction range, conventionalised fluctuation and a naturalistic degree of absorption and directionality (van Leeuwen, 1999: 181). Second, the naturalistic modality is based on the criteria of verisimilitude, normality and everydayness, and represents sounds as if hearers had been present at the scene where it was produced: it is related to the truth of perception and obviously implies systems like loudness and perspective. Third, the sensory modality shows a high degree of emotive impact, for example the sound effects in horror films. Its aim is less to faithfully reproduce sounds than to represent the emotive temperature of a type of sound or action, the truth of emotion. As such, sensory modality is high if a sound is intended to affect the listener emotionally.

All the discussed mode-specific elements (see Figure 4.4) explain the semiotic potential of voice, music and sound, which the following sections apply to tourism and travel discourse.

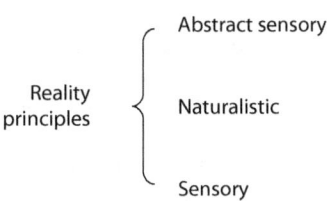

Figure 4.3 Reality principles

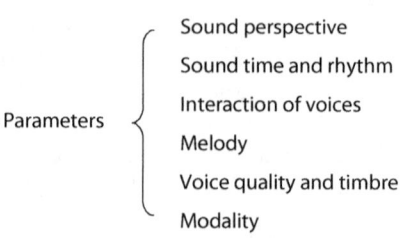

Figure 4.4 Parameters for soundscape assessment

Sound in Tourism and Travel Texts

The critical debate within tourism studies is only starting to turn to the auditory dimension of the holiday and to the need to properly address communication systems for people with restricted or no hearing (Dann, 2012a). Soundscapes both in travel and tourist domains and in contexts indirectly dealing with such situations have not yet been given sufficient theoretical and analytical attention. Music, for instance, should be explored as a mood creator and in relation to both the tourism segment and to targeted audiences. Instrumental, oriental, meditative music could accompany a video promoting a spa, while a contemporary ska piece would be perfect for a video on snowboarding and adventure holidays. In order to understand this potentiality, a tourism promotional text could be watched with a different soundtrack: an adventure travel video would totally lose its power with a slow, romantic soundtrack.

Alongside that of music, the connotative value of voice quality needs substantial exploration within tourism texts. For instance, a vibrant, energetic, male voice is normally adopted for promoting adventure tourism, while a soft, breathy, sensuous voice is preferred for spa tourism; the opposite would create weird effects. Acknowledging this, the following sections examine two different authentic audio text genres within travel and tourism, which realise distinct communication functions, involve diverse actors and adopt different audio strategies.

A radio travel programme on England

The first audio text is an episode from a BBC Radio 4 series entitled *Excess Baggage*. Conducted by either Sandi Toksvig or John McCarthy, *Excess Baggage* deals with travel tales from around the world. Unfortunately, it was suspended after many years during which it was broadcast on Saturdays from 10:00 to 10:30. Eighty-five episodes are available on the

BBC website for free download (www.bbc.co.uk/programmes/b006qjds, accessed January 2013).

In the episode 'England', broadcast on Saturday 31 December 2011, John McCarthy looks at the changing nature of the traditional attractions of England with historian, travel writer and television and radio presenter John Julius Norwich, curator and television presenter Lucy Worsley and *Guardian* journalist Martin Wainwright. They discuss the English heritage, from castles to cottages, that makes Englishness an attraction for visitors worldwide. According to the WTO website, there was a positive trend in arrivals in the UK in 2012, with an increase of 6% in receipts. Needless to say, the London Olympics that year played a major role in attracting visitors on a global scale, notwithstanding the economic crisis. However, the speakers address here the attractiveness of cultural symbols from Stonehenge to the Gherkin, from the Tower of London to Kew Gardens, and the appealing stories these sites tell.

In this 30-minute audio text, the speakers mainly provide information on sites to visit and opinions on general travel attitudes, preferences and trends. In so doing, genre values vary substantially. Description is generally used for monuments and itineraries, and it normally develops through the selection of catchy and memorable items. Narration is sometimes deployed by the three special guests to tell stories of interesting English sites but more often to tell their personal stories as travellers and experts on the topic, as if to sustain and legitimise their position. This enables them to express their personal views and opinions. Produced and broadcast by the national corporation, the audio text has a clear informative function. However, a component of entertainment can be appreciated, used in order to capture and hold the public's attention.

As for tenor in the whole text, all the speakers use a dialogic attitude: register is friendly; they often use humour and positively react to each other's funny comments and tales. No direct reference is made to enact a relationship between interactive participants, but numerous strategies are deployed to generate a natural, vibrant and pleasant dialogue among friends. As the transcript below demonstrates, turn-taking occurs in a polite and ordered way and the brief overlapping never disturbs communication.

The soundscape in the audio text is composed of four adult voices, three male and one female. No background music or sound effects accompany the voice as text. This is because the audio text is not meant to target the listeners' emotions and feelings. In the downloaded version of the episode, for the first 20 seconds a male voice introduces the episode and refers to the website for terms and conditions of use. Voices sequentially interact through turn-taking. The turns are very clear and distinct, even though sometimes speakers laugh together. This gives an impression of authentic speech and friendly talk, and invites listening. Moreover, voice interaction is varied and creates a sort of rhythmic patterning that encourages, sustains and accompanies listening.

The voice of the presenter has an organising function but never predominates over the others. In fact, the presenter acts as mediator between the travel writer and the audience. Sometimes, he intrudes in the travel writer's speech with items like 'Yeah', 'So' and 'Right', which establish a more informal tone and make the interview more conversational. Being authorities in the field and having published extensively on travel, the respondents are not positioned as a formal, distant, academic experts: they use sound affordances in order to minimise power distance.

By means of the technologies of amplification and recording, sound arrives loud and clear, the audio text can be easily followed and the voices establish a personal distance with listeners. All interactants speak in an energetic and dynamic way. The conversation between the four intertwining voices always seems natural, even though its progression is well structured and organised. At this point, a closer look at the verbal text is necessary. For space reasons, the following extract is from the first part of the episode, lasts 3 minutes 15 seconds and comprises 658 words. It features an exchange between the presenter John McCarthy (JM) as questioner and Julius Norwich (JN) as respondent.

JM: Thanks and good morning. New Year's Eve [the day of the broadcast] is of course seen first and foremost to be a Scottish affair, with Hogmanay being the main night of the year north of the border. However, rather than exploring Scotland's culture, today we're staying south of the border to celebrate England's heritage. The country is full of quintessentially English attractions, from castles to cottages, but do we appreciate the uniqueness of what is on our doorstep?

To see if we can pin down the Englishness of England, and where to find it, I'm joined by John Julius Norwich, the historian, presenter and travel writer who has written *The History of England in 100 Places*, in which, as the title suggests, he selects a hundred places across the centuries which typify, or were the site of, historically significant events or developments in England. John Julius, the history of England is all around us, in the sense you don't have to travel far to find it.

JN: No, you don't. I mean, England is such a gloriously small country and at the same time immensely varied, I mean, you can't drive for more than an hour without finding yourself face to face with some magnificent monument of one kind or another.

JM: So, how did you choose your one hundred places?

JN: With enormous difficulty. John Murray suggested that the subtitle should be *from Stonehenge to the Gherkin*.

JM: Right.

JN: So at least I had number one to do and I started off, off on Stonehenge long before I knew what the other 99 were going to be.

JM: And they all had to be places that one can still visit and, and really identify rather than just places that were in the historical record, so to speak?

JN: Oh yes. They had to be places you could still go to if you wanted, but it's not in any sense a guidebook....

JM: Right.

JN: It's not saying that you must go here, you must go there. It's just that each place has got a particular story to tell and the hope is that when all those stories are put together you do have a sort of vague picture of, of, of the march of English history for the last thousand years.

JM: So you've got some fantastic castles and stuff – we'll come back to those in a little while – but you also include something like Watford Gap service station. Where does that feature?

JN: Well, you see Watford Gap is a very interesting place because all the roads that have ever been built in that area, I mean since road building began, they all went through Watford Gap and nowadays we don't even notice Watford Gap. I mean Watford Gap is just a very slight declivity between two hills.

JM: Yeah.

JN: But, if you are building a road, you want to make a road as straight and on the level as you possibly can. So, the Romans went through Watford Gap. The old toll roads went through Watford Gap ... every – the turnpikes went through Watford Gap. They all go through Watford Gap. And therefore there is a story of the whole English road building ... on Watford Gap.

JM: Right in that spot. So, have you been to all one hundred places in the book?

JN: Just about yes, I think I have. Not, not specially for the book, but I mean I, I, I did a long book thirty odd years ago called *The Architecture of Southern England* and I went to a lot of places then.

JM: So they're places that....

JN: I mean in the old days, erm, we did do an awful lot of just touring for the fun of it, staying in, if possible, in a Landmark Trust property over the weekend, you know. And, as you say, I mean, the country is so small and so compact that you get an awful lot done.

In terms of field, this short passage presents a volume on English cultural attractions, identified by an authoritative scholar in the area. Placing emphasis on the non-tourist nature of his work, John Julius Norwich explains why and how he has selected the places. He discusses the case study of Watford Gap service station, as an alternative, unexpected site in such a volume. Concerning represented participants, out of 86 processes, the text features: 38 material processes, like 'to go', 'to drive', 'to travel'; 22 mental, like 'mean', 'want', 'know'; 7 verbal, like 'say', 'call', 'speak'; 0 behavioural; 6 attributive; 2 experiential; and 11 of identification. The last three processes heavily rely on the verb 'to be'. As for clause relations, some simplexes are present, especially in the questioner's turns. The respondent's text is more articulated, being composed of complexes and of subordinated clauses. This makes him an authoritative speaker. Consistent with the oral nature of the text, embedding is rare.

In terms of interaction, the dialogic exchange is that of giving and demanding information, articulated across questions and statements. Both speakers intrude in the message through the system of modalisation, expressing positive attitudes and judgements. Clearly, the spoken variety is BBC English, which intermingles aspects of standardisation and prestige. What follows is a transcript of the excerpt presented with the conventions of the GAT 2 (Selting *et al.*, 2011) transcription system and highlighting the text's prosodic features. Accordingly, the whole transcript follows the temporal unfolding of speech and indicates both linguistic and non-linguistic actions. The text is divided into numbered intonation phrases and is presented essentially in lower case throughout, as upper case is here used to indicated stress. Highly sophisticated and articulated, this transcription system is used by specialists in conversation analysis. It is adopted here only to provide evidence of the complexity of the sound system.

Key:

[xxxx]: overlaps / .h:inbreath / (.): micro pause (up to 0.2 seconds) / (-): pause 0.2–0.5 seconds.
Pitch movements at the end of intonation phrases:
¿ high rising / , rising / – level31/ ; falling / . low falling/ =: latching/ YE:S vowel lengthening
<<f> > forte, loud/ <<ff> > fortissimo, very loud / <<p> > piano, soft / <<pp> > pianissimo, very soft
<<all> > allegro, fast / <<len> > lento, slow / <<cresc> > crescendo, becoming louder
<<dim> > diminuendo, becoming softer / <<acc> > accelerando, becoming faster / <<rall> > rallentando, becoming slower/ !YES!

strong accent/ WHIle: main accent of the intonation phrase/ whIle: secondary accent

001 **JM**: thanks and good MORning.
002 new year's Eve is of course seen first and foremost to be a SCOTtish affair;
003 with hogmanay being the mAin night of the YEAR-
004 .h north of the BORder.
005 howEver .h,
006 rather than exploring SCOTland's culture,
007 today we're staying SOUTH of the border;
008 to celebrate ENgland's heritage.
009 (.) the country is full of (.) quIntessentially English atTRACtions;
010 from cAstles to COTtages;
011 but we appreciate the unIqueness (.) of what is on our DOORstep.
012 (.) to see if we can pin DOWN the Englishness of England,
013 and where to FIND it;
014 i'm joined by jOhn jUlius NORwich;
015 the hisTOrian,
016 preSENter,
017 and TRAvel writer.=
018 =who has written (.) the HIStory of england in hundred plAces;=
019 =in WHICH,
020 <<p>as the title> sugGESTS;
021 he selects a HUNdred places across the centuries-
022 which TYpify-
023 or WEre the site of-
024 historically siGNIficant events-
025 or developments in ENgland.
026 john julius (.) the history of england-
027 is all aROUND us.
028 in the sense you don't have to travel far to FIND it.
029 **JN**: no you DON'T.
030 i mean england is such a GLOriously small country;
031 and at the same time im!MEN!sely varied;
032 I mean, you can't drive for more than an HOUR;
033 <<p>without finding yourself FAce to face with some magnificent monument of one kind or another.>
034 **JM**: so how did you CHOOse your one hundred places;
035 **JN**: with e!NOR!mous difficulty.

036		john MURray;
037		sugGESted;
038		that the SUBtitle;
039		should be from STOnehenge;
040		to the GHERkin.
041	JM:	RIGHT.
042	JN:	SO;
043		at least i had number One to do.
044		So and I started off off on stonehenge lOng before I knew what the other ninety-nine were going to BE.
045	JM:	and they all had to be places that one can still VIsit;
046		and, and really iDENtify;
047		rather than just places that were in the historical REcords so to speak.
048	JN:	OH yes.=
049		=they hAd to be plAces (.)you COULD still go to
050		(.) !I!f you WANted;
051		but it's not in Any sense a GUIdebook.
052	JM:	[RIGHT.]
053	JN:	[it's not saying that you MUST] go here-
054		you must go THEre.
055		it's just that EAch (.)PLAce;
056		(.) has got a parTIcular story to tell.
057		and the HOpe is;
058		that when all those stories are (.) put toGEther;
059		you do have a sort of vague PICture
060		of of of the march of english history for the last thousand YEARS.
061	JM:	so you've got some fantastic CAStles,
062		and stuff <<all>we'll come back to those in a in a little WHIle.
063		but you ALso include something like-
064		watford gap SERvice station.
065		WHEre does that feature>.
066	JN:	well you see watford GAP-
067		is a very interesting PLAce;
068		because ALL the roads-
069		that have ever been BUILT in that area;=
070		=i mean since road building beGAN,
071		they All went through watford GAP.
072		and nowadays we don't even NOtice watford gap.
073		I mean Watford Gap is just (.) a very slight deCLIvity
074		between two HILLS.

075 **JM**: YEah.
076 **JN**: but If you are building a ROAD,
077 you want to make a road as STRAIGHT (.) and on the level as you possibly can.
078 .h so the ROmans went through watford gap.
079 (.) .h the old (.) TOLL roads went through watford gap.=
080 =even the TURNpikes went through watford gap.
081 they !ALL! go through watford gap.
082 and THErefore;
083 there is a story of the WHOle english road building.
084 <<p>on watford gap.>
085 **JM**: right in that SPOT.
086 so have you bEEn to ALL one hundred places in the book;
087 **JN**: just about YE:S.
088 i think i HAve.=
089 =ahh not not specially for the BOOK.
090 but i mean i i i did a LONG book.
091 thirty ODD years ago.=
092 =called the (.) Architecture of southern ENgland
093 .h and i went to a LOT of places;
094 THEN. .h
095 **JM**: [So they're PLAces that]
096 **JN**: [erm i mean (.) in the OLF days]
097 erm we did do a:n AWful lot;
098 of just touring for the (.) for the FUN of it;
099 staying in-
100 if possible-
101 in a LANDmark-
102 (.) TRUST-
103 (.) PROperty;
104 over the WEEKend;
105 you KNOW-
106 And, as you say,
107 I mean, the country is so small and so comPACT;
108 (-) .h that you get an awful lot DOne.

Radio text transcription casts light on salient prosodic features. First, sentences are systematically segmented into smaller intonation units, as in the case of lines 036–040, with five intonation phrases in a very simple sentence, or lines 099–105, with even higher fragmentation. Another interesting aspect concerns fast speech, which is peculiar of the radio situation and which confers dynamism and energy to speech. Stressing is typically used to mark participants, in particular artistic and architectural elements like Stonehenge, Gherkin, castles, cottages and service station, whereas it is rarely adopted for processes. Finally, the spoken text features frequent loudness variation: it often tends to change from soft to loud.

The following section examines a completely different text genre in terms of structure and aims, yet it shares with the BBC text the radio medium.

A radio commercial promoting India

The second text is the radio commercial 'Incredible India', part of an international marketing campaign, launched in 2002 by the government of India for global tourism promotion (www.incredibleindia.com, accessed December 2012). Aiming to promote India as a travel destination, the project addressed the discerning traveller and focused on the national culture and history, from architecture to food, through spirituality. In 2012 the second phase of the campaign followed, this time focused on the consumer. Called 'Find what you seek', it aimed to show that visitors to India from all over the world can find heritage, spirituality, wellness and adventure there. These institutional campaigns proved to be successful for tourism in India: the WTO reported a 22% increase in international tourism receipts in the first nine months of 2012 (www2.unwto.org).

The 'Incredible India' audio text lasts 30 seconds, the average length of a radio commercial. It features a male voice, friendly but determined, speaking in Indian English. This voice acts as figure in the commercial soundscape, accompanied by an instrumental soundtrack as ground. The music is produced by the interaction of flute, Indian drums and bells. In the first part, voice and music interact in a very direct, almost mutual way, while in the central section the relation is more contrastive, since the music calms down while the voice is still vibrant. In the end, with the Indian chimes and the voice giving the website address, sound interplay becomes harmonious once more. Clearly, this is not a melodic piece, although the voice prosody and the flute can be perceived as melodic elements.

With a vibrant, intense, stimulating, persuasive tone, the male voice starts speaking very slowly, stressing all the following words:

Explore ancient temples!
Enjoy our music concerts!
Shake your legs at a grand Indian Wedding!
Rich heritage, diverse culture, luxurious events: find what you seek!
Incredible India. For more information log on to incredibleindia.org

The speech unit represents India as a country that offers its visitors a unique cultural heritage and experience. The system of Transitivity is constructed via material processes like 'explore', 'enjoy', 'shake' and 'find', expressing dynamism, implying recipients as actors and Indian cultural symbols as goals. Tenor is mainly established by the means of the recurrent imperative mood in theme position alongside possessive adjectives and the personal pronouns 'our', 'your', 'you'. Mode is achieved via syntax parallelisms in the three imperative clauses and in the complement structure and position in the fourth sentence. Unmarked Thematisation of the abovementioned material verbs achieves a function of emphasis and rhythm. As already mentioned, the slogan 'Incredible India' is built on the immediate alliteration of the [i] vowel, which evokes and anchors the country's name and makes it memorable as inextricably associated with its predetermining qualifying adjective 'incredible'.

As for voice quality, the text is uttered by a tense, smooth and clean voice, whose vibrant pitch register expresses enthusiasm. Spacious, resonating and reverberating sounds then connote India as vast and a holiday to India as an intense experience. As the whole commercial configures a sensory reality principle, emotional value is also realised by maximal pitch extent, by various degrees of duration with purposefully extended sounds and by intense perspectival depth. Consistently, the soundscape is highly dynamic, being characterised by increasing speech speed with important breaks between intonation lines and by a sequence of pitch values. The beginning of this audio text shapes a vivid and vibrant image of India, while the central part frames a quieter, more meditative horizon, even though the voice tone remains positive, direct and inviting throughout the whole segment. Time and rhythm are regular, periodic and tenacious in the sound of the traditional Indian drum, the *tabla*, and of the Indian bell at the beginning, and become more rapid, sharp and articulated in the second part, when more rhythms are juxtaposed over a unifying pulse. The human voice adds further rhythm. Subsequently, the tempo slows and musical instruments change, with the entrance of a flute and piano, which engenders a highly meditative atmosphere. The first part of the traditional, percussive piece does not feature any particular modality or tonality, while the second part becomes more tonal and reassuring, therefore inviting.

These aural communication strategies serve the purpose of attracting and capturing the listeners' attention: in contrast to the *Excesses Baggage* programme, the commercial is not chosen by faithful followers who regularly wait for it and switch the radio on when it starts. It is a 'parasitic text' (Cook, 2001: 29; Santulli, 2007: 33), living within other radio programmes and 'borrowing' their followers. As such, text recipients tend to coincide with the actual listener of the hosting programme (Santulli, 2007: 33): the producer of a travel commercial is likely to select a travel programme within which to position its text. Since attention in the audience may decrease during commercials, parasitic texts need to find attention-capturing and attention-holding communication solutions.

Summary

The two radio texts show both similarities and differences. Although both broadcast via the radio, the two text units differ in length, topic, composition, modes and forms of sound interaction, target and function. As for topic, the BBC programme presents a hidden, 'anti-tourist' 'attraction', while the commercial celebrates the main symbols of Indian heritage. In the first, the referential function is predominant, while the second is a persuasive text, aimed to convince listeners to visit India. Language and sound are used accordingly. In the first instance, human voices are the exclusive component of the soundscape, while in the second they crucially interact with the soundtrack. Alongside soundscape composition, dynamism and rhythm are the main elements that make the two texts distinct, the second being a much more varied and dynamic instance, with maximal pitch extent and various degrees of duration. This is strictly related to the intended audience, only apparently juxtaposed: while the first text relies on regular and faithful programme listeners, the 'parasitic' commercial needs to capture the attention of people who consider it only a break, a pause within a radio programme, during which their attention can be lowered.

Conclusion

This chapter has addressed the semiotic system of sound, deriving meaning-making potential from sound materiality. After defining the soundscape as the co-existence and interaction of speech, music and sound in a sound system, it has then outlined a descriptive analytical framework for the mapping of sound resources and sound perspective based on the six parameters of time and rhythm, interaction of voices, melody, voice quality and timbre, and modality. It has finally concentrated on the use of sound resources within two tourist and travel radio texts that have distinct communication functions. The following chapter examines audio and visual semiotic resources interacting in multimodal artefacts.

5 Multimodal and Intermodal Analysis

Semiotic Resources

Following two chapters devoted to, respectively, visual and aural modes, this chapter centres on multimodal and intermodal semiosis, as deriving from the integration of different modes. First, it affirms the use of multi-modality in contemporary communication systems and defines modes as semiotic resources with specific semantic properties, cognitive orientation and semantic potential. Second, it contextualises multimodality in the tourism and travel discourse and explains its high communication potential and appeal. Third, it illustrates and compares: static pages as space-based texts, making meaning through the simultaneous co-deployment and perception of semiotic items; time-based texts, making meaning through sequential unfolding of textual items; and hypertextual artefacts, as hybrid genres integrating both logics and signifying via the hypertextual link.

According to O'Halloran (2011: 120), **semiotic resources** describe those modes (such as language, image, music, gesture and architecture) integrating across sensory modalities (such as visual, auditory, tactile, olfactory, gustatory, kinaesthetic) in multimodal texts, discourses and events called multimodal phenomena. Questioning logocentrism and the predominance of writing in our system of thought and communication, multimodal discourse analysis (henceforth MDA) defines the semiotic resources of typography or layout, for instance, not as ancillary to writing but as having the same dignity and deserving specific critical attention and analytical approach. In turn, writing is not denied but questioned, redefined and reoriented, addressed as one semiotic resource among others and as making meaning in combination with other modes (Kress, 2010: 79).

From a multimodal perspective, semiotic resources feature distinct semantic properties, cognitive orientation and semantic potential (Stöckl,

2004: 16). First, semantic properties signal modal internal structures. Writing is constructed through the combination of graphemes into words, words into sentences and sentences into paragraphs, whereas images cannot be neatly divided into compositional units. The integration of such discrete units establishes a different relation with reality: writing is a symbolic code, as it deploys two-dimensional arbitrary graphic forms, while images are an analogue one, as they represent three-dimensionality (Stöckl, 2004: 16; see Chapters 2 and 3).

Second, cognitive orientation refers to the specific cognitive operations performed thanks to given semiotic systems. If language is a linear mode that unfolds sequentially, images are based on simultaneous perception. More polysemous than language, the latter boast a higher communicative power and impact than verbal language does, which increases their pervasiveness in promotional texts. Hence, visuals are attention-catching, evoke feelings and emotions, provide richer information, raise a range of connotative meanings and are more easily remembered (Stöckl, 2004: 17).

Third, semantic potential suggests what users can do with distinct semiotic resources. As their perception is based on the simultaneous display on the page, canvas or screen (Kress, 2003: 20), images are well suited to description. By contrast, temporal relations of time-based modes like speech, dance and music can better express relations of sequentiality or causality typical of narrative patterning (Kress, 2003: 57).

Variability in terms of semantic properties, cognitive orientation and semantic potential raises, at the same time, sociocultural, affective and cognitive issues (Jewitt, 2009: 22; Kress, 2003: 59; Kress, 2009: 54). Indeed, semiosis encompasses sociocultural norms and rules operating at the moment of sign-making as affected by the sign-maker's individual motivations and interests. For example, rap, blues, jazz, country and folk music express the peculiarities of different ages, countries and cultural and social contexts. Such music genres are then performed by individual musicians, with their own techniques, ideas and emotions (van Leeuwen, 1999). That acknowledged, the webpage analysis in this Chapter examines the specific adoption of reggae music in tourism promotion of Jamaica, used ideationally as a symbolic cultural icon, interpersonally for positive mood creation but also textually as a cohesive device.

Cultural and historical contexts imply changes not only in modal configurations but also in the media. The history of travel and tourism has variously recorded the affirmation of the printed guide or brochure, the material art piece or miniature souvenir, the live festival or exhibition or the technological iPhone or iPad (see Chapter 1). In these media, modes materialise and integrate, acquire meaning and realise their communication function as shaping and being shaped by their diverse historical and sociocultural contexts. The following section considers multimodality and intersemiosis in tourism and travel texts.

Multimodality and Intersemiosis

The concept of multimodality marks and signals the simultaneous co-deployment of resources within a single communication process for meaning-making purposes. From a social semiotic perspective, all semiosis is multimodal, monomodality being perceived as an abstraction (Baldry, 2000; Baldry & Thibault, 2006; Kress, 2010; Kress & van Leeuwen, 2001, 2006; Lemke, 2002; Royce & Bowcher, 2007). Even the apparently monomodal written page of a novel performs meaning by exploiting the tactile–visual semiotic potential of paper and of typography (see Chapter 1).

If all texts are multimodal, it is yet contemporary communication that makes substantial and pervasive use of multimodality. Modes and forms of communication have rapidly become more sophisticated since the advent of interactive and participatory digital media, and this has led to the increasing use of and interest in multimodality, on the part of the general public, institutions and academics.

A critical debate on multimodal phenomena has developed over the last 30 years, with the examination of a variety of domains, classrooms (Clarke, 2001; Jewitt, 2006; O'Halloran, 2011), homes (Ventola, 2011), museums (Stenglin, 2009) and hospitals (Iedema, 2001) being just a few examples. Consequently, many disciplines are involved in multimodal analysis, such as linguistics, media studies, education, psychology, cognitive studies and information technologies (Jewitt, 2009; O'Halloran & Smith, 2012: 10). Besides enormously enriching the discussion, multidisciplinary and interdisciplinary convergence could explain the general reluctance to conceptualise multimodal studies as an academic discipline, with its distinct theoretical challenges, analytical techniques and institutional space (O' Halloran & Smith, 2012: 10). It can be better defined as a 'domain of inquiry' (Kress, 2009: 54), a 'field of application' (Jewitt, 2009: 2), with reference to an area of scientific exploration within literacy studies.

Jewitt (2009: 28) remarks that literacy studies have shown three main perspectives associated with multimodality, each foregrounding specific aspects:

- Kress and Van Leeuwen's social semiotic approach, based on Halliday's social semiotics;

- O'Halloran, Baldry and Thibault, and O'Toole's MDA, drawing on Halliday's SFL;
- Scollon and Scollon, and Norris's multimodal interactional analysis, based on interactional sociolinguistics.

The differences between these approaches are due to historical influences, the degree of emphasis given to the context and the relations within modes or modal systems.

As for text analysis, Jewitt (2009: 29–33) identifies two main approaches in MDA: contextual and grammatical. These developed in the 1980s and 1990s, through the application of Halliday's SFL to the visual mode. First, adopting a functional view, the top-down contextual approach was proposed by Kress and van Leeuwen (2006) for the exploration of images and visual design (see Chapter 3), with a focus on ideological potential of communication. Second, an anatomistic perspective, the bottom-up grammatical approach outlined by O'Toole (2010) was for the analysis of displayed art, paintings, sculpture and architecture. Jewitt (2009) relates these, respectively, to social semiotic multimodality and to MDA.

All three perspectives and both approaches cast light on multisemiosis, albeit that the third one more specifically foregrounds intersemiotic patterns. Accordingly, analytical separation of different resources in multimodal artefacts is seen as an abstraction (Baldry & Thibault, 2006: 18), since the meaning and function of each mode cannot be identified and described on its own, but only in relation to the overall semiotic system in which it is inscribed. As such, text analysts should never exclude any text elements during the examination process, in order to avoid partial or biased interpretation (see Afterword).

An emerging field of interest in multimodal studies is, thus, **intersemiosis**, which addresses how and why modes interact. As Kress and van Leeuwen assert, it draws attention to:

> the use of several semiotic modes in the design of a semiotic product or event, together with the particular way in which these modes are combined – they may for instance reinforce each other (say the same thing in different ways), fulfil complementary roles or be hierarchically ordered. (Kress & van Leeuwen, 2006: 18)

Hence, conceptualisations and examination of multimodal semiosis should overcome an 'additive' view, interested in the juxtaposition of the different meanings expressed by the distinct modal systems and nourishing a perception of the realised meanings deriving from co-integrations of semiotic modalities as the sum of the parts (Baldry & Thibault, 2006: 18; Kress, 2010). According to an 'integrative' perspective, intersemiosis is rather to be observed as 'intersemiotic complementarity' (Royce, 2007: 63), as it subtly associates and integrates modes that mutually balance weaknesses and strengths. From here originates a 'multiplicative' view of the function of intersemiosis, which addresses modal relations as mutually enhancing the semiotic potential of each mode and invites the examination of the multiplied meaning derived from the interaction of modal resources (Baldry & Thibault, 2006; Lemke, 1998; Stöckl, 2004: 9).

In light of integrative and multiplicative multimodal semiosis, artefacts can be divided between space-based and time-based texts. The former include static texts, such as writing, pictures, postcards and guides, and realise meaning through the simultaneous co-deployment of visual and verbal items. The latter encompass dynamic texts, such as speech, dance, commercials and films, and are articulated upon the unfolding in time of various integrated semiotic resources. In between these is the hypertext, which combines and exploits properties of both static and dynamic texts. Within tourism and travel domains, this chapter examines the meaning-making process of static, dynamic and hypertextual text genres, by taking into consideration a website homepage and its structure, some postcards and a safety announcement.

Multimodal Tourism Communication

The tourist industry has increasingly exploited the multimodal interaction of more than one semiotic resource in the same text, at the service of visibility and appeal to the public (Antelmi *et al.*, 2007: 223). Hence, dynamic images, vivid colours, vibrant sound effects and appealing fonts have cognitive and emotional effects on text recipients – tourists or travellers-to-be. Overall, intersemiosis captures and holds the reader's attention, engenders a pleasant psychological attitude, assists concentration, places emphasis and thus leaves a lasting mnestic trace (Francesconi, 2011a).

In multimodal static artefacts, writing, images and colour interact to build a coherent text, where the boundaries between distinct modes are blurred (Antelmi *et al.*, 2007: 227). An example is the Maltese Tourism Authority logo, shown in Figure 5.1, used by the official tourist board for all its informative and promotional texts and material. The visual–verbal text shows an upper section devoted to the symbolic visual text and a lower section devoted to writing. The visual part juxtaposes the Maltese cross on the left and the Eye of Osiris on the right. The most recognised

Figure 5.1 The logo used by the official Maltese tourist board

symbol of Malta, the Maltese cross is known globally as the Cross of the Knights of St John and evokes the European religious and military order. The Eye of Osiris, also present on the local colourful fishing boats, the *luzzu*, symbolises the Egyptian goddess of the underworld and evokes Malta's North African heritage. The combination of these two iconic items frames Malta as a multicultural place, where a Semitic and a Germanic language meet (Maltese and English), where the Sicilian cookery tradition is mixed with Maltese and Gozitan dishes, and where megalithic temples co-exist with baroque palaces. At the crossroads of ancient trade routes, Malta is represented as an encounter between different worlds (Francesconi, 2011b).

Associated and integrated with the visual text, the lower part of the icon shows the writing, in turn divided into two items: 'Malta' and 'Malta Gozo Comino'. These are distinct in terms of font and size, the first being bigger and in a cursive font, the second smaller and in a more formal and regular sans serif font. A highly cohesive strategy is colour, the writing being in blue, one of the three colours used in the visual text. Integration is also achieved through careful and balanced disposition of elements. In this multimodal ensemble, each semiotic resource has a specific potential: layout composes, colour evokes mood, writing names and image connotes. Thanks to symbol choice, item arrangement, vivid colours, colour repetition, font size and type, the logo thus achieves visibility, recognition and memorability. Worthy of note, the logo never appears in isolation in authentic multimodal artefacts. It is visible within a wider textual context where it makes meaning in co-occurring and integrating with other text elements such as banners, pictures or headings. This process is the focus of the following section.

Clustering and Reading Paths

In the past, the traditional page tended to be organised as a unique and dense block of written text. Over recent decades, text configuration has been changing with the evolution of society, varieties of domain, modes and forms of expression, and, in particular, with the affirmation of digital communication (Garzone, 2007). The page we are familiar with today is systematically broken up into smaller, coherent segments, namely textual units variously called 'lexias' (Barthes, [1970] 1975), 'frames' (Antelmi et al., 2007: 169), 'clusters' (Baldry & Thibault, 2006: 31; Santulli, 2007: 34), 'segments' (Stöckl, 2004: 26) or 'modules' (Kress, 2010). **Clusters** need to be assessed in number, size, shape, dynamism, mode, placement, orientation and function.

Identified by Barthes as expressing 'the plural nature of the text' ([1970] 1975: 20), the property of textual fragmentation is termed **granularity** and it increases as the number of clusters grows (Garzone, 2007): it is low in a poorly fragmented traditional page but high in a marketing website rich in textual units. Cluster number is related to size, a value which applies to the single cluster and not to the page: clusters' size on a page is not homogeneous and different units have a different size. Shape is a further parameter, tourist pictures being typically rectangular in shape: the Italian-style photograph, generally used for landscape representation, has a horizontal orientation, while the French-style photograph, generally adopted for portraits and castle battlements, has a vertical orientation (Dann, 1996b). A medium-related parameter is that of dynamism: clusters in a printed document are necessarily static, while the electronic page may include dynamic units such as animated advertisements or a picture slideshow.

As for mode, clusters may be verbal, visual or both (Baldry & Thibault, 2006: 11), such as, respectively, titles, pictures or logos. Far from being randomly organised and distributed, these textual units also follow specific rules in terms of grouping, distribution, interaction within superclusters and orientation (Francesconi, 2012: 73). Clusters' *dispositio* follows the meaning potential of specific 'zones': left and right, top and bottom, centre and margins. Their corresponding informational values are given and new, ideal and real, centrality and marginality (see Chapter 3). This implies textual orientation. In brochures, the page develops along the horizontal axis of the two-page spread and exploits the salience and information value of the right zone, where the most prominent element is positioned (Francesconi, 2011b). In the case of travel websites, the homepage is structured along a vertical axis, with the upper section visually configuring the values of glamour, adventure or relaxation promised by the holiday experience and the lower section verbally offering practical information on packages and the tour operator (Kress & van Leeuwen, 2006: 219).

Hence, granularity frames genre configurations. If the verbal text in a travel novel is generally displayed as a continuous textual block, in a magazine it is vertically divided into columns, whereas on a website it is composed of visually distinct paragraphs. Within the various generic instances, textual clusters act as graphically separated 'blocks of signification' and 'units of reading', thus fulfilling specific communication functions (Barthes, [1970] 1975: 13). Clustering also outlines page orientation and invites privileged reading paths.

The **reading path** indicates the trajectory followed by the gaze while reading a text and it may be described in terms of directionality, continuity and predictability. Paths may be linear, discontinuous, multisequential or, again, horizontal, vertical, circular, diagonal, zigzagging, spiralling, and so on (Kress & van Leeuwen, 2006: 219). 'Different readers may follow different paths' (Kress & van Leeuwen, 2006: 212) and the same reader reads differently in specific situations, domains, moments and places. Albeit potentially infinite, reading trajectories do not reflect random, ungraspable and individual behaviours and a certain degree of predictability can be detected (Kress & van Leeuwen, 1998). As Coelho argues (2008), every text is produced with an ideal reader in mind, thus providing a certain reading position to the real viewer and outlining plausible viewing directions.

Acknowledging the value of cultural, cognitive and emotional variables, the social semiotic approach indicates plausible text organisation on the basis of layout and, in particular, salience and text orientation. Holsanova *et al.* (2006: 71) have extracted the following seven assumptions on reading practices from Kress and van Leeuwen:

(1) Readers prefer new information and expect this to be on the right in the semiotic space.
(2) Readers prefer the most general information at the top and the most specific information at the bottom of the semiotic space.
(3) Readers look for the most important information in the centre of the page and less important information on the periphery.
(4) Readers look for graphically salient elements.
(5) Readers look for paratexts.
(6) Readers follow elements connected to each other by framing devices such as lines and arrows.
(7) Readers scan the semiotic space before taking a closer look at certain units.

Accordingly, readers' attention is generally captured by the biggest picture (assumption 4), positioned on the top-right of the semiotic space (assumptions 1 and 2), which acts as the 'entry point' for the reading process. The next most salient element is the paratextual cluster composed of title and subtitle (assumption 5). The main image and title are often related by spatial proximity. From here, vectors lead to other parts of the text space and invite further exploration. According to Kress and van Leeuwen (1998), many newspaper layouts do not yet prescribe a clear sequence of reading or a reading path to their audience, and this relative openness gives the reader the possibility of choosing a strategy of reading. Kress and van Leeuwen (2006: 205) thus describe 'the most plausible reading path' being taken when users 'begin by glancing at the photo, and then make a new start from left to right, from headline to photo, after which, optionally, they move to the body of the verbal text'.

Alongside these general cognitively driven rules, every reading is determined by variables in terms of culture, age, attitude, attention, genre, medium and mode. First, reading is culturally oriented. For example, the Western reading path follows linear left-to-right and top-to-bottom modes (Kress & van Leeuwen, 1996, 2006). This is generally reflected in highly coded texts based on the densely written page. Second, age has been identified as implying different dispositions towards text directionality (Kress, 2003: 165). In a controlled study of front-page reading paths, Coelho (2008: 13) observes that younger readers are more visually oriented and follow non-linear reading paths, whereas older readers prefer writing and tend to adopt a traditional, linear reading directionality.

Considering reading attitude and attention, Holsanova *et al.* (2006: 71) have detected three main categories:

- The 'editorial' reader avoids advertisements and follows only written text.
- The 'focused' reader is highly selective and reads only what she/he is interested in.
- The 'overview' reader is more superficial reader of the verbal text but also pays attention to paratextual items such as headlines, images and advertisements.

Clearly, the third profile is closer to the reader of tourist promotional texts, who appreciates breathtaking pictures and subtle verbal solutions rather than densely written textual blocks. This is especially valid at the pre-trip stage, when the emotional appeal of multimodal texts is most powerful and most effective. At the on-trip stage, the most plausible reader is instead 'focused', looking for that piece of information on a certain monument or advice on the restaurant that is the best value for money. Different text genres, then, imply different readers: if the brochure primarily attracts the overview reader, the guide predominantly targets the focused reader.

Reading path configurations also derive from medium-based constraints or possibilities with space-based printed texts such as brochures, catalogues or guides, presupposing a predominantly linear, page-by-page fruition. Non-linear hypertexts like tourism webpages are typically composed of often overlapping clusters that force viewers to hop backwards and forwards, thus inviting an open, plural and discontinuous reading process termed 'cluster hopping' (Baldry & Thibault, 2006: 26). The time-based sequential arrangement of shots in a video leads to linearly coded fruition, which is yet further affected by contextual conditions. If at the cinema the film-viewing process is pre-established, on an electronic support, the same multimodal artefact can be variously consumed in terms of viewing continuity, attention and exclusivity: unlike with an uninterrupted view, users can stop, pause, backtrack, fast-forward and review; they can also select a mute option or listen to sound without looking at the visual.

To sum up, various textual and contextual factors affect the reading trajectory and the meaning-making process: sociocultural background, readers' cognitive and emotional profiles, text genre, layout, salience and text orientation. The following section provides an example of homepage clustering.

Visit Jamaica website homepage

It has been argued that digital texts are marked by substantial granularity and by unpredictable reading paths. Official travel and tourism webpages are exemplary of this growing tendency (Fodde & van den Abbeele, 2012). Figure 5.2 shows the syntagmatic integration of visual and verbal clusters and plausible reading path(s) on the Visitjamaica homepage, the official national portal for the island's tourism.

As the website states, Jamaica attracts over one million visitors every year, which makes tourism the major source of income on the island. The third largest island of the Greater Antilles, Jamaica has English as its official language, having been under British rule until 1962 and being today part of the Commonwealth (Crystal, 2003; Kachru, 1985; McArthur, 1998). The website is in English, but offers the options of Chinese, Dutch, French, German, Italian, Japanese and Spanish. As soon as users open the homepage, they are welcomed by a dynamic, colourful page accompanied by vibrant, entertaining reggae music. Visual and aural interaction creates an appealing

Multimodal and Intermodal Analysis   137

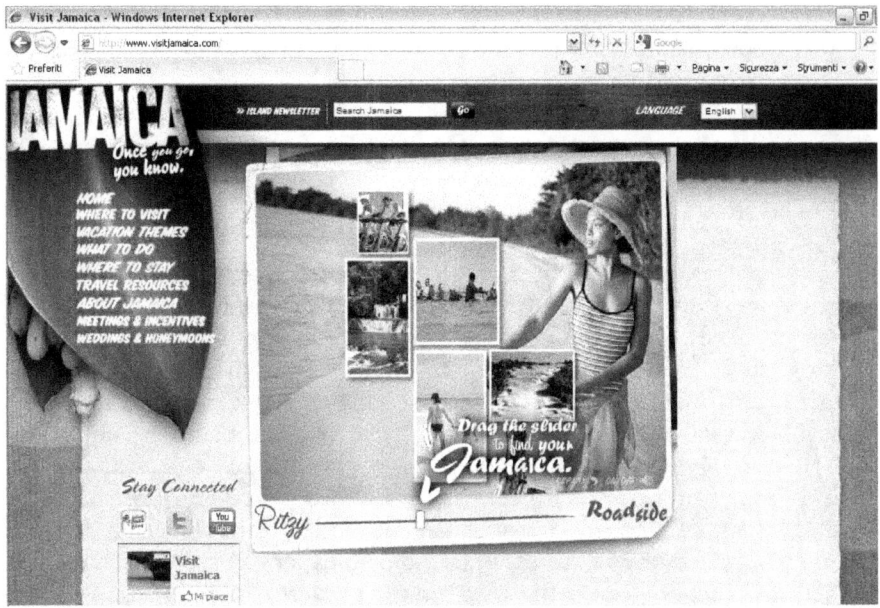

Figure 5.2 The Visit Jamaica homepage, www.visitjamaica.com (accessed January 2013)

atmosphere that invites further exploration. Differently from standard travel websites, the page does not show an extremely high granularity: clusters are relatively sparse and divided by relevant spacing. This creates an effect of light-heartedness, confirmed by the use of colourful writing, a colourful background and unusual fonts. Instead of the Times New Roman or Arial normally used in professional and institutional websites, a more personal, friendly, intimate font is adopted, between print and handwriting (Boardman, 2005: 47). From the top left corner, clockwise, these are the clusters on the Jamaica homepage (not all shown in Figure 5.2):

(1) Jamaica slogan;
(2) Island newsletter icon;
(3) the search button;
(4) the language option button;
(5) the main picture;
(6) the weather forecast;

(7) the special event cluster;
(8) the bottom cluster with contact, site map, terms of use, privacy policy, press room, JTB information portal;
(9) Hot travel deals;
(10) The logo for the destination Jamaica blog;
(11) Social network cluster;
(12) The navigation menu.

The central and main section shows a big square image acting as a salient super-cluster with superimposed smaller postcard-like images of Jamaican scenes. The user can select the set of images by simply dragging a yellow slider back and forth: the appearance and positioning of the small images on the main one keep varying, creating an effect of dynamism. This unusual strategy of interactivity makes the site visit amusing and entertaining (Held, 2004; and see Chapter 1).

Far from being the common flat, monochromatic solution, the background, then, is a composition of superimposed plans: the first layer is given by a shaded brown tint, the second by a paper-like sheet with uneven borders and then a green banana leaf on the top left corner. A warm-yellow bar traces a wide, horizontal line through the upper section of the website. These superimposed plans create an effect of depth and a positive and pleasant atmosphere. Symbolically, the deep space and warm tints invite both entry into the space and website navigation. The homepage, in fact, acts as a 'gateway', from which the user moves to connected pages within the website (Baldry & Thibault, 2006: 118).

Coherently, image appreciation is accompanied by the vibrant reggae soundtrack, which heavily relies on percussion and saxophone. Against the highly rhythmic music, a male choir sings 'Come and feel the spirit, the spirit of Jamaica', followed by a female voice:

> Booking Jamaica is easy and affordable. Just enter your departure city, travel dates, select the vacation resort, then see the great values available. Come feel the spirit of Jamaica: we have something for everyone! So book now!

This verbal text confirms and multiplies the notions of 'accessibility' and 'lightness' already framed by the layout and music.

Various multimodal devices like sound, images and writing make the official tourism page appear less marketing-oriented, less informative and more entertaining, thus proving an effective generic innovation process (see Chapter 1). Hence, the webpage is a hybrid text, in between the static, space-based text and the dynamic, time-based text. It uses 'pagey properties' (Baldry & Thibault, 2006: 105) like writing, depiction and special arrangement of items alongside 'screeny properties' such as moving objects, soundtrack and hypertextuality. All these co-concur in the performance of the homepage's plural function. At the ideational and textual levels, it presents and structures basic and preliminary information on the destination's natural and sociocultural profile. At the interpersonal level, it invites affective responses, indexes social values and creates a pleasant and welcoming atmosphere (Baldry & Thibault, 2006: 119). At the textual level, it achieves cohesion thanks to the high level of intramodal and intermodal coherence and realises multiplicative semiosis.

Due to the multiple and multimodal effects, this homepage can be freely and variously read. It invites a privileged trajectory, starting from the main, central image as the entry point. It then goes up to the title, to the top left slogo (logo + slogan), to the menu below and again to the centre, where it further explores the small pictures, to the social network cluster and to the lower section. Clearly, the pathway is unlikely to be followed in a linear and continuous path and rather implies cluster hopping. The same will happen with reference to website navigation, explored later in this chapter.

As webpage analysis has revealed, clustering and reading paths encode modes and forms of textual configuration and consumption. The following sections more specifically investigate three types of textual structure, namely static, dynamic and hypertextual.

Intersemiosis in Static Texts

Although individual modes have recently been given critical attention, research in cross-modal interplay is still under-represented (Stöckl, 2004: 10). Yet, a critical debate on intersemiotic complementarity started with Roland Barthes himself ([1961] 1977), who observed visual–verbal inter-relation in printed advertisements as bimodal static texts. The semiotician developed a framework of analysis in order to assess this relation type and function, and identified two main options, of relay and elaboration (Figure 5.3).

The relay function is grounded upon a complementary relationship between words and images: the verbal text can 'extend' the visual text, adding new and different meanings. What happens is that the former enhances the latter, extending the interpretations conveyed by the visual component. This is the case, for instance, with cartoons, comic strips and film. Conversely, elaboration takes place when the verbal text elaborates the image, or vice versa, restating the same meaning. It can be further divided into illustration (performed by the image when the verbal comes first) and

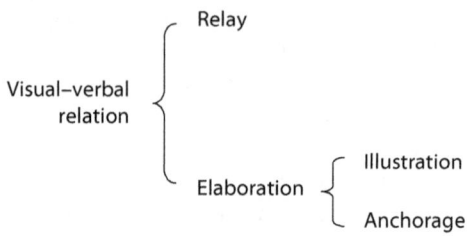

Figure 5.3 Barthes's framework for intersemiosis in static texts

anchorage (fulfilled by the verbal to fix the visual text, when the image comes first). In anchorage, the linguistic components allow the reader to choose and foreground the 'right' signified among the numerous interpretations the image invites: this is why this form of intersemiosis is predominant in printed advertisements. In this light, language seems not only to help the viewer but actually to control and affect understanding, through the use of culturally defined ideologies (Barthes, [1970] 1977: 274). It is worth noting that the two functions of relay and elaboration can co-exist within the same message, but one will always be dominant for the general economy of the work.

It should be emphasised that Barthes recognised the increasing role of multimodal messages in mass communication but he ascribed to the visual mode a relation of submission to the verbal code. The author preferred to use the expression 'civilisation of writing' rather than 'civilisation of the image', granting the main communication function exclusively to writing and speech (Barthes, [1970] 1977: 274).

Kress and van Leeuwen (2006: 18) consider their multimodal communication model antithetical to Barthes's, on the basis that they place the visual and verbal modes on the same level. Recently, scholars interested in intersemiosis have acknowledged this position and, starting from Halliday's metafunctional system, have been developing frames for assessing modes and forms of semiotic interplay (Marissa *et al.*, 2011; Martinec & Salway, 2005; Royce, 1998, 2002; Stöckl, 2004; Tsakona, 2009; Unsworth & Cléirigh, 2009). Among these, Martinec and Salway (2005) transposed the SFL clause relation system to image–text relations, with particular attention to the two systems of relative status and logico-semantics. Their framework is illustrated and exemplified below, with the use of some humorous postcards targeting Englishness.

Humorous British postcards

Curiously, in this age of participatory digital communication, printed postcards are still used in travel and tourist domains, especially if innovative. Alongside more traditional picture postcards, the tourist industry is offering more alternative texts, featuring unusual size, shape, materials and texts (Cohen, 2007; Pritchard & Morgan, 2005; Thurlow *et al.*, 2005; Yüksel & Olcay, 2007). Among these, humorous postcards are best-selling titles, perceived and purchased by travellers more as entertaining than as tourist texts. Rather than the celebratory attitude of picture postcards, they adopt a funny tone. Evoking the well-known Donald McGill's seaside resort postcards, such texts thus rewrite the solid British tradition of humorous postcards which had been celebrated by George Orwell (Francesconi, 2011a, 2012).

From a multimodal viewpoint, these texts make meaning through the interaction of visual and verbal systems. Image and text are related in a specific and meaningful way, mapped by Martinec and Salway through the system of relative status, retrieved from SFL. As seen in Chapter 2, Halliday has identified paratactic and syntactic clauses, the former encompassing independent adjacent clauses, the latter including dependent hypotactic adjacent clauses. Similarly, the relative status of images and texts is considered equal when they are joined on an equal footing and they can both stand on their own; or, alternatively, unequal when one cannot stand on its own and is dependent on the other. In the first case (equal status), the image and text may be independent if the messages they convey do not need to be combined; alternatively, the participants are complementary when they are part of a larger system and the information they provide makes sense by their combination (see Figure 5.6). Equal relative status in visual–verbal intersemiosis is exemplified in the humorous postcard commenting on English food in Figure 5.4, composed of a colourful drawing and a caption.

The drawing shows a Swiss tourist sitting at a table, with a fork and knife in his hands and ready to enjoy his meal, an enormous fish placed upon a mountain of chips. Ketchup, salt and pepper are available to make the overwhelming dish more savoury. Placed along the superior central section of the card, the caption reads: 'Eat fish & chips if it's the last thing you do!' The sentence is composed of two clauses: an imperative clause acting as head and a subordinate, conditional clause. The first part, the invitation to eat the typical English food, is subverted in the second section, which hyperbolically warns of its unhealthy properties and humorously forewarns death. If considered separately, both units are meaningful in themselves, that is, they autonomously engender mirth. They have thus an equal status

Figure 5.4 Equal and independent relative status in visual–verbal intersemiosis (copyright LGP)

and are independent chunks. If semantically unnecessary, their interconnection still plays a pragmatic function of illustration and emphasis.

The alternative to equal status is the unequal, indicating a relationship of subordination between participants. In bi-modal texts, the visual component can be subordinated to the verbal one, or the verbal component can be subordinated to the visual one. An unequal visual–verbal relation is represented in Figure 5.5, entitled 'British Beer or Instant English!', which humorously deals with the role of beer in the English learning process.

Central to meaning-making, the verbal text features a variation grid demonstrating that the more pints of beer one drinks, the better one's English becomes. With one pint, 'no change to your English' is observable and with five pints, 'you discover you can sing in English, and are brilliant at karaoke'. The adoption of quantitative criteria in order to support the humorous thesis enables the parody of the scientific genre to achieve a highly comic effect. Alongside writing, a visual text is visible in the postcard's central section, displaying an impeccable English man on the left, a pint of beer in the middle, with a drunken Swiss tourist hanging on the glass to the right. Albeit funny, the vignette alone does not articulate the connection

Multimodal and Intermodal Analysis 143

Figure 5.5 Unequal relative status with image subordinate to text (copyright LGP)

between beer drinking and English learning and is not meaningful itself. This postcard thus exemplifies a relation of subordination, with the image subordinate to text (Figure 5.6).

After relative clause status, the second system considered by Martinec and Salway is logico-semantics (Figure 5.7). In SFL, two logico-semantic relations have been identified between clauses: projection and expansion (see Chapter 2). Projection is common in two bimodal contexts: comic strips and in text–diagram combinations in textbooks and academic texts. It is subclassified into two types: locution (a projection of wording, usually by a verbal process) and idea (a projection of meaning, most often by a mental process) (see Figure 5.7). Examples can be found in comic strips,

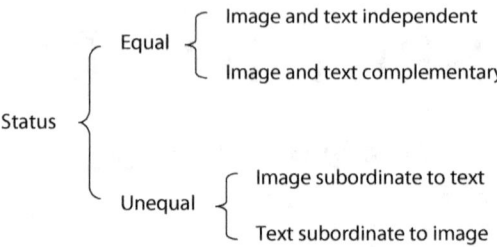

Figure 5.6 Relative status in visual–verbal intersemiosis

with speech bubbles containing locutions, while thought bubbles enclose ideas (Martinec & Salway, 2005: 354–355). Figure 5.8 exemplifies the relation of locution, with the verbal text being projected inside the speech bubble. The postcard features a couple of visitors walking in a town centre and immersed in ancient ruins, medieval monuments and antiques stores. The naïf male tourist asks: 'Excuse me, is there anything *new* to see around here?' As for relative status, this postcard provides an example of equal status, with visual and verbal texts fulfilling a complementary role. Neither the visual nor the verbal alone are self-sufficient: in order to generate humour, they need to be taken together.

The logico-semantic relation of expansion is further divided into three subgroups (Martinec & Salway, 2005: 352–353).

- In elaboration two cases can be discerned: exposition, when image and text have the same level of generality; and exemplification, where either the text or the image can be more general.
- Extension occurs when one participant, either image or text, adds new information; it extends the message by conveying new content.

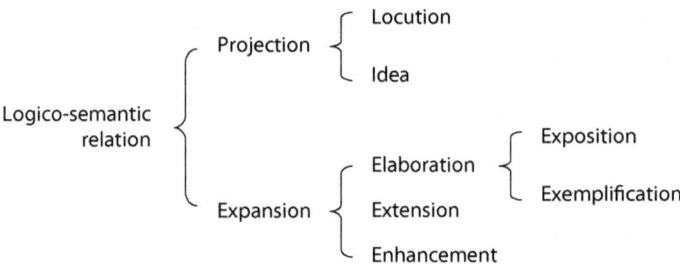

Figure 5.7 Logico-semantic relation in visual–verbal semiosis

Figure 5.8 The logico-semantic relation of locution (copyright LGP)

- The relation of enhancement deals with circumstantial relations of time, place and reason/purpose that qualify either image or text.

Figure 5.9 exemplifies the relation of expansion, since the verbal text adds new content to the information provided by the visual in 'Brain of Britain'. The postcard features a brain section made salient through vivid colours, relevant size and central placement, with straight lines locating precise points in the brain. The verbal text adds necessary, not circumstantial, information on the composition of the British brain, as made up of a long list of items like 'Royal Family recognition centre', 'mistrust of Europe ventricle' and 'national pride gland'. In this case, relative image–text status is problematic: it could seem one of inequality, the written list of Brain of Britain components being sufficient to generate the mirth. Yet, the text is based on both identification and location of brain items, which relies on the parody of the visual text genre to make meaning. Accordingly, the status is of equality, and the text and image complement each other.

Intersemiosis becomes more complex in sequential texts like comic strips, which are static texts combining visual and verbal semiotic resources

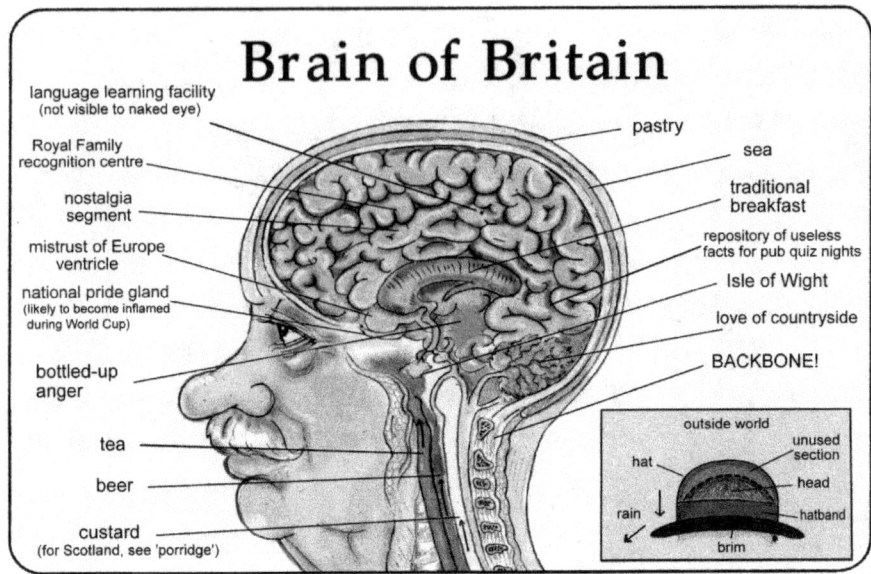

Figure 5.9 The logico-semantic relation of extension (copyright LGP)

(Figure 1.3 in Chapter 1). Comic strips encompass a series of panels, each of which contains images plus text. Yet, the single panel is insufficient to make meaning, that is, in generating humour. Only the sequential ordering of multimodal panels allows the unfolding of the narrative line and the realisation of the humorous message. Interestingly, comic strips can be positioned at the crossroads between static and dynamic texts, which introduces the following section.

Intersemiosis in Dynamic Texts

In contrast to space-based static texts, dynamic texts display sequential images unfolding in time and include television commercials, videos and films. Within tourism and travel domains, a very basic dynamic text is the slideshow; many websites display one in the ideal zone of their homepages. This is normally a slow sequence of images, which may be accompanied by background instrumental music. More articulated texts are short promotional videos available on the internet, on television, on DVDs and on screens in public places like airports and stations. In museums, more extended informative videos are visible that introduce, contextualise, enrich or accompany an exhibition. To this category may also be added travel-related lectures, conferences and radio programmes (see Chapter 4), as well as visits to tourism sites, exhibitions and fairs. The last group includes live events, occurring in real life, that therefore need to be recorded for multimodal analysis.

Following the logic of time, dynamic texts make meaning through their chronological succession (Kress, 2003: 33). Films, videos and commercials are not still but are 'a wave-like pattern' (Baldry & Thibault, 2006: 47), a 'system in flux', governed by 'patterns of change' (O'Halloran, 2004: 109). Such configurations perfectly combine the paradigms of the dynamic tourist gaze (see Chapter 3) and of mobility: multimodal dynamic textuality reflects the complexity, plurality and fluidity of reality and gives the viewer an impression of visiting and exploring the destination. Yet, space and time in film texts do not correspond to the dimensions we experience in real life: they are re-presented, compressed, constructed and edited in the form of continuity (Iedema, 2001: 187).

Filmic diegesis development in time can be first observed as structurally composed of ranks (Baldry, 2004; Baldry & Thibault, 2006; Bateman & Schmidt, 2012; Iedema, 2001; O'Halloran, 2004). These correspond to grapheme, word, group and clause in writing and to phoneme, syllable, foot, tone group in speech (see Chapter 4). According to Iedema (2001), multimodal audio-visual texts like a documentary, video or film can be analysed according to six levels: frame, shot, scene, sequence, generic stage and work as a whole (Figure 5.10). The first is the still of a shot, whereas the second is an uncut video unit. The shot is thus generally taken by film text analysts as the basic meaningful video unit, its role and function corresponding to those of the clause in SFL. Made up of more than one shot, the scene is still a one time–space unit, while the sequence embraces multiple space sequences. The level of generic stage embraces diegetic units like beginnings, middles and endings, while the work as a whole may be identified according to text genre.

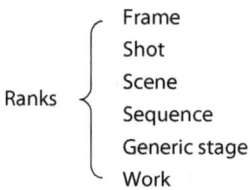

Figure 5.10 Ranks for film analysis

From the viewpoint of **modal resources**, film-video analysis can be thus undertaken addressing: first, the syntagmatic co-patterning within the shot of visual track and sound track; and second, the modal sequential paradigmatic interaction unfolding as choice through the shots. In order to decodify the intra-shot visual imagery, frame participants, camera scale, movement, point of view, depth, colour types, cohesion, contrast, light intensity, source, direction, flow, special effects, focus, duration of image, speed of motion and changes in all these items need to be observed (Iedema, 2001). In order to examine the aural resources, attention should be drawn to the soundscape, composed of given sounds such as voice in or off shot, music and sound effects, each with specific degrees of relevance to the listener, roles and functions (van Leeuwen, 1999).

Shots unfold in time and are mutually related via transitions that mark the shift from one segment to the next. Acting as linking adjuncts between paragraphs or sentences, transitions play a crucial cohesive role, since they weave the text together (Bateman & Schmidt, 2012). As such, conjunctive shot–shot transitions enact the logical metafunction, concerned with relations of causal, temporal interdependency among clauses, and can thus express different syntactic solutions (see Chapter 2). Cuts, cross-fades and fades vary in terms of length, the cut being the shortest and the cross-fade the longest type of transition (Baldry, 2004; Baldry & Thibault, 2006; Iedema, 2001; O'Halloran, 2004). In tourism and travel-related dynamic texts, such solutions carry semantic implications: slow cross-fading may be adopted to encode values of relaxation and peace, while immediate and clear cuts may express adventure and rhythm.

Yet, dynamism pertains to both intra-shot and inter-shot movements: the first involves camera movements, participants' movements, gestures, speech, light and colour changes, while the second involves shot transition and sound continuity via either music or voice-over. Camera movement is of particular interest. It may be fixed and represent either a horizontal movement, called panning, or a vertical movement, called tilting. The fixed camera may also slowly move in on the subject, via a zoom. The mobile camera may move forward, backward or in a circle, or follow a moving item. In tourism and travel texts, an interesting effect of on-the-road adventure is given by the hand-held camera, which offers a blurred vision (Francesconi, 2011c).

To sum up, the multimodal and dynamic ranks variously enact a metafunctional role. As regards the ideational strand of meaning, attention should be given to the represented participants' identity and actions, music type and speech topic. The interpersonal metafunction is fulfilled through systems like depth, dynamism, angle, scale and distance (see Chapter 3), while structure and rhythm are patterns of textual organisation realised across the interaction of sound and images (van Leeuwen, 2009).

In order to show how time-based texts make meaning, a sample video will be considered hereafter, a brilliant and popular safety announcement displayed by Air New Zealand on its flights. Aimed to provide instructions on how to adopt security measures, the Air New Zealand safety announcement features characters from Tolkien's *The Hobbit*.

The Air New Zealand safety video

In November 2012, shortly before the release of the fantasy adventure movie *The Hobbit: An Unexpected Journey* by Peter Jackson, New Zealand's national carrier launched the Hobbit-themed video for its flights. Curiously, actors include Peter Jackson himself and two great grandsons of *The Hobbit* author J.R.R. Tolkien, Mike and Royd Tolkien. The video, which lasts 4 minutes 17 seconds, attracted more than one million hits per day in the first week of its release and images from it are available for download at www.airnzhobbitmedia.com.

Given the complex structure of video texts, an accurate practice of multimodal transcription is necessary, which enables identification of the many elements and their integration into larger-scale units. Transcriptions should simultaneously reveal the multimodal nature of the video – that is, how moving images and sound are integrated within the shot – and its dynamic component – that is, how shots are related to and integrated into bigger units, like scenes and sequences (Baldry & Thibault, 2006: 50). Tables 5.1 and 5.2 present the integrated transcription of image track and sound track of the safety video's first 12 shots.

Excluding the opening section in the first two shots, the video features 10 shots in 20 seconds. Reduced duration of image, participant alternation and the use of cuts as exclusive transition types help the text achieve a dynamic effect. Variety is also expressed through different camera positions and angles and sizes of frame. Conversely, camera movements tend to be constant and extremely slow, regardless of the horizontal, vertical, frontal or oblique direction and on the setting or character focus. Reminiscent of an airy dimension, the music supplies mood and ambience. Produced by flute, violins and strings, featuring a constant allegro–moderato tempo, it starts at a relatively high volume, since it acts as figure in the soundscape. Then its volume lowers and acts as ground when the female voice enters as figure. Subsequently, volume remains constant throughout the whole video. Music and voice combined engender a slow, pleasant rhythm, distinct from the more hectic pace of standard safety videos.

Table 5.1 Transcription of the Air New Zealand safety video: Image track

Image track Shot no. and length	Shot	Main represented participants	Size of frame	Angle and movement	Written text	Transition
1. 00:01–00:05		Company logo	Close-up		Company logo	Cut
2. 00:06–00:10		Written texts	Long shot	Eye-level, item approaching at slow speed	Your guide to safety aboard this 777-300ER	Fade
3. 0:11–0:15		Female elf stewardess	Long shot	Eye-level, slow forward tracking	X	Cut
4. 0:16–0:18		Female elf stewardess	Close-up	Eye-level, extremely slow forward tracking	X	Cut
5. 0:19–0:22		Hobbits, dwarfs and orcs as passengers	Medium shot	Oblique angle, slow forward tracking	X	Cut

6. 0:23		Female elf stewardess	Medium-long shot	Eye-level, extremely slow forward tracking	X Cut
7. 0:24–0:26		A group of passengers	Medium shot	Oblique, high angle, slow side tracking	X Cut
8. 0:27		Female elf stewardess	Close-up	Eye-level, extremely slow pan	X Cut
9. 0:28		A group of passengers	Medium shot	Oblique, eye-level, stationary camera	X Cut
10. 0:29		Female passenger	Medium shot	Oblique, low angle, hand-held camera	X Cut
11. 0:30		Male passenger	Medium shot	Oblique, eye-level, low pan	X Cut
12. 0:31		Male passenger's feet	Close-up	Oblique, high angle, slow pan	X Cut

Table 5.2 Transcription of the Air New Zealand safety video: Sound track

Shot no. and length	Spoken text	Music	Volume	Sound
1. 00:01–00:05	X	Instrumental		X
2. 0:06–00:10				
3. 0:11–0:15	Welcome aboard this Middle Earth flight. Before we set out on our journey	Instrumental	↓	X
4. 0:16–0:18	I would like to impart this story of safety	Instrumental	↔	X
5. 0:19–0:22	X	Music	Extremely low	Passengers' chats, laughs, whistles
6. 0:23	Even if you flight with us often	Instrumental	↔	Lower chatting
7. 0:24–0:26	Be sure to keep a sharp eye on the briefing.	Instrumental	↔	X
8. 0:27	Be sure your belongings	Instrumental	↔	X
9. 0:28	are hidden away in the compartments	Instrumental	↔	X
10. 0:29	above	Instrumental	↔	X
11. 0:30	or under the seat before you.	Instrumental	↔	X
12. 0:31	X	Instrumental	↔	X

Made salient through close-ups and eye-level shots, the female elf stewardess is framed as the main represented participant in the scene, who imparts security instructions. These visual strategies interact with her appealing but clear and reliable voice and invite viewers to listen to and trust her. This predominance becomes more evident if contrasted with shots depicting hobbits, dwarfs, elves and orcs as passengers, making use of medium size of frame and oblique camera angle. From the viewpoint of logico-semantic relations, this video realises a projection and, more specifically, locution: if we could make a drawing, we could resort to a comic strip with speech bubbles (Bateman & Schmidt, 2012). The main speaker is introduced in shots 3 and 4, while shots 6–12 feature the message of locution itself. Interestingly, instructions are not vertically delivered from an authoritative speaker to a silent, often invisible audience. To the contrary, reverse angle is used to depict and include the represented audience in shots 5, 7, 9–12 as interactive participants: elves and dwarfs co-participate in message delivery, showing how to safely behave onboard (shots 9–12).

This audio-visual text provides an insightful example of generic innovation (see Chapter 1). Undoubtedly, this instance exemplifies generic integrity in terms of message content and main communication function: it effectively provides instructions on security measures to be taken onboard. Innovation occurs as for represented participants, an 'unexpected' solution which proves to be extremely catchy and holds passengers' attention, making a highly technical, specialised and boring announcement on safety belts and oxygen masks an extremely pleasant and entertaining clip. Passengers recognise the famous story and its protagonists, are captured by the charm of the characters and the atmosphere, and pay attention to the instructions delivered by the elf in her sweet, airy voice.

An indirect communication function can still be identified alongside the pragmatic safety information provision. The highly evocative story is deeply rooted in Middle Earth culture and the video indirectly performs a promotional function. It represents New Zealand as a fascinating, entertaining environment that also takes care of its visitors'/passengers' security. The airline's manager, Mike Tod, explains that this video was only the beginning of a wider Air New Zealand two-year global marketing programme dedicated to *The Hobbit* trilogy. This will act in conjunction with Tourism New Zealand and aims to significantly increase the number of tourist arrivals to 'Middle Earth' (www.airnzhobbitmedia.com). Given this, Air New Zealand passengers have some experience of unusual safety videos, having been offered instructions onboard by New Zealand's famous All Blacks rugby union team, a pilot and cabin crew dressed only in body paint made to resemble their normal uniforms, and US rapper Snoop Dogg.

Having seen how multisemiosis develops in space and time, the following section discusses and exemplifies hypertextuality as combining static and dynamic strategies of communication. The case study refers to the Jamaica tourism website we have already looked at.

Intersemiosis in Hypertextual Texts

The hypertext is a text composed of a network of visual and verbal clusters and, in turn, of mutually connected pages. **Hypertextuality** thus shows a two-dimensional development: a syntagmatic functioning on the page and a paradigmatic functioning across pages. The former relies on the combination of co-occurring textual units within the screen space, while the latter functions through selection among possible options across further pages (Adami, 2013).

The hypertext link is the most fundamental structural property of the web, without which the medium would not exist (Crystal, 2006: 210). Inscribed inside clusters, the link used to be visually identified by the graphic convention of blue underlined text. The colour generally used to change when the link had been used, expressing a dynamic textuality that is possible only in web publishing (Boardman, 2005: 14). Underlining is progressively disappearing and the user now generally needs to actively look for hyperlinks, hovering the mouse around the page and waiting for the cursor to change into a graphical pointing finger (Boardman, 2005: 19). Potentially, any still or dynamic area of the page – like title, logo, map or toolbar – is a hyperlink and can be clicked or touched to be activated (Francesconi, 2012).

Crucially important for the interpersonal metafunction, the hypertextual link invites interactivity (Kress, 2003), asks users to act upon the digital text in order to access further text on other pages, to add their own text in the form of feedback, to transfer text to other spaces like email, online social communities or download and print it (Adami, 2013). With the development of Web 1.0 into Web 2.0 and Web 3.0 (see Chapter 1), opportunities for interactivity constantly and substantially grow and diversify.

As for the textual metafunction, the hypertextual link generates multiple, potentially infinite 'pathways' (Boardman, 2005: 14), 'trajectories' (Baldry & Thibault, 2006: 116) or 'traversals' (Lemke, 2002: 300) across clusters and across pages. This means that in hypertextuality there is no starting point, nor unifying narrative or sequential development. Moreover, the time-unfolding surfing process across pathways may have a varying duration, from seconds, to minutes, to hours; it may be simultaneous to other activities and may be interrupted or not (Lemke, 2002: 301). Like reading, surfing is in fact an individual and contingent process affected by specific and contextual aspects, which make it unpredictable, open, fluid and multiple (Francesconi, 2012).

However, as with static pages, the trajectory is suggested by authors, in this case by web-masters, through multimodal strategies functioning on cognitive and emotional levels. Variously salient devices are designed to catch the readers who surf the internet and let them explore the website without difficulties (Antelmi *et al.*, 2007: 173–174). The hypertext thus pre-organises and pre-codifies traversals, establishing meaningful cross-associations among clusters and documents and building a proper 'hypertext semantics' (Lemke, 2002: 306). Paradigmatically, cohesion chains across pages reflect clause relations identified by Halliday for language and realise in hypertexts the main semantic processes of expansion or projection (Lemke, 2002: 307). In webpages, meanings mainly offer a subcategorisation structure: the homepage generally presents the main theme and links allow access to categories which further develop previously mentioned topics (Lemke, 2002: 318). The paths suggested to the users can meet different standards but are generally chronological, alphabetical or by category (Antelmi *et al.*, 2007: 173–174).

The following section examines the Visitjamaica website structure (Figure 5.11) in terms of hypertextuality across pages.

The Visit Jamaica website structure

The Visitjamaica site map is visually presented as a list of contents, organised as chapter titles ('home', 'where to visit', 'vacation themes', 'what to do', 'where to stay', 'travel resources', 'about Jamaica', 'meeting and incentives', 'login', 'my Jamaica', 'newsletter', 'booking and travel deals', 'contact us', 'site map', 'terms of use'). The central points of the list are further divided into sub-chapters: the 'where to visit', for example, is followed by the 'main Jamaica locations' and, in turn, each one has further sections of 'attractions', 'activities', 'lodging', 'dining' and 'events'. Clearly, such informative units are organised following a logical progression, offering a conceptual map of the given arguments (Antelmi *et al.*, 2007: 172). In this case, relations are by categories and logical ties indicate expansion, in terms either of enhancement or of extension (see Chapter 2). By the means of such relations, the website thus configures a strictly interwoven textual system.

According to Lemke (2002: 323), hypertextuality foregrounds crucial political issues. The hypertext affords the website author/designer the opportunity not only to establish a dialogue with the user, enacting a systematic form of 'interpersonal interactivity' but it also to include multiple texts (Kress, 2003: 5) and various social voices, in the Bakhtinian sense of

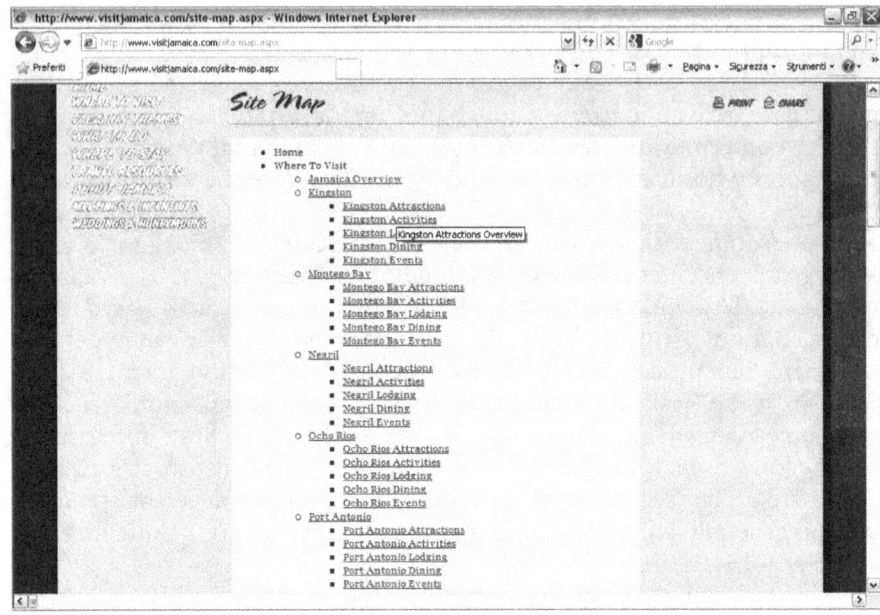

Figure 5.11 The structure of the Visit Jamaica website, www.visitjamaica.com (accessed January 2013)

heteroglossia (see Chapter 1). The unquestioned authoritative voice of the author wanes and disappears (Kress, 2003: 172) and the hypertextual space is inhabited by discursive diversity and conflict. The same happens with multimodality, which questions and subverts the strenuous logocentrism in Western society and forces an examination of the dialogue among a plurality of resources.

Lemke (2002: 300) further discusses the combination of multimodality and hypertextuality to produce the paradigm of hypermodality. Showing more complex configurations than multimodality does, hypermodality does not juxtapose semiotic affordances but designs potential and explicit interconnections among multimodal text units of various scales. Epistemically, if multimodality challenges logocentrism and hypertextuality challenges linearity, hypermodality subverts monologism across the multiplication of modal affordances alongside the linking to various texts, styles and registers. Ultimately, it invites a more open and critical thinking.

Conclusion

This chapter has addressed modes and forms of communication configured by space-based, time-based and hypermodal text instances. The multimodal unit of the cluster is seen as subverting logocentrism and providing a useful conceptual and analytical paradigm for multimodal text examination. Multiple cluster relations have been explored in visual–verbal static texts and in a hypertextual network of pages as meaning-making devices. Audio and visual temporal patterns of semiosis have been observed in dynamic film texts.

With a focus on syntagmatically and paradigmatically organised intersemiosis, this last chapter has contributed to the general aim of the volume, that of outlining a methodological framework for the analysis of tourism and travel texts, within the even broader scope of fostering the development of textual and tourism awareness. This should be achieved on the one hand by questioning, deconstructing and subverting rigid, simplistic and biased approaches to textuality, genre, mode and language, and on the other hand by overcoming a snobbish and hypocritical 'touristophobia' (Canestrini, 2001: 49). Tourism should thus be seen as defined by the WTO Global Code of Ethics for Tourism: 'when practised with a sufficiently open mind, it is an irreplaceable factor of self-education, mutual tolerance and for learning about the legitimate differences between peoples and cultures and their diversity' (www.unwto.org).

Afterword: Methods of Multimodal Analysis

Throughout the five main chapters, the volume has presented theories and frameworks for multimodal analysis. This conclusion seeks to briefly outline the main aspects, methods and tools used in multimodal studies.

Overall, the investigation of multimodal textuality has a tradition of qualitative, heuristic and deductive analysis. Extensively exemplified throughout the chapters, qualitative exploration describes a multimodal text employing Halliday's SFL frameworks outlined for different modes: O'Toole (2010) and Kress and van Leeuwen (2006) for the visual text; and van Leeuwen (1999) for audio systems. The metafunctional principle is also used as a starting point for studying the interaction between semiotic resources, as demonstrated with the frameworks developed by Martinec and Salway (2005), Royce (2007), Stöckl (2004) and Unsworth and Cléirigh (2009), among others.

In the tradition of case study research, qualitative analysis is based on text instance observation and the subsequent formulation of hypotheses for general rules. This means the social semiotic approach points out plausible text interpretations by the ideal reader. Text decodification practices are indeed recognised as potentially infinite in number, since they result from sociocultural and psychological personal history, habits, attitudes, tastes, mood, alongside variables like ethnicity, gender and age. However, generic conventions and constraints mainly deriving from modal choices are seen as substantially influencing the fruition process, thus enabling the identification of probable reading directions and modalities.

In recent years, scholars of multimodal phenomena following this trend have felt the urgent need to empirically check and confirm hypotheses on a larger scale through quantitative investigation. In order to pursue this aim, more consistent corpora of multimodal texts are being compiled, that go beyond the single case study and that need to meet requirements of balance, representativeness and quality (Bateman, 2008: 251). In fact, they are constructed as reflecting authentic and natural language, used for specific purposes or, more frequently, show given generic configurations like printed car advertisements, television make-up commercials or institutional webpages. Meanwhile, recent research is developing computer-driven tools for the exploration of such extended corpora, which should collect, tag and store a high quantity of multimodal material.

This empirical and computer-based tendency reflects what has happened in research in linguistics, where the development of digital technology was based on the need to investigate naturally occurring linguistic data – written, spoken and signed, as represented by a collection of texts put together for linguistic analysis (Bateman, 2008: 249). The British National Corpus, for instance, collects 100 million words used in written and spoken British English in a variety of fields, registers and genres (www.natcorp.ox.ac.uk). The most established and widespread tool for language corpora analysis is Wordsmith Tools. Developed by Mike Scott (2008) and today widely used by students, teachers and researchers in its fifth edition, Wordsmith Tools is an integrated suite of programs for looking at how words behave in texts. Its available features of Wordlist, Concord, and Keyword generate statistical information such as average sentence length, provide a list of all the words contained in the texts chosen for analysis, show the linguistic co-text of a word with a list of recurring clusters or phrases and create a list of all those words and word forms that, according to certain statistical criteria, are significant in the text corpus.

In contrast to corpus linguistic analysis, multimodal analysis needs to explore semiotic systems other than the verbal, their static or dynamic integration on the page, screen or space or their temporal unfolding. Multi-modal corpora are thus used for identifying configurations of co-occurring patterns in multimodal phenomena like the still visual and verbal text or the audio and moving image. Such intersemiotic 'collocates', in turn, are used to construct and test hypotheses that seek to explain why the information is configured as it is. The construction of interactive digital technologies for multimodal analysis is the primary aim of specialised research centres like the Multimodal Analysis Lab at the Interactive and Digital Media Institute of the National University of Singapore directed by Kay O'Halloran (http://multimodal-analysis-lab.org). What follows is a brief illustration of the main projects and tools I am aware of, first concerned with static texts, then with dynamic ones.

A valid framework for empirical analysis of space-based multimodal documents has been outlined through the GeM project (genre and multi-modality), run by the Universities of Stirling and Bremen (1999–2002) and directed by John Bateman (www.fb10.uni-bremen.de/anglistik/langpro/webspace/jb/info-pages/multi-root.htm). As the name suggests, the project has focused on generic configurations, with specific attention to webpages, illustrated books, instruction manuals and newspapers. Assuming social practices as the context of production of multimodal artefacts, this model defines a 'virtual artefact' in terms of its physical form, its production and its consumption. Alongside traditional tags used by corpus linguistics, the GeM project proposes several levels of transcription for distinct text genres, namely base, layout, rhetorical structure and navigational. First, the base layer is used to distribute verbal and visual elements into recognisable base units, for instance, headings, captions or photographs. These may be grouped together into the second layer, layout, for example, a paragraph, forming a single layout unit to be defined according to the principle of visual similarity. Third, the rhetorical layer is used to describe the rhetorical relationship between multimodal elements on a page, developed from models for verbal relations. Fourth, the navigational layer is used to describe navigational structures present in a multimodal artefact, defining pointers and entries (Bateman, 2008).

Further developing the GeM model, studies by Hiippala (2012a, 2012b) on tourist brochures are of particular interest to the present research. The researcher proposes the notion of prototype in order to examine the generic, thus prototypical, structure of such static multimodal artefacts. Advocating a shift from detailed analysis focused on case studies to abstract descriptions of the semiotic system, which may map possible configurations of the semiotic resources, he eventually aims to provide conceptualisations for the meaningful integration of visual–verbal semiotic modes in tourist brochures.

Multimodal text analysts who need to annotate a corpus of multimodal static texts may find UAM Image Tool useful. Freely available online at www.wagsoft.com/ImageTool, this software allows the annotation of multimodal text instances like advertisements, brochures or magazine pages and multiple images at various levels. A second interactive program for examining similar images is the Multimodal analysis image, developed by the Multimodal Analysis Lab of the National University of Singapore, which supports a variety of file formats: png, jpg, jpeg, tif, tiff, bmp, gif. Information and video tutorials may be found on the already mentioned Lab website.

As for multimodal video data annotation, the main systems are MMAX2, ANVIL, ELAN, MCA and Multimodal analysis video. Developed at the European Media Laboratory in Heidelberg, MMAX2 is a tool for multimodal annotation in XML and supports stand-off annotation. Born in the context of real-world annotation projects in computational linguistics, MMAX2 is a specialised annotation tool employed for creating, browsing, visualising and querying linguistic annotations on multiple levels (http://mmax2.sourceforge.net). Originally designed for gesture research in 2000 at the University of Saarland, ANVIL is now being used in many research areas, including human–computer interaction, linguistics, ethology, anthropology, psychotherapy, embodied agents, computer animation and oceanography. Written in Java and running on Windows, Macintosh and Unix platforms, this free video annotation tool is now in its newest version of ANVIL 5 (www.anvil-software.org). Developed at the Institute for Psycholinguistics in Nijmegen, ELAN enables combined text, video and audio annotation. The textual content of annotations is always in Unicode and the transcription is stored in an XML format. ELAN provides several different views on the annotations; each view is connected and synchronised to the media playhead (http://tla.mpi.nl/tools/tla-tools/elan). Produced at the University of Pavia, MCA is an online multimodal concordancing system that aims to analyse multimodal interplay in film texts, intended as time-based multimodal texts such as television documentaries, cartoons and recording of children's classroom activities (Baldry, 2005). In Baldry's terms, the challenge was to balance an *in vitro* approach and an *in vivo* approach: dissecting a film into frames is undoubtedly a useful task for scholars and students to understand the co-deployment of semiotic resources but fails to capture the temporal, dynamic, living unfolding of textual units (Baldry, 2005: xvii; http://mca.unipv.it). Finally, Multimodal analysis video has been created by the Multimodal Analysis Lab of the National University of Singapore for annotation and analysis of videos and supports the following video formats: mpg, avi, mov, mp4, wmv, flv and m4v.

Alongside the development of computer-based tools enabling the understanding of how texts are constructed, attention is being devoted to empirical studies on how texts are actually read. If Chapter 5 has illustrated plausible reading paths resulting from the application of SFL assumptions, instruments in cognitive sciences are being implemented that measure the actual perception of the text by the reader through controlled experiments (Hiippala, 2012a, 2012b, 2012c). Often, readers are unaware of the reading trajectories they follow, which motivates the need for controlled analysis. Empirical eye-tracking studies are thus being conducted within the cognitive framework in order to measure visual behaviour. For the analysis of reading paths, for instance, videos were used in the past to monitor the process: analysis implied viewing the record in slow motion through frame-by-frame observation (Holsanova *et al.*, 2006: 73). Subsequently, studies and data processing were computer-based and conducted through a helmet on the reader's head equipped with a head-tracking and eye-tracking device. These supports allow an inductive, empirical approach to multimodal text exploration, showing how texts are actually interpreted by readers and suggesting a plurality of readers' profiles.

Glossary

Actor: agent in the communication system, such as a sender or a recipient.
Affordance (modal): potentialities and limits of a semiotic system.
Bending (generic): the process of adaptation of an existing genre, giving rise to a new one with a different communicative purpose.
Clause complex: in SFL, sentence consisting of more than one clause.
Cluster: in visual analysis, the semiotic unit of the static multimodal text.
Colony (generic): a group of closely related genres in different discourse communities (e.g. promotional genres).
Communication function: the aim of a text or utterance, for example promotional or informative.
Contact: in visual analysis, relation between interactive participants realised through direct gaze (contact) or its absence (offer).
Discourse: language use in institutional, professional and social settings.
Embedding (generic): a form of generic innovation, the use of a genre as a template to give expression to another conventionally distinct generic form.
Family (generic): group of texts sharing a socio-professional context and communication purpose.
Field: in SFL, what the text deals with, including topic and processes.
Framing: in visual analysis, patterns of continuity or discontinuity.
Genre: group of texts sharing patterns of structure, style, content, intended audience and communication function.
Genre value: basic forms of linguistic communication, which include descriptive, narrative, expositive, argumentative and regulative values.
Grammar intricacy: in SFL, degree of syntax complexity.
Granularity: in visual analysis, the property of texts constituted by graphically distinct functional units.

Hybridisation (generic): the losing of clear-cut generic constraints and boundaries.
Hypertextuality: cross-links between electronic documents.
Ideational: in SFL, the metafunction concerned with environment representation.
Identification: in visual analysis, meaning projected through the presence of represented human beings.
Information value: in visual analysis, meaning projected by placement of elements of an image on the page or screen.
Innovation (generic): natural or induced dynamic generic configurations.
Integrity (generic): standardised generic configurations.
Interaction of voices: in aural analysis, how voices interact, which may be either sequential or simultaneous.
Interdiscursivity (generic): appropriation of generic resources.
Interpersonal: in SFL, the metafunction concerned with relations among actors.
Intersemiosis: the static or dynamic co-deployment of semiotic resources.
Invitation: in a tourist picture, meaning projected through absence of represented human beings.
Lexical density: in SFL, the proportion of lexical words to all the words in a text.
Lexico-grammar: in SFL, the intermediate level of language content in Bhatia's three-level system.
Logico-semantic relations: in SFL, semantic links among sentences, of projection or expansion.
Macro-genre: a composite text identified in terms of communication function and medium.
Medium: the material substance that realises communication, e.g. printed, vocal or electronic.
Metafunction: distinct ways in which language is used in order to create meaning.
Mixing: a form of generic innovation, where the genres involved in the process are no longer distinguishable.
Modal resource: the semiotic resources used in the act of communication, e.g. visual, audio or gustatory.
Modality: in SFL, the grammar system realising the ideational metafunction and expressing degrees of either probability/usuality or obligation/inclination in an exchange; in visual texts, it is determined by colour, light, depth, representation and contextualisation, whereas in aural texts by pitch range, durational variation, dynamic range, absorption range, perspectival depth, degree of fluctuation, friction and directionality.

Mode: in SFL, the contextual role played by language as writing or speech.
Modulation: in visual analysis, variety of chromatic nuances.
MOOD: in SFL, an element of Mood, including Subject and Finite.
Mood: in SFL, the grammar system realising the interpersonal metafunction, declarative, interrogative or imperative.
Move: in SFL, verbal unit of meaning.
Netspeak: the verbal language of the internet.
Perspective: in visual analysis, the angle of vision (low, eye level or high); in aural analysis, figure, ground and field division.
Reading path: the trajectory followed by the gaze while reading a text, which can be horizontal, vertical, spiral or zigzag.
Reality principle: reality orientation in terms of truth; may be naturalistic, sensory or abstract.
Residue: in SFL, in the system of Mood, includes Predicator, Complement and Adjunct.
Rheme: in SFL, the new element in the Theme system.
Salience: in phonology, the strong syllable in the foot; in visual analysis, prominence achieved by size, colour, placement, light etc.
Semiotic resources: meaning-making mode.
Size of frame: in visual analysis, displayed portion of body/monument/landscape.
Social distance: in visual analysis, relation of closeness or distance between interactive participants.
Social semiosis: the process of socially contextualised meaning-making.
Soundscape: the co-existence and interaction of different types of sound.
Stage (of trip): period before, during or after a holiday.
Sub-genre: further definition of genre, on a thematic level.
Systemic functional linguistics: a theory of language and a methodological framework based on language as contextually based making-meaning.
Taxis: in SFL, the grammar system realising the ideational metafunction and indicating clause linkages.
Tenor: in SFL, interpersonal relations in communication.
Text: a meaningful act of communication.
Textual: in SFL, the metafunction concerned with the text message.
Theme: in SFL, the grammar system realising the textual metafunction, composed of Theme and Rheme.
Time: in aural analysis, determines the tempo, the rhythm of a sound event.
Transitivity (or process type): in SFL, the grammar system realising the ideational metafunction and indicating processes.
Voice quality: in aural analysis, voice tension, roughness, breathiness, loudness and pitch register.

Bibliography: Genre-Based Critical Works on the Language of Tourism

Blogs

Cappelli, G. (2008) Expats' talk: Humour and irony in an expatriate's travel blog. *Textus: English Studies in Italy* 21 (1), 9–26.

Dann, G. (1992) Travelogues and the management of unfamiliarity. *Journal of Travel Research* 30 (4), 59–63.

Dann, G. (2007) Revisiting the language of tourism: What tourists and tourees are saying. In C. De Stasio and O. Palusci (eds) *The Languages of Tourism: Turismo e mediazione* (pp. 15–32). Milan: Unicopli.

Dann, G. and Liebman Parrinello, G. (2007) From travelogue to travelblog: (Re)-negotiating tourist identity. *Acta Turistica* 19 (1), 7–29.

Mack, R.W., Blose, J.E. and Pan, B. (2008) Believe it or not: Credibility of blogs in tourism. *Journal of Vacation Marketing* 14 (2), 133–144.

Pan, B., MacLaurin, T. and Crotts, J. (2007) Travel blogs and their implications for destination marketing. *Journal of Travel Research* 46 (1), 35–45.

Brochures

Bandyopadhyay, R. and Morais, D. B. (2005) Representative dissonance: India's self and Western image. *Annals of Tourism Research* 32 (4), 1006–1021.

Buck, J. (1977) The ubiquitous tourist brochure: Explorations in its intended and unintended use. *Annals of Tourism Research* 4, 195–207.

Dann, G. (1993) Advertising in tourism and travel: Tourism brochures. In M.A. Kahn, M.D. Olsen and V. Turgut (eds) *VNR'S Encyclopedia of Hospitality and Tourism* (pp. 893–901). New York: Van Nostrand Reinhold.

Dann, G. and Johanson, L. B. (2009) Lost in translation: The changing verbal imagery of Norwegian 'Lapland'. *Estudios y Perspectivas en Turismo* 18, 449–475.

Dilley, R. (1986) Tourist brochures and tourist images. *Canadian Geographer* 30 (1), 59–65.

Echtner, C.M. (2002) The content of Third World tourism marketing: A 4A approach. *International Journal of Tourism Research* 4 (6), 413–434.

Francesconi, S. (2007) *English for Tourism Promotion: Italy in British Tourism Texts*. Milan: Hoepli.

Francesconi, S. (2011) Images and writing in tourist brochures. *Journal of Tourism and Cultural Change* 9 (4), 341–356.
Getz, D. and Sailor, L. (1993) Design of destination and attraction-specific brochures. *Journal of Travel and Tourism Marketing* 2 (2/3), 111–131.
Henderson, J. (2001) Presentations of the Orient: Singapore and UK tour operator brochures compared. *Tourism, Culture and Communication* 3, 71–80.
Hiippala, T. (2012) The localisation of advertising print media as a multimodal process. In W.L. Bowcher (ed.) *Multimodal Texts from Around the World: Linguistic and Cultural Insights* (pp. 97–122). London: Palgrave Macmillan.
Mocini, R. (2009) The verbal discourse of tourist brochures. *Annals of the Faculty of Foreign Languages and Literatures of the University of Sassari* 5, 153–164.
Molina, A. and Esteban, A. (2006) Tourism brochures: Usefulness and image. *Annals of Tourism Research* 33 (4), 1036–1056.
Nelson, V. (2005) Representation and images of people, places and nature in Grenada's tourism. *Geografiska Annaler* 8 (2), 131–143.
Papen, U. (2005) Exclusive, ethno and eco: Representations of culture and nature in tourism discourses in Namibia. In A. Jaworski and A. Pritchard (eds) *Discourse, Communication and Tourism* (pp. 79–97). Clevedon: Channel View Publications.
Selwyn, T. (1990) Tourist brochures as post-modern myths. *Problems of Tourism* 12 (3/4), 13–26.
Selwyn, T. (1993) Peter Pan in South-East Asia: Views from the brochures. In M. Hitchcock *et al.* (eds) *Tourism in South-East Asia* (pp. 117–137). London: Routledge.
Viallon, P. (2004) La Méditerranée au risque de la communication touristique. In F. Baider, M. Burger and D. Goutsos (eds) *La communication touristique: Approches discursives de l'identité et de l'altérité [Tourist Communication: Discursive Approaches to Identity and Otherness]* (pp. 191–214). Paris: L'Harmattan.
Wicks, B. and Schuetts, M. (1991) Examining the role of tourism promotion through the use of brochures. *Tourism Management* 12, 301–312.
Wicks, B. and Schuetts, M. (1993) Using travel brochures to target frequent travellers and big-spenders. *Journal of Travel and Tourism Marketing* 2 (2/3), 77–90.
Yui Ling Ip, J. (2008) Analyzing tourism discourse: A case study of a Hong Kong travel brochure. *LCOM Papers* 1, 1–19.

CDs

Poli, M.S. (2000) Stéréotypes culturels et multimédia: Le musée de la Galerie des Offices à Florence sur cédérom interactif. In M. Margarito *et al.* (eds) *L'Italie en stereotypes: Analyse de textes touristiques* (pp. 37–64). Paris: L'Harmattan.

Guides

Antelmi, D., Held, G. and Santulli, F. (2007) *Pragmatica della comunicazione turistica*. Rome: Editori Riuniti.
Barthes, R. [1957] (1972) Blue guide. In *Mythologies* (A. Lavers, transl.) (pp. 74–77). London: Paladin.
Bova, S. (2000) Histoire récente de l'Italie à travers trois guides de tourisme français. In M. Margarito *et al.* (eds) *L'Italie en stéréotypes. Analyse de textes touristiques* (pp. 65–70). Paris: L'Harmattan.

Cappelli, G. (2012) Travelling in space: Spatial representation in English and Italian tourism discourse. *Textus: English Studies in Italy* 25 (1), 19–36.
Denti, O. (2012) The Island of Sardinia from travel book to travel guides: The evolution of a genre. *Textus: English Studies in Italy* 25 (1), 37–50.
Fodde, L. and Denti, O. (2008) The dialogic dimension in tourist discourse. In G. Garzone and P. Catenaccio (eds) *Language and Bias in Specialised Discourse* (pp. 155–175). Milan: CUEM.
Fodde, L. and Denti, O. (2005) Cross-cultural representations in tourist discourse: The image of Sardinia in English tourist guides. In M. Bondi and N. Maxwell (eds) *Cross-cultural Encounters: Linguistic Perspectives* (pp. 116–129). Rome: Officina Edizioni.
Giannitrapani, A. (2010) *Viaggiare: Istruzioni per l'uso. Semiotica delle guide turistiche.* Pisa: ETS.
Giannitrapani, A. and Ragonese, R. (eds) (2010) *Guide turistiche: Spazi, percorsi, sguardi* 4 (6), available online at www.ec-aiss.it/monografici/6_guide_turistiche.php
Gritti, J. (1967) Les contenus culturels du Guide Bleu: Monuments et sites 'à voir'. *Communications* 10, 51–64.
Kerbrat-Orecchioni, C. (2004) Suivez le guide! Les modalités de l'invitation au voyage dans les guides touristiques: L'exemple de l'île d'Aphrodite. In F. Baider, M. Burger and D. Goutsos (eds) *La communication touristique: Approches discursives de l'identité et de l'altérité* [Tourist Communication: Discursive Approaches to Identity and Otherness] (pp. 132–150). Paris: L'Harmattan.
Margarito, M. (2000) La *bella Italia* des guides touristiques: Quelques formes de stereotypes. In M. Margarito *et al.* (eds) *L'Italie en stéréotypes: Analyse de textes touristiques* (pp. 9–36). Paris: L'Harmattan.
Moirand, S. (2004) Le même et l'autre dans les guides de voyage au XXIe siècle. In F. Baider, M. Burger M. and D. Goutsos (eds) *La communication touristique: Approches discursives de l'identité et de l'altérité* [Tourist Communication: Discursive Approaches to Identity and Otherness] (pp. 151–172). Paris: L'Harmattan.
Nigro, M.G. (2006) *Il linguaggio specialistico del turismo.* Rome: Aracne.
Nigro, M.G. (2006) The language of tourism as LSP? A corpus-based study of the discourse of guidebooks. In H. Picht (ed.) *Modern Approaches to Terminological Theories and Applications* (pp. 187–198). Bern: Peter Lang.
Ramm, W. (2000) Textual variation in travel guides. In E. Ventola (ed.) *Discourse and Community: Doing Functional Linguistics* (pp. 147–168). Tübingen: Gunter Narr Verlag.
Vestito, C. (2005) The tourist representation of the Italian South. *Textus: English Studies in Italy* 18 (2), 369–379.
Visentin, C. and Frediani, F. (2002) *La Lombardia vista dagli altri: L'immagine della Lombardia nelle guide turistiche internazionali.* Milan: Angeli.

Magazines

Belenguer J.M. (2002) *Periodismo de Viaje. Análisis de una especialización periodística.* Seville: Comunicación Social.
Berger, A.A. (2004) *Deconstructing Travel: Cultural Perspectives on Tourism.* Walnut Creek, CA: Altamira Press.
Calvi, M.V. (2000) *Il linguaggio spagnolo del turismo.* Viareggio: Baroni.
Chiavetta, E. (2007) 'Heritage' and 'modernity': A discourse analysis of the in-flight magazine articles in Italian cities. In L. Jottini, G. Del Lungo and J. Douthwaite (eds) *Cityscapes: Islands of the Self. Language Studies* (pp. 309–326). Cagliari: CUEC.

Fancher, M. (1988) The state of travel journalism in newspapers today. In *Tourism Research: Expanding Boundaries. Proceedings of the Travel and Tourism Research Association* (pp. 23–26). Salt Lake City, UT: University of Utah Press.

Schomaker, J. and Morck, V. (1986) Representation of outdoor recreation in magazine advertisements. In *Proceedings of Southeastern Recreation Research Conference* (pp. 135–144). Asheville, NC: University of North Carolina.

Small, J., Harris, C. and Wilson, E. (2008) A critical discourse analysis of in-flight magazine advertisements: The 'social sorting' of airline travellers? *Journal of Tourism and Cultural Change* 6 (1), 17–38.

Steward, J. (2005) 'How and where to go': The role of travel journalism in Britain and the evolution of foreign tourism, 1840–1914. In J.K. Walton (ed.) *Histories of Tourism: Representation, Identity and Conflict* (pp. 39–54). Clevedon: Channel View Publications.

Thurlow, C. and Jaworski, A. (2003) Communicating a global reach: Inflight magazines as a globalizing genre in tourism. *Journal of Sociolinguistics* 7 (4), 579–606.

Thurlow, C. and Jaworski, A. (2006) The alchemy of the upwardly mobile: Symbolic capital and the stylization of elites in frequent-flier programmes. *Discourse and Society* 17 (1), 131–167.

Werly, N. (2000) De clichés en fil d'Ariane: Voyage à travers l'Italie des revues de tourisme. In M. Margarito et al. (eds) *L'Italie en stereotypes: Analyse de textes touristiques* (pp. 71–126). Paris: L'Harmattan.

Performance

Adler, J. (1989) Travel as performed art. *American Journal of Sociology* 94, 1366–1391.

Edensor, T. (2001) Performing tourism, staging tourism: (Re)producing tourist space and practice. *Tourist Studies* 1 (1), 59–81.

Jaworski, A. and Thurlow, C. (2009) Gesture and movement in tourist spaces. In C. Jewitt (ed.) *The Routledge Handbook of Multimodal Analysis* (pp. 253–262). London: Routledge.

Pictures

Dann, G. (1996) The people of tourist brochures. In T. Selwyn (ed.) *The Tourist Image: Myths and Myth Making in Tourism* (pp. 61–81). Chichester: John Wiley.

Dann, G. (1996) Images of destination people in travelogues. In R. Butler and T. Hinch (eds) *Tourism and Native Peoples* (pp. 349–375). London: Routledge.

Jenkins, O.H. (2003) Photography and travel brochures: The circle of representation. *Tourism Geographies* 5 (3), 305–328.

Hunter, W.C. (2008) A typology of photographic representations for tourism: Depictions of groomed spaces. *Tourism Management* 29 (2), 354–365.

Li, X., Pan, B., Zhang, L. and Smith, W.W. (2009) Online information search and image development: Insights from a mixed method study. *Journal of Travel Research* 48 (1), 45–57.

Pritchard, A. (2001) Tourism and representation: A scale for measuring gendered portrayals. *Leisure Studies* 20 (2), 79–94.

Sirakaya, E. and Sonmez, S. (2000) Marketing gender images in state tourism brochures: An overlooked area in socially responsible tourism. *Journal of Travel Research* 38 (4), 353–362.

Postcards

Ady, M. (2011) The symbolic role of postcards in representing a destination image: The case of Alanya, Turkey. *International Journal of Hospitality and Tourism Administration* 12 (2), 144–173.
Cohen, E. (2007) From benefactor to tourist: Santa Claus on cards from Thailand. *Annals of Tourism Research* 34 (3), 690–708.
Edwards, E. (1996) Postcards: Greetings from another world. In T. Selwyn (ed.) *The Tourist Image* (pp. 197–221). Chichester: John Wiley.
Francesconi, S. (2011) Multimodally expressed humour shaping Scottishness in tourist postcards. *Journal of Tourism and Cultural Change* 9 (1), 1–17.
Hornstein, S. (2006) Architectural voyages through postcards. In O. Palusci and S. Francesconi (eds) *Translating Tourism: Linguistic/Cultural Representations* (pp. 95–106). Trento: Trento University Press.
Kennedy, C. (2005) 'Just perfect!' The pragmatics of evaluation in holiday postcards. In A. Jaworski and A. Pritchard (eds) *Discourse, Communication and Tourism* (pp. 223–246). Clevedon: Channel View Publications.
Markwich, M. (2001) Postcards from Malta: Image, consumption, context. *Annals of Tourism Research* 28, 417–438.
Östman, J.O. (2004) The postcard as media. *Text* 24 (3), 423–442.
Pritchard, A. and Morgan, N. (2005) Representations of 'ethnographic knowledge': Early comic postcards of Wales. In A. Jaworski and A. Pritchard (eds) *Discourse, Communication and Tourism* (pp. 53–75). Clevedon: Channel View Publications.
Robinson, M. and Ploner, J. (eds) (in preparation) *Cultures Through the Post: Essays on Tourism and Postcards*. Bristol: Channel View Publications.
Thurlow, C., Jaworski, A. and Ylänne, V. (2005) 'Half-hearted tokens of transparent love': 'Ethnic' postcards and the visual mediation of host–tourist communication. *Tourism, Culture and Communication* 5 (2), 93–104.
Thurlow, C., Jaworski, A. and Ylänne-McEwen, V. (2010) Transient identities, new mobilities: Holiday postcards. In C. Thurlow and A. Jaworski (eds) *Tourism Discourse: Language and Global Mobility* (pp. 91–128). London: Palgrave.
Wall, R. (2007) Family relationship in comic postcards 1900–1930. *History of the Family* 12 (1), 50–61.
Whittaker, E. (2000) A century of indigenous images: The world according to the tourist postcard. In M. Robinson *et al.* (eds) *Expressions of Culture, Identity and Meaning in Tourism* (pp. 425–437). Newcastle upon Tyne: Centre for Travel and Tourism.
Yüksel, A. and Akgül, O. (2007) Postcards as affective image makers: An idle agent in destination marketing. *Tourism Management* 28 (3), 714–725.

Souvenirs

Canestrini, D. (2001) *Trofei di viaggio: per un'antropologia dei souvenir*. Turin: Bollati Boringhieri.
Cave, J., Jolliffe, L. and Baum, T. (eds) (2013) *Tourism and Souvenirs: Glocal Perspectives from the Margins*. Bristol: Channel View Publications.
Francesconi, S. (2005) The language of souvenirs: The use of humour in London t-shirts. *Textus: English Studies in Italy* 18 (2), 381–396.
Gordon, B. (1986) The souvenir: Messenger of the extraordinary. *Journal of Popular Culture* 20 (1), 135–146.

Graburn, N.H.H. (ed.) (1976) *Ethnic and Tourist Arts: Cultural Expressions from the Fourth World*. Berkeley, CA: University of California Press.

Hitchcock, M. and Teague, K. (eds) (2000) *Souvenirs: The Material Culture of Tourism*. Aldershot: Ashgage.

Peters, K. (2012) Negotiating the 'place' and 'placement' of banal tourist souvenirs in the home. *Tourism Geographies* 13 (3), 234–256.

Shenhav-Keller, S. (1994) The Israeli souvenir: Its 'text' and 'context'. In J. Jardel (ed.) *Actes du Colloque International 'Le tourisme International entre Tradition et Modernité'* (pp. 89–93). Nice: Université de Nice.

Stewart, S. (1984) *On Longing: Narratives of the Miniature, the Gigantic, the Souvenir, the Collection*. Baltimore, MD: Johns Hopkins University Press.

Television Programmes

Jaworski, A., Virpi Y., Thurlow, C. and Lawson, S. (2003) Social roles and negotiation of status in host–tourist interaction: A view from British television holiday programmes. *Journal of Sociolinguistics* 7 (2), 135–164.

Mapelli, G. (2012) Tourism in television: The case of Buscamundos. Viajes por la vida. *PASOS: Revista de Turismo y Patrimonio Cultural* 10 (4), 97–104.

Websites

Bonelli, E.T. and Manca, E. (2004) Welcoming children, pets and guests: Towards functional equivalence in the languages of 'agriturismo' and 'farmhouse holidays'. In K. Aijmer and B. Altenberg (eds) *Advances in Corpus Linguistics: Papers from the 23rd International Conference on English Language Research on Computerised Corpora* (pp. 371–386). Amsterdam: Rodopi.

Cappelli, G. (2008) The translation of tourism-related websites and localization: Problems and perspectives. In A. Baicchi (eds) *Voices on Translation: RILA Rassegna Italiana di Linguistica Applicata* (pp. 97–115). Rome: Bulzoni Editore.

Denti, O. (2005) The representation of Sardinia in its tourism websites: A multimodal analysis. *Annali della Facoltà di Economia di Cagliari* 21, 599–620.

Hallett, R.W. and Kaplan-Weinger, J. (2010) *Official Tourism Websites: A Discourse Analysis Perspective*. Bristol: Channel View Publications.

Jiménez, F.S. (2012) The 2.0 tourist as recipient of touristic promotion: Linguistic strategies and importance of its study. *PASOS: Revista de Turismo y Patrimonio Cultural* 10 (4), 143–153.

Maci, S.M. (2007) Virtual touring: The web language of tourism. *Linguistica e Filologia* 25, 41–65.

Maci, S.M. (2012) Click here, book now! Discursive strategies of tourism on the web. *Textus: English Studies in Italy* 24 (1), 137–156.

Manca, E. (2004) The language of tourism in English and Italian: Investigating the concept of nature between culture and usage. *ESP Across Cultures* 1, 53–65.

Manca, E. (2007) Beauty and tranquillity in the language of tourism: Linguistic and cultural reasons. In C. De Stasio and O. Palusci (eds) *The Languages of Tourism: Turismo e mediazione* (pp. 113–128). Milan: Unicopli.

Manca, E. (2012) Translating the language of tourism across cultures: From functionally complete units of meaning to cultural equivalence. *Textus: English Studies in Italy* 25 (1), 51–68.

Nigro, M.G. (2012) From words to keywords: The journey from general language to the language of tourism. *Textus: English Studies in Italy* 25 (1), 105–120.

Pan, B. and Fesenmaier, D.R. (2000) A typology of tourism related web sites: Its theoretical foundation and implications. *Information Technology and Tourism* 3 (3/4), 155–176.

Pierini, P. (2006) Comunicazione turistica e multilinguismo in internet. In M. Rocca Longo and M. Leproni (eds) *La Babele mediatica. Multiculturalità e comunicazione* (pp. 79–101). Rome: Edizioni Kappa.

Pierini, P. (2007) La comunicazione turistica in Rete: Peculiarità e tendenze. In M. Rocca Longo, C. Pierantonelli and G. Liebman Parrinello (eds) *La comunicazione turistica: Viaggi reali e virtuali tra storia e futuro* (pp. 385–401). Rome: Edizioni Kappa.

Pierini, P. (2007) Quality in web translation: An investigation into UK and Italian tourism web sites. *Journal of Specialised Translation* 8, available online at www.jostrans.org/issue08/art_pierini.pdf.

Plastina, A.F. (2012) Tourism destination image: Distortion or promotion? An analysis of web-based promotional discourse about Calabria. *Textus: English Studies in Italy* 25 (1), 121–136.

References

Adami, E. (2013) *A Social Semiotic Multimodal Analysis Framework for Website Interactivity*. NCRM Working Paper. London: National Centre for Research Methods. Online preprint version at http://eprints.ncrm.ac.uk/3074 (accessed November 2013).
Aime, M. (2000) *Diario dogon*. Turin: Bollati Boringhieri.
Alighieri, D. [1302–05] (1996) *The vulgari eloquentia* (S. Botterill, ed. and transl.) Cambridge: Cambridge University Press.
Antelmi, D. and Santulli, F. (2012) Travellers' memories: The image of places from literature to blog chatter. *Pasos: Revista de Turismo y Patrimonio Cultural* 4 (10), 13–24.
Antelmi, D., Held, G. and Santulli, F. (2007) *Pragmatica della comunicazione turistica*. Rome: Editori Riuniti.
Ashworth, G. and Goodall, B. (eds) (2012a) *Marketing Tourism Places*. London: Routledge.
Ashworth, G. and Goodall, B. (eds) (2012b) *Marketing in the Tourism Industry*. London: Routledge.
Austin, J. (1962) *How to Do Things With Words*. Cambridge, MA: Harvard University Press.
Bakhtin, M.M. (1986) *Speech Genres and Other Late Essays* (C. Emerson and M. Holquist, eds). Austin, TX: University of Texas Press.
Baldry, A. (ed.) (2000) *Multimodality and Multimediality in the Distance Learning Age*. Campobasso: Palladino.
Baldry, A. (2005) *A Multimodal Approach to Text Studies in English: The Role of MCA in Multimodal Concordancing and Multimodal Corpus Linguistics*. Campobasso: Palladino.
Baldry A. (2004) Phase transition, type and instance: Patterns in media texts as seen through a multimodal concordancer. In K. O'Halloran (ed.) *Multimodal Discourse Analysis: Systemic Functional Perspectives* (pp. 83–108). London: Continuum.
Baldry, A. and Thibault, P.J. (2006) *Multimodal Transcription and Text Analysis*. London: Equinox.
Barthes, R. [1970] (1975) *S/Z: An Essay* (R. Miller, transl.) New York: Hill and Wang.
Barthes, R. [1961] (1977) Rhetoric of the image. In *Image, Music, Text* (pp. 32–51). New York: Hill and Wang.
Barthes, R. [1970] (1977) *Image–Music–Text* (S. Heath, ed. and transl.). New York: Hill and Wang.
Bateman, J. (2008) *Multimodality and Genre: A Foundation for the Systematic Analysis of Multimodal Documents*. London: Palgrave Macmillan.
Bateman, J.A. and Schmidt, K.H. (2012) *Multimodal Film Analysis: How Films Mean*. London: Routledge.

Beeton, S. (2005) *Film-Induced Tourism*. Clevedon: Channel View Publications.
Belenguer, J.M. (2002) *Periodismo de Viaje: Análisis de una especialización periodística*. Seville: Comunicación Social.
Benjamin, W. [1936] (1969) The work of art in the age of mechanical reproduction (H. Zoon, transl.). In *Illuminations* (pp. 217–251). New York: Schocken Books.
Berger, A.A. (2004) *Deconstructing Travel: Cultural Perspectives on Tourism*. Walnut Creek, CA: Altamira Press.
Berger, J. (1972) *Ways of Seeing*. London: Penguin.
Bhatia, V.K. (1993) *Analysing Genre. Language Use in Professional Settings*. London: Longman.
Bhatia, V.K. (1997) Genre-mixing in academic introductions. *English for Specific Purposes* 16 (3), 181–195.
Bhatia, V.K. (2002) Applied genre analysis: A multi-perspective model. *Iberica* 4, 3–19.
Bhatia, V.K. (2004) *Worlds of Written Discourse: A Genre-Based View*. London: Continuum.
Bhatia, V.K. (2010) Interdiscursivity in professional communication. *Discourse and Communication* 4 (1), 32–50.
Boardman, M. (2005) *The Language of Websites*. London: Routledge.
Bolter, J.D. and Grusin, R. (2000) *Remediation: Understanding New Media*. Cambridge, MA: MIT Press.
Bondi, M. (1999) *English Across Genres*. Il Fiorino: Modena.
Boorstin, D. [1987] (1992) *The Image: A Guide to Pseudo-Events in America*. New York: Atheneum.
Buzard, J. (1993) *The Beaten Track: European Tourism, Literature, and the Ways to Culture, 1800–1918*. New York: Oxford University Press.
Calvi, M.V. (2010) Los generos discursivos en la lengua del turismo: Una propuesta de clasificación. *Iberica* 19, 9–32.
Canals, J. and Liverani, E. (eds) (2010) *Viaggiare con la parola*. Milan: Franco Angeli.
Canestrini, D. (2001) *Trofei di viaggio: Per un'antropologia dei souvenir*. Turin: Bollati Boringhieri.
Cappelli, G. (2008) Expats' talk: Humour and irony in an expatriate's travel blog. *Textus: English Studies in Italy* 21 (1), 9–26.
Castello, E. (2001) *Tourist-Information Texts: A Corpus Based Study of Four Related Genres*. Padova: Unipress.
Chandler, D. (1997) An introduction to genre theory. At www.aber.ac.uk/media/Documents/intgenre/intgenre.html (accessed 12 January 2013).
Clarke, D. (ed.) (2001) *Perspectives on Practice and Meaning in Mathematics and Science Classrooms*. Dordrecht: Kluwer Academic.
Coelho, P.Z. (2008) Front page layout and reading paths: The influence of age on newspaper reading. *Communication Studies* 4, 1–14.
Cohen, E. (1993) The study of touristic images of native people. Mitigating the stereotype of the stereotype. In D. Pearce and R. Butler (eds) *Tourism Research: Critiques and Challenges* (pp. 36–69). London: Routledge.
Cohen, E. (2004) *Contemporary Tourism: Diversity and Change*. Amsterdam: Elsevier.
Cohen, E. (2007) From benefactor to tourist: Santa Claus on cards from Thailand. *Annals of Tourism Research* 34 (3), 690–708.
Cohen, E. and Cooper, R. (2004) Language and tourism. In E. Cohen (ed.) *Contemporary Tourism: Diversity and Change* (pp. 205–228). Amsterdam: Elsevier.
Coleman, S. and Crang, M. (eds) (2002) *Tourism: Between Place and Performance*. New York: Bengham Books.
Cook, G. (2001) *The Discourse of Advertising* (2nd edn). London: Routledge.

Crouch, D. and Lübbren, N. (eds) (2003) *Visual Culture and Tourism*. Oxford: Berg.
Crouch, D., Jackson, R. and Thompson, F. (eds) (2005) *The Media and the Tourist Imagination: Converging Cultures*. London: Routledge.
Crystal, D. (2003) *English as a Global Language* (2nd edn). Cambridge: Cambridge University Press.
Crystal, D. (2006) *Language and the Internet* (2nd edn). Cambridge: Cambridge University Press.
Culler, J. (1989) The semiotics of tourism. In *Framing the Sign: Criticism and Its Institutions* (pp. 153–167). Norman, OK: University of Oklahoma Press.
Danesi, M. (2002) *Understanding Media Semiotics*. London: Edward Arnold.
Dann, G. (1993) Advertising in tourism and travel: Tourism brochures. In M.A. Kahn, M.D Olsen and V. Turgut (eds) *VNR's Encyclopedia of Hospitality and Tourism* (pp. 893–901). New York: Van Nostrand Reinhold.
Dann, G. (1996a) *The Language of Tourism: A Sociolinguistic Perspective*. Oxford: CAB International.
Dann, G. (1996b) The people of tourist brochures. In T. Selwyn (ed.) *The Tourist Image: Myths and Myth Making in Tourism* (pp. 61–81). Chichester: John Wiley.
Dann, G. (2007) Revisiting the language of tourism: What tourists and tourees are saying. In C. De Stasio and O. Palusci (eds) *The Languages of Tourism: Turismo e mediazione* (pp. 15–32). Milan: Unicopli.
Dann, G. (2012a) Traditional and recent media of the language of tourism: Crises of credibility or new forms of dialogic communication? In M. Agorni (ed.) *Comunicare la città: Turismo culturale e comunicazione. Il caso di Brescia* (pp. 31–54). Milan: Franco Angeli.
Dann, G. (2012b) Remodelling a changing language of tourism: From monologue, to dialogue to trialogue. *Pasos: Revista de Turismo y Patrimonio Cultural* 4 (10), 59–70.
Dann, G. and Parrinello, G.L. (2007) From travelogue to travelblog: (Re)-negotiating tourist identity. *Acta turistica* 19 (1), 7–29.
Davies, C. (2002) *The Mirth of Nations*. New Brunswick, NJ: Transaction Publishers.
Derrida, J. [1997] (2000) *Of Hospitality* (R. Bowlby, transl.). Stanford, CA: Stanford University Press.
Descartes, R. [1637] (2006) *A Discourse on the Method of Correctly Conducting One's Reason and Seeking Truth in Science* (I. Maclean, transl.). Oxford: Oxford University Press.
Eggins, S. (2011) *An Introduction to Systemic Functional Linguistics* (2nd edn). London: Continuum.
Enkvist, N.E. (1991) Discourse strategies and discourse types. In E. Ventola (ed.) *Functional and Systemic Linguistics: Approaches and Uses* (pp. 3–22). Berlin: Mouton de Gruyter.
Fairclough, N. (1989) *Language and Power*. London: Longman.
Fairclough, N. (1995) *Critical Discourse Analysis*. London: Longman.
Ferreira, A.A. (2007) Japanese semiotic vernaculars in ESP multiliteracies projects. In T.D. Royce and W.L. Bowcher (eds) *New Directions in the Analysis of Multimodal Discourse* (pp. 299–329). Mahwah, NJ: Lawrence Erlbaum Associates.
Fodde, L. and van den Abbeele, G. (eds) (2012) Tourism and Tourists in Language and Linguistics (special issue). *Textus: English Studies in Italy* 1.
Fodde, L. and Denti, O. (2008) The dialogic dimension in tourist discourse. In G. Garzone and P. Catenaccio (eds) *Language and Bias in Specialised Discourse* (pp. 155–175). Milan: CUEM.
Fodde, L. and Denti, O. (2012) Il discorso turistico: Peculiarità linguistico-comunicative nella didattica dell'inglese specialistico. In M. Agorni (ed.) *Comunicare la città: Turismo culturale comunicazione. Il caso di Brescia* (pp. 23–46). Milan: Franco Angeli.

Forster, E.M. [1908] (1995) *A Room with a View*. New York: Dover Publications.
Foucault, M. [1969] (2002) *The Archaeology of Knowledge* (A.M. Sheridan Smith, transl.). London: Routledge.
Foucault, M. [1963] (1973) *The Birth of the Clinic: An Archaeology of Medical Perception* (A.M. Sheridan Smith, transl.). New York: Pantheon Books.
Francesconi, S. (2005) The language of souvenirs: The use of humour in London T-shirts. *Textus: English Studies in Italy* 18 (2), 381–395.
Francesconi, S. (2007) *English for Tourism Promotion: Italy in Tourism Texts*. Milan: Hoepli.
Francesconi, S. (2011a) Multimodally expressed humour shaping Scottishness in tourist postcards. *Journal of Tourism and Cultural Change* 9 (1), 1–17.
Francesconi, S. (2011b) Images and writing in tourist brochures. *Journal of Tourism and Cultural Change* 9 (4), 341–356.
Francesconi, S. (2011c) New Zealand as 'the youngest country on earth': A multimodal analysis of a tourist video. *Textus: English Studies in Italy* 24 (2), 323–340.
Francesconi, S. (2012) *Generic Integrity and Innovation in Tourism Texts in English*. Trento: Tangram.
Frye, N. (1957) *Anatomy of Criticism*. Princeton, NJ: Princeton University Press.
Fussel, P. (1987) *The Norton Book of Travel*. New York: Norton.
Gage, J. (1993) *Colour and Culture: Practice and Meaning from Antiquity to Abstraction*. London: Thames and Hudson.
Gage, J. (1999) *Colour and Meaning: Art, Science and Symbolism*. London: Thames and Hudson.
Garzone, G. (2007) Genres, multimodality and the world-wide-web: Theoretical issues. In G. Garzone, P. Catenaccio and G. Poncini (eds) *Multimodality in Corporate Communication: Webgenres and Discursive Identity* (pp. 15–30). Milan: Franco Angeli.
Garzone, G., Catenaccio, P. and Poncini, G. (eds) (2007) *Multimodality in Corporate Communication: Webgenres and Discursive Identity*. Milan: Franco Angeli.
Giannitrapani, A. (2010) *Viaggiare: Istruzioni per l'uso. Semiotica delle guide turistiche*. Pisa: ETS.
Goddard, A. (2002) *The Language of Advertising: Written Texts* (2nd edn). London: Routledge.
Gotti, M. (2003) *Specialised Discourse*. Bern: Peter Lang.
Gotti, M. (2005) *Investigating Specialised Discourse: Linguistic Features and Changing Conventions*. Bern: Peter Lang.
Gotti, M. (2006) The language of tourism as specialized discourse. In O. Palusci and S. Francesconi (eds) *Translating Tourism: Linguistic/Cultural Representations* (pp. 15–34). Trento: Trento University Press.
Graburn, N. (ed.) (1976) *Ethnic and Tourist Arts: Cultural Expressions from the Fourth World*. Berkeley, CA: University of California.
Hall, D. (2000) *Tourism and Sustainable Community Development*. London: Routledge.
Hall, S. (ed.) (1997) *Representation: Cultural Representations and Signifying Practices*. London: Sage.
Hallett, R.W. and Kaplan-Weinger, J. (2010) *Official Tourism Websites: A Discourse Analysis Perspective*. Bristol: Channel View Publications.
Halliday, M.A.K. (1978) *Language as Social Semiotics: The Social Interpretation of Language and Meaning*. London: Edward Arnold.
Halliday, M.A.K. (2004) *An Introduction to Functional Grammar* (3rd edn, revised by C. Matthiessen). London: Arnold.
Halliday, M.A.K. (1989) *Spoken and Written Language* (2nd edn). Oxford: Oxford University Press.

Halliday, M.A.K. and Hasan, R. (1985) *Language, Context and Text: Aspects of Language in a Social-Semiotic Perspective*. Oxford: Oxford University Press.

Held G. (2004) L'annuncio pubblicitario di destinazione. In P. D'Achille (ed.) *Generi, architetture e forme testuali* (pp. 257–274). Firenze: Cesati Editore.

Hiippala, T. (2012a) The localisation of advertising print media as a multimodal process. In W.L. Bowcher (ed.) *Multimodal Texts from Around the World: Linguistic and Cultural Insights* (pp. 97–122). London: Palgrave Macmillan.

Hiippala, T. (2012b) The interface between rhetoric and layout in multimodal artefacts. *Literary and Linguistic Computing* 28 (3), 461–471.

Hiippala, T. (2012c) Reading paths and visual perception in multimodal research, psychology and brain sciences. *Journal of Pragmatics* 44, 315–327.

Holsanova, J., Holmqvist, K. and Rahm, H. (2006) Entry points and reading paths on newspaper spreads: Comparing a semiotic analysis with eye-tracking measurements. *Visual Communication* 5 (1), 65–93.

Iedema, R. (2001) Analysing film and television. A social semiotic account of hospital: An unhealthy business. In T. van Leeuwen and C. Jewitt (eds) *Handbook of Visual Analysis* (pp. 183–204). London: Sage.

Jack, G. and Phipps, A. (2005) *Tourism and Intercultural Exchange: Why Tourism Matters*. Clevedon: Channel View Publications.

Jamal, T. and Robinson, M. (eds) (2009) *The Sage Handbook of Tourism Studies*. Los Angeles, CA: Sage.

James, H. [1881] (1998) *The Portrait of a Lady*. Oxford and New York: Oxford University Press.

Jameson, F. (1991) *Postmodernism, or, The Cultural Logic of Late Capitalism*. Durham, NC: Duke University Press.

Jaworski, A. and Coupland, N. (eds) (1999) *The Discourse Reader*. London: Routledge.

Jaworski, A. and Thurlow, C. (2009) Gesture and movement in tourist spaces. In C. Jewitt (ed.) *The Routledge Handbook of Multimodal Analysis* (pp. 253–262). Abingdon: Routledge.

Jenkins, O.H. (2003) Photography and travel brochures: The circle of representation. *Tourism Geographies* 5 (3), 305–328.

Jenks, C. (ed.) (1995) *Visual Culture*. London: Routledge.

Jennings, G.R. (2009) Methodologies and methods. In T. Jamal and M. Robinson (eds) *The Sage Handbook of Tourism Studies* (pp. 673–693). Los Angeles: Sage.

Jewitt, C. (2006) *Technology, Literacy, Learning: A Multimodal Approach*. New York: Routledge.

Jewitt, C. (ed.) (2009) *The Routledge Handbook of Multimodal Analysis*. London: Routledge.

Jonathan, B. (ed.) (1984) *The Complete Works of Aristotle*. Princeton, NJ: Princeton University Press.

Kachru, B.B. (1985) *The Alchemy of English*. Oxford: Pergamon.

Kress, G. (2003) *Literacy in the New Media Age*. London: Routledge.

Kress, G. (2009) What is mode? In C. Jewitt (ed.) *The Routledge Handbook of Multimodal Analysis* (pp. 54–67). London: Routledge.

Kress, G. (2010) *Multimodality: A Social Semiotic Approach to Contemporary Communication*. London: Routledge.

Kress, G. and van Leeuwen, T. (1998) Front pages: (The critical) analysis of newspaper layout. In A. Bell and P. Garrett (eds) *Approaches to Media Discourse* (pp. 186–219). Oxford: Blackwell.

Kress, G. and van Leeuwen, T. (2001) *Multimodal Discourse*. London: Arnold.

Kress, G. and van Leeuwen, T. (2006) *Reading Images: The Grammar of Visual Design* (2nd edn). London: Routledge.
Leech, G. (1966) *English in Advertising: A Linguistic Study of Advertising in Great Britain*. London: Longman.
Leed, E.J. (1991) *The Mind of the Traveler: From Gilgamesh to Global Tourism*. New York: Basic Books.
Lemke, J. (1998) Multiplying meaning: Visual and verbal semiotics in scientific text. In J.R. Martin and R. Veel (eds) *Reading Science: Critical and Functional Perspectives on Discourses of Science* (pp. 87–113). London: Routledge.
Lemke, J. (2002) Travels in hypermodality. *Visual Communication* 1 (3), 299–325.
Ling Ip, J.Y. (2008) Analyzing tourism discourse: A case study of a Hong Kong travel brochure. *LCom Papers* 1, 1–19. At www.hku.hk/english/LCOM%20paper/LCOM%20papers%20new,%20rev/2008%20vol1/1%20Tourism%20Discourse.pdf.
Long, P. and Robinson, M. (2009) Tourism, popular culture and the media. In T. Jamal and M. Robinson (eds) *The Sage Handbook of Tourism Studies* (pp. 98–114). Los Angeles, CA: Sage.
MacCannell, D. [1976] (1989) *The Tourist: A New Theory of the Leisure Class*. New York: Schocken Books.
MacCannell, D. (1992) *Empty Meeting Grounds: The Tourist Papers*. London: Routledge.
Maci, S. (2007) Virtual touring: The web-language of tourism. *Linguistica e Filologia* 25, 41–65.
Maci, S. (2010) *The Language of Tourism*. Bergamo: CELSB.
Maci, S. (2012) Glocal features in in-flight magazines: When local becomes global. An explorative study. *Altre Modernità* 2, 196–210.
MacLellan, R. and Smith, R. (eds) (1998) *Tourism in Scotland*. London: Thomson Business Press.
Malta Tourism Authority (2009) *Malta, Gozo and Comino*. Valletta: MTA.
Mangiapane, F. (2010) La città sul web: Il caso dell'*urban blog* Rosalio. In G. Marrone (ed.) *Palermo: Ipotesi di semiotica urbana* (pp. 259–285). Rome: Carocci.
Marissa, E., O' Halloran, K.L. and Judd, K. (2011) Working at cross-purposes: Multiple producers and text-image relations. *Text and Talk* 31 (5), 579–600.
Martin, J.R. (1992) *English Text: System and Structure*. Amsterdam: John Benjamins.
Martinec, D. and Salway, A. (2005) A system for image–text relations in new (and old) media. *Visual Communication* 4 (3), 339–374.
McArthur, T. (1998) *The English Languages*. Cambridge: Cambridge University Press.
McLuhan, M. (1967) *The Medium Is the Message: An Inventory of Effects*. New York: Random House.
Meethan, K. (2001) *Tourism in a Global Society: Place, Culture, Consumption*. New York: Palgrave.
Meyer, G. (1994) *Words in Ads*. London: Edward Arnold.
Meyer, G. (1999) *Ad Worlds: Brands, Media, Audiences*. London: Edward Arnold.
Mills, S. (1997) *Discourse*. London: Routledge.
Mirzoeff, N. (ed.) (1998) *The Visual Culture Reader*. London: Routledge.
Mirzoeff, N. (1999) *An Introduction to Visual Culture*. London: Routledge and Kegan Paul.
Mocini, R. (2009) The verbal discourse of tourist brochures. *Annals of the Faculty of Foreign Languages and Literatures of the University of Sassari* 5, 153–164.
Molina, A. and Esteban A. (2006) Tourism brochures: Usefulness and image. *Annals of Tourism Research* 33 (4), 1036–1056.

Morrison, A. (2008) Blogs and blogging: Text and practice. In S. Schreibman and R. Siemens (eds) *A Digital Literary Studies* (pp. 369–387). Oxford: Blackwell.
Myers, G. (2010) *The Discourse of Blogs and Wikis*. London: Continuum.
Nielsen, C. (2001) *Tourism and the Media: Tourist Decision-Making, Information, and Communication*. Melbourne: Hospitality Press.
Norris, S. (2004) *Analysing Multimodal Interaction: A Methodological Framework*. New York: Routledge.
O'Halloran, K.L. (2004) Visual semiosis in film. In K. O'Halloran (ed.) *Multimodal Discourse Analysis: Systemic Functional Perspectives* (pp. 110–130). London: Continuum.
O'Halloran, K.L. (2011) Multimodal discourse analysis. In K. Hyland and B. Paltridge (eds) *Companion to Discourse Analysis* (pp. 120–137). London: Continuum.
O'Halloran, K. and Smith, B.A. (2012) *Multimodal Studies: Exploring Issues and Domains*. New York: Routledge.
O'Toole, M. (2010) *The Language of Displayed Art* (2nd edn). London and New York: Routledge.
Ong, W. (2002) *Orality and Literacy: The Technologizing of the Word* (2nd edn). London: Routledge.
Östman, J.O. (2004) The postcard as media. *Text* 24 (3), 423–442.
Palusci, O. and Francesconi, S. (eds) (2006) *Translating Tourism: Linguistic/Cultural Representations*. Trento: Trento University Press.
Pearce, P.L. (2009) Now that is funny: Humour in tourism settings. *Annals of Tourism Research* 36 (4), 627–644.
Pinnavaia, L. (2001) *The Italian Borrowings in the Oxford English Dictionary: A Lexicographical, Linguistic and Cultural Analysis*. Rome: Bulzoni.
Pritchard, A. and Morgan, N. (2005) Representations of 'ethnographic knowledge': Early comic postcards of Wales. In A. Jaworski and A. Pritchard (eds) *Discourse, Communication and Tourism* (pp. 53–75). Clevedon: Channel View Publications.
Ragonese, R. (2010) Guide turistiche: Un'introduzione. In A. Giannitrapani and R. Ragonese (eds) *Guide turistiche: Spazi, percorsi, sguardi, EIC IV* (6), 5–18.
Ramm, W. (2000) Textual variation in travel guides. In E. Ventola (ed.) *Discourse and Community: Doing Functional Linguistics* (pp. 147–168). Tübingen: Gunter Narr Verlag.
Robinson, M. and Andersen, H.C. (eds) (2011) *Literature and Tourism*. Andover: Cengage Learning.
Robinson, M. and Picard, D. (eds) (2009) *The Framed World: Tourism, Tourists and Photography*. Farnham: Ashgate.
Royce, T.D. (1998) Synergy on the page: Exploring intersemiotic complementarity in page-based multimodal text. *JASFL Occasional Papers* 1 (1), 25–49.
Royce, T.D. (2002) Multimodality in the TESOL classroom: Exploring visual–verbal synergy. *TESOL Quarterly* 36 (2), 191–205.
Royce, T.D. (2007) Intersemiotic complementarity: A framework for multimodal discourse analysis. In T.D. Royce and W.L. Bowcher (eds) *New Directions in the Analysis of Multimodal Discourse* (pp. 63–109). Mahwah, NJ: Lawrence Erlbaum.
Royce, T.D. and Bowcher, W. (eds) (2007) *New Directions in the Analysis of Multimodal Discourse*. Mahwah, NJ: Erlbaum.
Said, E.W. (1978) *Orientalism*. London: Routledge and Kegan Paul.
Santulli, F. (2007) The rhetoric of multimodality: The persuasive power of verbal–visual interplay. In G. Garzone, P. Catenaccio and G. Poncini (eds) *Multimodality in Corporate Communication: Webgenres and Discursive Identity* (pp. 31–54). Milano: Franco Angeli.

Schaaf, L.J. (2000) *The Photographic Art of Henry William Fox Talbot*. Princeton, NJ: Princeton University Press.
Scott, M. (2008) *Wordsmith Tools Version 5*. Liverpool: Lexical Analysis Software Ltd.
Selting, M., Auer, P., Barth, D., *et al*. (2011) A system for transcribing talk-in-interaction: GAT 2. *Gesprächsforschung* 12 (2011), 1–51. At www.gespraechsforschung-ozs.de/heft2011/px-gat2-englisch.pdf (accessed 13 December 2012).
Searle, J. (1969) *Speech Acts*. Cambridge: Cambridge University Press.
Sontag, S. [1971] (2002) *On Photography*. London: Penguin.
Stenglin, M. (2009) From musing to a/musing: Semogenesis and Western museums. In E. Ventola and A.J. Moya (eds) *The World Told and the World Shown: Multisemiotic Issues* (pp. 123–145). London: Macmillan.
Stewart, S. (1984) *On Longing: Narratives of the Miniature, the Gigantic, the Souvenir, the Collection*. Baltimore, MD: Johns Hopkins University Press.
Stöckl, H. (2004) In between modes: Language and image in printed media. In E. Ventola, C. Charles and M. Kaltenbacher (eds) *Perspectives on Multimodality* (pp. 9–30). Amsterdam: John Benjamins.
Stubbs, M. (1996) *Text and Corpus Analysis*. Oxford: Blackwell.
Sturken, M. and Cartwright, L. (2009) *Practices of Looking: An Introduction to Visual Culture* (2nd edn). New York: Oxford University Press.
Swales, J. (1990) *Genre Analysis*. Cambridge: Cambridge University Press.
Talbot, W.H.F. [1844–46] (1969) *The Pencil of Nature*. New York: Da Capo Press.
Thurlow, C. and Jaworski, A. (2010) *Tourism Discourse: Language and Global Mobility*. London: Palgrave.
Thurlow, C., Jaworski, A. and Ylänne-McEwen, V. (2005) 'Half-hearted tokens of transparent love': 'Ethnic' postcards and the visual mediation of host–tourist communication. *Tourism, Culture and Communication* 5 (2), 93–104.
Todorov, T. [1978] (1990) *Genres in Discourse* (C. Porter, transl.). Cambridge, New York: Cambridge University Press.
Todorov, T. [1989] (1994) *On Human Diversity: Nationalism, Racism and Exoticism in French Thought* (C. Porter, transl.). Cambridge, MA: Harvard University Press.
Trask, R.L. (1998) *A Dictionary of Phonetics and Phonology*. London: Routledge.
Tsakona, V. (2009) Language and image interaction in cartoons: Towards a multimodal theory of humor. *Journal of Pragmatics* 41 (6), 1171–1188.
Turner, L. and Ash, J. (1976) *The Golden Hordes*. New York: St Martin's Press.
Unsworth, L. and Cléirigh, C. (2009) Multimodality and reading: The construction of meaning through image–text interaction. In C. Jewitt (ed.) *The Routledge Handbook of Multimodal Analysis* (pp. 151–163). London: Routledge.
Urry, J. (2002) *The Tourist Gaze: Leisure and Travel in Contemporary Societies* (2nd edn). London: Sage.
Urry, J. (1995) *Consuming Places*. London: Routledge.
Urry, J. and Larsen, J. (2011) *The Tourist Gaze 3.0* (3rd edn). London: Sage.
Urry, J. and RojeK, C. (1997) *Touring Cultures: Transformation of Travel and Theory*. London: Routledge.
van Leeuwen, T. (1999) *Speech, Music, Sound*. London: Macmillan.
van Leeuwen, T. (2009) Parametric systems: The case of voice quality. In C. Jewitt (ed.) *The Routledge Handbook of Multimodal Analysis* (pp. 68–77). London: Routledge.
van Leeuwen, T. (2011) *The Language of Colour*. London: Routledge.
Ventola, E. (2011) Semiotization processes of space: From drawing our homes to styling them. In K. O'Halloran and B.A. Smith (eds) *Multimodal Studies: Exploring Issues and Domains* (pp. 220–238). New York: Routledge.

Wahab, S. and Cooper, C. (2001) *Tourism at the Age of Globalization*. London: Routledge.
Waugh, E. (1930) *Labels: A Mediterranean Journal*. London: Duckworth.
Wenger, A. (2008) Analysis of travel bloggers' characteristics and their communication about Austria as a tourism destination. *Journal of Vacation Marketing* 14 (2), 169–176.
Werlich, E. (1982) *A Text Grammar of English*. Heidelberg: Quelle and Meyer.
Wilson, N. (ed.) (2000) *Lonely Planet Guide to Malta and Gozo*. Melbourne: Lonely Planet.
Wilson, N. and Murphy, A. (2009) *Lonely Planet Guide to Scotland*. Melbourne: Lonely Planet.
Wordsworth, W. (1981) *The Poems*. J.O. Hayden (ed.). New Haven, CT: Yale University Press.
Yüksel, A. and Olcay, A. (2007) Postcards as affective image makers: An idle agent in destination marketing. *Tourism Management* 28 (3), 714–725.

Websites

ANVIL 5, accessed December 2012. http://www.anvil-software.org
BIT website, accessed 10 September 2012. www.bit.fieramilano.it/.
British National Corpus, accessed March 2013. www.natcorp.ox.ac.uk
ELAN, accessed December 2012. http://tla.mpi.nl/tools/tla-tools/elan
Excess Baggage, England episode, BBC4, radio programme. accessed 23 February 2013. http://www.bbc.co.uk/programmes/b01gng56.
GeM project, accessed December 2012 http://www.fb10.uni-bremen.de/anglistik/langpro/webspace/jb/info-pages/multi-root.htm
Hobbit media kit website, accessed 3 February 2013. www.airnzhobbitmedia.com
Incredible India, radio commercial, accessed 12 February 2013. http://www.incredible-india.org/
Lee Gone publication website, accessed 10 September 2012. www.lgpcards.com.
MCA, accessed December 2012. http://mca.unipv.it
MMAX2, accessed December 2012. http://mmax2.sourceforge.net.
Multimodal Analysis Lab, National University of Singapore, accessed march 2013. http://multimodal-analysis-lab.org/
Oxford English Dictionary, www.oed.com (accessed 8 February 2013).
Pegasus Airlines safety announcement, accessed 19 February 2013. www.youtube.com/watch?v=HPLJV6YcvUE
UAM Image Tool useful, accessed December 2012. http://www.wagsoft.com/ImageTool
Wikitravel webpage, accessed 10 September 2012. www.wikitravel.org.
World Tourism Organization website, accessed 14 September 2012. www.unwto.org/index.php.

Author Index

Abbeele 5, 136, 175
Adami 154, 173
Agorni 175
Andersen 22, 24, 27, 179
Antelmi 131, 133, 155, 167, 173
Arnold, Edward 175–6, 178
Ashworth 173
Austin 23, 173

Baedeker 1–2, 53
Baider 167–8
Baldry 23, 129–31, 133, 136, 138–9, 147–9, 154, 161, 173
Barthes 133–4, 140, 167, 173
Bateman 13, 147–8, 153, 159–60, 173
Belenguer 14, 16, 168, 174
Benjamin 73–4, 174
Berger 14, 71, 73, 168, 174
Bhatia 5, 11–15, 25–6, 28–31, 164, 174
Boardman 137, 154, 174
Bowcher 167, 175, 177, 179
Burger 167–8
Buzard 1–2, 174

Calvi 5, 15–16, 19, 21–3, 28, 31–2, 57, 64, 168, 174
Cappelli 64–5, 166, 168, 171, 174
Carrier 45–6, 59–60, 86
Cartwright 71, 73, 74, 180
Castello 56, 174
Catenaccio 168, 175–6, 179
Coelho 134–5, 174
Cohen 4, 82, 141, 170, 174
Cook 57, 111, 125, 174

Crouch 25, 72, 75, 77, 175
Crystal 10, 33, 65, 106, 136, 154, 175
Culler 1–2, 4, 58, 175

Dann 3–5, 11, 19–24, 28, 32–3, 58, 62, 64–5, 81–2, 86, 116, 133, 166, 169, 175
Denti 26, 37, 62, 168, 171, 175
Descartes 72, 175

Eggins 14–15, 41, 43, 45, 47–9, 51, 53–5, 69, 175
Enkvist 25–6, 38, 175
Esteban 57, 58, 167, 176

Fairclough 29, 175
Fodde 5, 26, 37, 62, 136, 168, 175
Forster 1–2, 75, 176
Foucault 12, 72, 176
Francesconi 2–6, 8, 15, 20–1, 24, 26, 29, 57–8, 75–6, 131–3, 154–5, 166–7, 170, 176, 179
Fussel 1–2, 176

Gage 94, 176
Garzone 32, 133, 168, 175–6, 179
Giannitrapani 79, 168, 176, 179
Goodall 173
Gotti 7, 11, 16, 19, 23, 27–8, 176
Goutsos 167–8

Hall 3, 6, 176
Halliday 6, 13, 41–3, 45, 47–8, 52–6, 94, 104, 129, 141, 155, 176–7

Hasan 41, 42, 167
Highveld 37
Hiippala 57–8, 160–1, 167, 177
Holsanova 134–5, 161, 177
Hudson 176

Iedema 129, 147, 148, 159, 160, 177

Jackson, P. 149
Jackson, R. 175
Jaworski 4, 11, 81, 169, 170, 171, 177, 180
Jamal 4, 177
James 1, 177

Larsen 23, 32, 75, 81, 173, 180
Lübbren 25, 72, 75, 77, 175

MacCannell 2, 23, 75, 78, 81, 178
Maci 6, 10, 14, 15, 22, 23, 24, 25, 26, 27, 81, 171, 178
Manca 171
Margarito 167, 168, 169
Martin 178
Martinec 140, 178, 141, 143, 148, 158, 178
McCarthy 116, 117, 118
McLuhan 20, 106, 111, 178
Meyer 27, 178, 181
Mirzoeff 71, 72, 74, 75, 178
Molina 57, 58, 167, 178
Murphy 79, 80, 181
Myers 28, 33, 64, 65, 179

Nigro 168, 172
Norwich 17, 118, 120, 121

O'Halloran 127, 129, 130, 147, 148, 159, 173
Olcay 141, 181
Olsen 166, 175
Ong 106, 179
Orwell 141
Östman 29, 170, 179
O'Toole 130, 158, 179

Palusci 8, 166, 171, 175, 176, 179
Pan 166, 167, 169, 172
Papen 167

Parrinello 22, 32, 64, 65, 166, 172, 175
Pearce 25, 174, 179
Perdue 8
Peters 171
Phipps ii, 8, 25, 177
Picard 74, 76, 179
Picht 168
Pierantonelli 172
Pierini 172
Pinnavaia 10, 179
Plastina 172
Plato 72, 106
Ploner 170
Poli 167
Poncini 176, 179
Porter 180
Pritchard 141, 167, 169, 170

Ragonese 12, 168, 179
Ramm 168, 179
Robinson ii, 4, 8, 22, 24, 27, 32, 35, 74, 76, 170, 177, 178, 179
Rocca Longo 172
Rojek 4, 180
Royce 43, 129, 131, 140, 158, 175, 179

Salway 140, 141, 143, 144, 158, 178
Santulli 6, 24, 65, 81, 125, 126, 133, 167, 173, 179
Schaaf 75, 180
Schmidt 147, 148, 153, 173
Schomaker 169
Schreibman 179
Schuetts 167
Scollon 130
Scott 159, 180
Searle 23, 180
Selwin 167, 169, 175, 180
Shakespeare 23
Shenhav-Keller 170
Siemens 179
Sirakaya 169
Smith 80, 129, 169, 178
Socrates 106
Sonmez 169
Sontag 74, 75, 76, 180
Stenglin 129, 180
Steward 169
Stewart 21, 171

Stöckl 102, 127, 128, 131, 133, 139, 140, 158, 180
Stubbs 55, 180
Sturken 71, 73, 74, 180
Swales 13, 27, 180

Thibault 23, 129–31, 133, 136, 138–9, 147–9, 154, 161, 173
Thurlow 4, 81, 141, 169, 170, 171, 180
Tod 153
Todorov 12, 20, 171, 180
Tolkien 149
Tsakona 140, 153, 180
Turner 2, 153, 180

Unsworth 140, 158, 180
Urry 3, 4, 7, 23, 32, 72, 74, 75, 76, 77, 81, 82, 180

Van Leeuwen 9, 23, 71, 81, 82, 83, 84, 86, 98, 90, 92, 93, 94, 95, 96, 97, 98, 99, 105, 107, 109, 110, 111, 112, 113, 114, 115, 128, 129, 130, 134, 135, 140, 148, 149, 158, 177, 178, 180

Ventola 129, 168, 175, 179
Vestito 168
Viallon 167
Visentin 178

Wahab 4, 181
Wall 170
Wallace 79
Walton 169
Waugh 2, 181
Wenger 32, 181
Werlich 25, 181
Werly 169
Whittacker 170
Wicks 167
Wilson 58, 79, 80, 169, 181

Yüksel 141, 170, 181

For Product Safety Concerns and Information please contact our EU Authorised Representative:

Easy Access System Europe

Mustamäe tee 50

10621 Tallinn

Estonia

gpsr.requests@easproject.com